Coaching Reimagined

Expanding Human Potential

COACHING REIMAGINED Expanding Human Potential

COACHING REIMAGINED Expanding Human Potential

Copyright © Dr Suzanne Henwood
All rights reserved.
ISBN: 9798316747351

The following chapters are Dr Suzanne Henwood & Co's intellectual property and the stories of the individuals. All rights reserved. No part of this book may be reproduced or modified in any form, including photocopying, recording, or by information storage and retrieval system, without written permission from the publisher/author.

Legal Notice: This book is for personal use only. You cannot amend, distribute, sell, use, quote or paraphrase any part of this book's content without the author's or copyright owner's consent. Legal action will be pursued if this is breached. The information provided herein is stated to be truthful and consistent in that any liability, in terms of inattention or otherwise, by any usage or abuse of any policies, processes, or directions contained within is the solitary and utter responsibility of the recipient reader. Under no circumstances will any legal responsibility or blame be held against the publisher for any reparation, damages, or monetary loss due to the information herein, either directly or indirectly.

Disclaimer Notice: The views, opinions, and advice expressed by other authors in this book are solely their own. This book is not providing medical advice; it is intended for informational purposes only. It is not a substitute for professional medical advice, diagnosis or treatment. Never ignore professional medical advice in seeking treatment. Every attempt has been made to provide accurate, up-to-date, reliable, and complete information. No warranties of any kind are expressed or implied. Readers acknowledge that the author is not engaging in the rendering of legal, financial, medical or professional advice. By reading this document, the reader agrees that under no circumstances are we responsible for any losses, direct or indirect, which are incurred as a result of the use of the information contained within this document, including, but not limited to, errors, omissions, or inaccuracies. These stories are written by real people in their own words.

COACHING REIMAGINED Expanding Human Potential

DEDICATION

To the many amazing mentors, teachers, and inspirers who saw our potential before we fully stepped into it—thank you. Your unwavering belief, guidance, support and wisdom shaped us into who we are today and for that, we are forever grateful. You laid the foundations for this book, we hope you feel your presence between the words.

To our family and friends, for being with us through our own learning. Thank you for your unwavering love and support.

And to our incredible, amazing clients, who entrust us with their stories, their dreams, and their transformation—thank you. It is a privilege and an honour to hold space for you, to witness your courage, and to walk beside you, even for a short while, on your journey of becoming. You remind us, every day, why this work matters.

With the deepest, heartfelt gratitude.

Thank You. The Authors.

COACHING REIMAGINED Expanding Human Potential

COACHING REIMAGINED Expanding Human Potential

CONTENTS

Introduction:	**Page: 9**
Chapter 1: Frances Lamb	**Page: 21**
Chapter 2: Sarah Carruthers	**Page: 33**
Chapter 3: Dr Suzanne Henwood	**Page: 47**
Chapter 4: Shelly Bean	**Page: 61**
Chapter 5: Jean de Bruyne	**Page: 75**
Chapter 6: Angèle Te Baerts – Fleurkens	**Page: 87**
Chapter 7: Henrietta Lait	**Page: 101**
Chapter 8: Tiffanee Cook	**Page: 113**
Chapter 9: Andrew Mills	**Page: 127**
Chapter 10: Fay Millington	**Page: 139**
Chapter 11: Rory Lemon	**Page: 153**
Chapter 12: Wendy Shaw	**Page: 173**
Chapter 13: Helen Oakwater	**Page: 189**
Chapter 14: Michelle Dalley	**Page: 203**
Chapter 15: Sue Frend	**Page: 217**

Chapter 16: Joanna Harper   **Page: 229**

Chapter 17: Frank van Nimwegen   **Page: 245**

Chapter 18: Michelle Comrie   **Page: 259**

Chapter 19: Colleen Lansdell   **Page: 273**

Chapter 20: Dee Dawson & Christine Mellor   **Page: 287**

Chapter 21: Kerry Smith   **Page: 299**

Chapter 22: Karl Sandland   **Page: 313**

Conclusion   **Page: 327**

bWISE   **Page: 331**

COACHING REIMAGINED Expanding Human Potential

INTRODUCTION
Coaching is changing - are we ready?
Dr Suzanne Henwood and Andrew Mills

"Here's to the bridge-builders, the hand-holders, the light-bringers, those extraordinary souls wrapped in ordinary lives who quietly weave threads of humanity into an inhumane world.

They are the unsung heroes in a world at war with itself. They are the whisperers of hope that peace is possible.
Look for them in this present darkness. Light your candle with their flame. And then go.

Build bridges. Hold hands. Bring light to a dark and desperate world. Be the hero you are looking for. Peace is possible. It begins with us."

-L.R. Knost

Think about the last time you truly felt heard. The kind of listening and witnessing that doesn't just nod along but shifts something deep inside you: thoughts, beliefs, perspectives, world views. That's coaching at its best - isn't it?

Isn't that what we want for all clients? And to achieve that - don't we as coaches need to keep pace with the world as it changes and evolves?

There can be no doubt that we are living in times of rapid, unpredictable change. The way we work, lead and live is shifting faster than ever, and uncertainty has become the norm. At the same time, stress, burnout, and anxiety are reaching critical levels – with many people feeling overwhelmed, disconnected, and searching for something more.

COACHING REIMAGINED Expanding Human Potential

If coaching is to remain relevant, impactful, and transformative, it too, must evolve.

This book is not just about coaching as it is - but re-imagining what coaching could be. It brings together a collective of master coaches and thought leaders, representing over 350 years of experience and wisdom, together exploring the edges of what's possible, integrating new modalities, and challenging traditional coaching frameworks.

Whether you're a coach, leader, or someone passionate about human potential, this book invites you into a new paradigm, one that is adaptive, embodied, systemic, and future-focused, with the potential to create a different future - one that is wise, courageous, deeply human, empowering us to navigate the complexities of modern life with insight, compassion and resilience.

Alongside these changes, AI technology continues evolving, reshaping industries, including coaching. AI can process vast amounts of data, identify patterns, and offer insights at an unprecedented scale and speed.

Yet, despite its capabilities, AI currently lacks intuition, presence, and the ability to access expanded states of human consciousness. True transformation, the kind that shifts not just what we do but who we are, and who we can be, requires something only human coaches can provide: deep listening, connection, compassion and the ability to hold space for the unknown.

Rather than replacing coaching, AI serves best as a personal assistant tool that enhances efficiency, supports reflective processes, and expands access to coaching insights. We have an opportunity to be leading it to determine how it can best serve humanity. We believe that the heart of coaching success is in the profound, human-to-human exchange—and that remains irreplaceable.

Beyond Traditional Coaching - A New Paradigm

COACHING REIMAGINED Expanding Human Potential

For decades, coaching has been dominated by structured, linear models and cognitive-based techniques. While effective at some level, many of these methods primarily focus on what and how we think, plan, analyse and problem solve. But true transformation happens when we go deeper - when we integrate the mind, body, and deeper intelligence within us, and beyond us. It is operating at a different level.

People today are looking for real, meaningful change.

- **Not** quick fixes.
- **Not** surface-level solutions.
- **Not** empty promises.
- **Not** memes and buzz words on social media.

They want to reconnect to themselves and to others to something beyond humanity. They want to be real, authentic and to contribute. People want to matter and to feel that they matter. They are questioning old narratives, tired methodologies and redefining what success, purpose, and fulfilment mean in an increasingly complex world. People are realising they have ONE precious life - and they want to make it count.

This shift is opening the door to new ways of coaching - ones that honour intuition, wisdom, embodiment, healing, energy, and the intelligence of interconnected systems.

Challenging Traditional Models

Coaching has a long and rich history of supporting transformation and playing a pivotal role in many arenas including: leadership, sports, psychology, health, well-being, and education, to name a few. With beginnings in academia in the 1830's, it was not until the late 20th Century that coaching found a place in professional circles and became established as a field of study in its' own right.

There is no doubt it has, and continues, to make a positive impact.
But we must ask ourselves:

COACHING REIMAGINED Expanding Human Potential

- Is it time to push the boundaries and reimagine what is possible?
- Is it time to integrate new modalities, update old ones, and challenge conventional coaching wisdom?
- Is it time to ensure that coaching stays relevant, effective, and deeply human in an evolving world?

Traditional coaching models that focused heavily on 'talk-based' methods and 'individual performance,' are no longer enough in an era of technological acceleration, workplace stress, increased awareness of trauma and shifting societal expectations.

As the world we live in evolves, coaching too is undergoing a profound metamorphosis, adapting to an increasingly fast paced, complex and interconnected world. People are looking for deeper, more holistic support that acknowledges the fluid and dynamic nature of their lives. People want approaches that embrace adaptability, self-discovery, and ongoing personal growth and healing and to tackle real issues in a real way.

Clients want coaching that fosters resilience, emotional intelligence, and a greater sense of meaning—helping them navigate uncertainty with confidence rather than simply striving for fixed outcomes. Embodied wisdom, neuroscience, systemic and holistic approaches are no longer optional. They are essential for deep, sustainable transformation.

Yet, if we reduce coaching to a formula, focusing only on individual problem-solving, we risk missing the opportunity for something greater: true systemic change.

It is not about rejecting existing coaching methodologies - it is about building on them and expanding them. It is about stepping into a new era of coaching.

For those who are ready, willing, and capable of stepping into a higher level of coaching mastery, there is an opportunity to evolve. To raise consciousness, to explore new ways of being and doing, and to coach in a way that is truly in service of humanity.

COACHING REIMAGINED Expanding Human Potential

The Future of Coaching and Our Invitation to You

This book is not a step-by-step manual.

It does not claim to offer a new universal framework to replace all others. Instead, it is an invitation - to question, explore, and expand.

Each chapter presents a unique perspective by an experienced coach, sharing how they use their wisdom and experience to navigate these crossroads - weaving together disciplines ranging from neuroscience and somatic practices to systems thinking and consciousness work.

Some of our musings may challenge conventional notions of traditional coaching approaches, and we invite you to join us with curiosity as we venture into uncharted territories of what's possible in the next paradigm of coaching evolution. We make no claims to definitive knowledge or absolute truth. We aren't proposing a singular framework to replace all others or suggesting we've discovered the one "right" path forward. Rather, we offer these reflections as fellow travellers on a journey of discovery—adding our voice to an evolving conversation about how we might better serve the magnificent complexity of human becoming.

Coaching is no longer just about helping people cope with problems or change. It is about empowering them to get to the root cause, to create new paths forward, to become way-makers, shaping the future for themselves and others.

- What if coaching became less about goal-setting and more about reconnection - to self, to purpose, and to collective wisdom?
- What if we embraced a degree of uncertainty in our coaching practice - allowing the work to evolve with the client rather than forcing it into a predefined framework?
- What if coaching moved beyond the individual - to honour the complexity of human experience within social, cultural, energetic, and systemic contexts?

These are the questions we invite you to explore.

COACHING REIMAGINED Expanding Human Potential

What an amazing time to be a coach.

The Bigger Picture: What If...?
We believe the time is ripe for this book.

- What if we had the courage to question old norms?
- What if we rewrite the narrative of what coaching can be?
- What if we could create new pathways that elevate how we do humanity - that raises consciousness and connectedness?

Coaching stands at the threshold of something new. A time of transformation, reinvention, and infinite possibility.

Coaching isn't just a profession—it's an organic movement, a transformational force that empowers individuals and organisations to break barriers and achieve extraordinary success. It is redefining how we grow, lead and thrive.

Today's coaching pioneers are boldly bringing new thinking, new science and importantly, a mind-body-soul connection to the practice. Possibilities are endless to rejuvenating the potential of the human being.

The question is not just: Are you ready? It is: What role will you play? Will you dare to make an impact?

If you are ready to explore new ways of being and doing coaching, welcome.

We are honoured to have you with us on this journey.

This is not just the beginning; it's an invitation. An opportunity to expand, challenge, and redefine what coaching can be as we step into new possibilities.

The future is shaped by those who dare to lead.

Will you join us?

Inviting Reflection: Deepening Your Learning and Insight

The journey from knowledge to wisdom rarely follows a straight line. As you engage with the ideas and approaches shared in this book, we invite you to travel beyond mere intellectual understanding into the rich territory of embodied knowing—where concepts become lived experience and theory transforms into practice beyond reading and into reflection, and beyond that into embodiment of your learning.

Coaching is an evolving, embodied practice—one that is shaped not just by concepts but by lived experience, felt sense, and action. Coaching at its most powerful is not something we merely do but something we become. It emerges from the integration of our whole being: our thoughts, emotions, physical sensations, intuitive wisdom, and relational presence.

Each chapter in this book offers a unique portal into coaching's emerging paradigm, inviting you to expand beyond conventional frameworks into more holistic and interconnected ways of being with clients. Each offers a unique perspective on coaching's new paradigm, exploring and expanding beyond traditional ways of thinking and being.

To support your personal learning and integration, we encourage you to pause at the end of each chapter and explore the following reflective questions. They are designed as thresholds—points of pause and possibility where you can deepen your relationship with the material. Choose which ones would be most helpful to explore.

They invite you to notice what resonates in your body, what challenges your assumptions, what awakens your curiosity, and what calls for integration and embodiment into your practice.

They invite you to engage at the levels of mind, body, and nervous system regulation—because learning is not just cognitive but somatic, emotional, social, environmental and deeply connected to who we are and how we show up in the world.

You can spend a few moments, in thought, or take time out to sit and journal your responses for maximum learning.

Cognitive Illumination: Expanding Mental Models

- What concepts or metaphors in this chapter resonate?
- Which ideas challenge any aspects of my existing coaching paradigm or philosophy?
- What hidden assumptions about coaching, healing, development and transformation did this chapter bring to light?
- How might these perspectives transform the questions I ask and the conversations I facilitate?
- Who can I share these ideas with or discuss them with to deepen my understanding?

Somatic Intelligence: The Body's Wisdom

- How did this chapter make me feel? What emotions arose as I read? What and where did any physical sensations arise—expansion, contraction, warmth, tension, tingling, heaviness, lightness?
- How does the content in this chapter align with my values, purpose and contribution, and what matters most to me in my work?
- In what ways does this approach invite more presence, connection, or compassion—toward myself and those I coach?
- What feels grounding or affirming in this approach? Where do I feel a sense of "yes" in my body?
- What resistance, discomfort, or uncertainty do I notice? What might that be telling me?
- How might I invite my clients into greater embodied awareness through this lens?

Nervous System Attunement: Regulation, Energy, and Attention

- How did my nervous system respond while reading this chapter? Did I feel at ease, energized, tense, or something else? What was

this alerting me to? What memories did I recall?
- Where am I directing my energy and attention as a coach? Is there anything I want to adjust?
- What helps me stay regulated and open to new ideas, even when they challenge me?

Relational Field: The Space Between

- How does this perspective shift my understanding of the coach-client relationship?
- What qualities of presence does this approach invite me to embody?
- How might I create a relational container that supports the emergence of what wants to be known?

Ecological Systems: Beyond Individual Change

- How does this chapter's perspective expand my understanding of human development beyond individual transformation?
- In what ways might the ideas presented help me recognize and honour my clients' connections to their wider systems (family, intergenerational, community, culture, nature)?
- In what ways could implementing these approaches allow my coaching to serve both individual growth and collective well-being?

Creative Edge: Beyond Conventional Methods

- What experiments, metaphors, or alternative approaches does this chapter inspire me to explore in my coaching practice?
- How might this chapter's perspectives help me embrace uncertainty or not-knowing as a potential strength in my coaching?
- How could these concepts help me recognize when conventional methods might be limiting what's possible with a client?
- What aspects of this chapter invite me to step beyond my

comfort zone as a coach to serve my clients even more effectively?

Personal Integration: Your Living Laboratory

- How have the patterns described in this chapter manifested in my own life and relationships?
- How does my own healing journey inform my capacity to facilitate this work?

Ethical Implications: Responsibility and Boundaries

- How does this approach challenge or expand my understanding of ethical coaching practice?
- What new considerations and responsibilities might arise from working at deeper levels with each individual and the wider system?
- How do I discern when to refer clients to complementary practitioners?
- What boundaries need to be tweaked or clarified when working in more holistic, integrative ways?
- How will I ensure ongoing support for myself when working at these edges?

Implementation: From Insight to Practice

- What is one small, immediate shift I could make in my coaching stance or methodology?
- What might stop me integrating new ideas in practice?
- How can I explain these concepts to clients in accessible, inviting language?
- What practices would help me to develop greater capacity to work at this level?
- What resources, training, or experiences would deepen my embodiment of this approach?

- How will I measure or sense the impact of integrating these perspectives into my work?
- What might be possible in your coaching practice that you haven't yet imagined?

Take a few moments after each chapter to journal your reflections, discuss with a colleague, or experiment with bringing an idea into your practice. Transformation doesn't happen through reading alone—it happens through engagement, curiosity, and lived experience. Let this book be more than information; let it be an invitation into deeper awareness, growth, and evolution in your work as a coach.

"Don't look for me in a human shape. I am inside your looking."

-Rumi

And the official bit

The publisher and the authors are providing this book and its contents on an "as is" basis and make no representations or warranties of any kind with respect to this book or its contents. The publisher and the author disclaim all such representations and warranties, including but not limited to warranties of healthcare for a particular purpose, legal consideration or financial implications. To the maximum extent permitted by law, the publisher and the author disclaim any and all liability in the event any information, commentary, analysis, opinions, advice and/or recommendations contained in this book prove to be inaccurate, incomplete unreliable, inconsistent, or result in any investment or other losses.

The content of this book is for informational purposes only and is not intended to diagnose, treat, cure, or prevent any condition or disease. Nor is it designed to offer any business or organisation advice. You understand that this book is not intended as a substitute for consultation with a licensed practitioner in the appropriate field. Please consult with your own expert services regarding the suggestions and recommendations made in this book and undertake your own research and due diligence before applying any concept to your practice. The use of this book implies your acceptance of this disclaimer.

The publisher and the author make no guarantees concerning the level of success you may experience by following the advice and strategies contained in this book, and you accept the risk that results will differ for each individual. The testimonials and examples provided in this book show exceptional results, which may not apply to the average reader, and are not intended to represent or guarantee that you will achieve the same or similar results.

CHAPTER 1
The Power of Presence
By Frances Lamb

Be an Isumataq: The keeper of the sacred space where wisdom reveals itself

It was back in 2015 that I first heard the word 'Isumataq' (Iz-zoo-ma-tak) an Inuit word, and it stayed with me. With over 20 years' experience working as a coach, mentor, and training facilitator, I have found that the biggest difference in my coaching came when I learned how to truly be present with the client.

Being present wasn't something that came naturally to me, however, when I took the time to develop the skill of presence, I became aware of how the simple act of being present was like a catalyst that changed the outcomes for my clients.

COACHING REIMAGINED Expanding Human Potential

My Journey to Presence

What does 'being present' actually mean? Well, for me, it means that you are
in a state of being where you are, aware and conscious of the moment, without judgement both in your mind and body; you are not distracted by the voice in your head or the things you have to do. When you focus solely on the other person it creates a deep connection. During a conversation with a dear friend of mine, Meredith Martinek, who is also a coach, she said "Presence is the soul's need for connection to others."

Over the years I have had the pleasure of working with hundreds of clients in a variety of settings. My primary tool is the Havening Techniques®, which are based in neuroscience, and I also use a raft of other techniques including Neuro-Linguistic Programming (NLP) and Emotional Freedom Technique (EFT) or Tapping. However, no matter what tool or technique I employ when coaching, delivering training or mentoring in a work environment, I know that when a client feels safe, they are more likely to allow their inner wisdom to reveal itself and transformation occurs due to the client's reconnection to self.

I believe it is a privilege to be a coach and should not be taken for granted. As coaches, we use our expertise, and skills such as listening, communication, questioning, and compassion to honour this privilege. However, in my opinion, arguably the most important one is to be present with the client who has entrusted you with their heart and is asking you to hold their pain. When collaborating with another individual, it is essential to be fully present, as coaching is inherently a collaborative process. Coaching is a relationship where it is all about them, the client, and not you. When we are absent from our clients, it shows disrespect to the privilege that we have been entrusted, and as a new coach I had unknowingly disrespected that privilege. Looking back, I realise how much I was in my head during sessions. By that I mean, whilst I was doing my best to apply my newfound knowledge of coaching, I wasn't really listening, so I wasn't really present with the client. I was busy thinking about what was coming next or what question I could ask from my list of questions from the question book I had created. It was my support tool as a new coach.

Often I found myself focusing more on choosing the NLP techniques I wanted to use rather than on the client's actual needs. Whilst my intention was to engage with the client to help and support them, I was in my head all the time. I had, and still do at some level, a deep-seated fear that I wasn't good enough as a coach and that they would see through me and realise that I didn't know what I was talking about. I focused so much on making sure the client had a beneficial session that I overthought things. I can only imagine now how disconnecting my inability to be present was for the client.

As a coach, when you are truly present with a client you are more able to witness their pain, grief, sadness, loss, joy, happiness, bliss, etc., that sits behind their thoughts and gives us the opportunity to understand their belief and value systems, amongst other things. When you are present and listening on a deep level, you can begin to notice the roots of their beliefs. Being present is a pathway to the body and during a session, pathways could open that provide access to forgotten memories, to unresolved trauma, and to core needs from childhood that were never met.

Being present creates safety in the client's world. When you are present and hold space for the client to honour their thoughts, accept their emotions and acknowledge their behaviours, without any judgement, just the gift of awareness, then you support them in accessing and connecting to their own inner wisdom. This is the power of presence.

Guides on the Journey to Presence

So, how did I learn to be present with the client? Well, to be honest, it took a while; however, I was lucky enough to have several mentors and guides along the way and there are two that come to mind.

The first is my coach from the early days, Rachel Anastasi, a poet, author, coach, Psychosomatic Therapist and so much more. I first met Rachel in 2012 when I attended a retreat for coaches at her place on Phillip Island.

After the retreat I began regular coaching supervision sessions with her, and it was during one of these sessions that she tasked me to run it without my coaching question book! I was so scared to do this. The book was my support mechanism and full of amazing questions. I didn't trust myself to know what to say, what techniques to offer, when to offer them, or how to run a session for a client. So, this time without my crutch I had no choice but to stay still, be present, and listen, intently. I also learnt how to just sit quietly, observe and listen with my head, heart, and gut, and it helped me get out of the client's way.

The second guide is my current coach and mentor, Jason Irving of the Wellness Breakthrough Academy: Founder, Practitioner and Facilitator. I have known Jason since 2012 when I went to him for holistic healing at the practice he used to run. He subsequently founded the Academy which I now attend. As part of the Academy, I receive regular coaching and mentoring from him. In one of the sessions we discussed my definition of transformation. In my head I had it as this huge thing that was like a light bulb moment that was dramatic and life changing. I was feeling frustrated that I could not give my clients these light bulb moments all the time and that I was failing as a coach.

Jason asked me "How do you feel when you leave a session with me and there hasn't been a light bulb moment?". I thought about this, and I realised that I always left the session feeling connected with myself. I would feel still, peaceful, calm, relaxed and grounded in my body and in who I was in that moment. It wasn't about light bulb moments each time, it was more how Jason was present with me that helped me connect back to myself. Connecting back to self *was* the transformation. His ability to hold that space that felt safe because he was so still himself, was the key to my connecting with my own inner wisdom. Jason showed me that being still and listening deeply allows transformation to unfold.

Jason was being an *Isumataq*.

Be an *Isumataq*

As mentioned earlier, in 2015 I attended a Psych-K® 'Divine Integration

Retreat' run by an amazing instructor, Duccio Locati. It was during this retreat that I first heard the word '*Isumataq*' (Iz-zoo-ma-tak.) *Isumataq* is an Inuit word that means: *The keeper of the sacred space where wisdom reveals itself.* To be a *'keeper of the sacred space'* you have to be present.

Another explanation I like related to presence is by Eckhart Tolle:

> *The stillness of your presence means you can look beyond the veil of form and separation with others. This is oneness. This is love.*

When you are being an *Isumataq* and creating a sacred space for the client to be present, then you give them permission to be their true self. That is love.

In her 2016 book called *Presence*, the American social psychologist and author, Amy Cuddy outlines the Ten Principles of Presence. Principle 6 states that, *"When we are present with others, we invite them to be present with us."*

Creating Presence

Whilst we have alluded to how a coach can create presence; I wanted to share with you some thoughts on how to create presence.

Personal Presence

Leave the cat outside the door.
As a coach, I often work from home, which is great, however, I had a beautiful cat called Moya, who just loved people! Whenever I ran training sessions or workshops in my home, or was working with a client, she would want to be in the room. Moya loved being cuddled, having her belly rubbed, and also liked to 'chat' to the clients. This sounds lovely, however, maybe not so much when a client is revealing their deepest trauma. So, unfortunately as cute as she was, and as loved as she was by clients, she was a distraction. So, Moya had to stay outside the door.

As a coach you must 'leave your own cat outside' the coaching room door to build trust with your client. Therefore, one way you can be present is to be aware of what distractions you might be bringing into the coaching environment. For example:

Internal Distractions
Those looping thoughts that you may have about things like hanging out the washing, calling so and so, paying that bill, sorting out the garage etc. Or maybe it might be that there is some stress about family, your partner, the business, finances etc. One way to handle the open loops in your mind is to make a list of everything or maybe even spend a moment doing some journalling. Writing things down helps clear those looping thoughts, which means you can be more focused, and therefore, more present, with the client.

External Distractions
There are many external distractions that can impact our ability to be present. A key one is technology, especially if you coach online, e.g. browsers open with content and images on them such as FB, WhatsApp, Messenger, YouTube. Other distractions could include a cluttered desk or your mobile phone. Before you begin coaching, taken a few minutes to tidy up your desk, close down those browsers, and check your notifications on your phone.

Your own practices
There are many ways to help yourself be present for the client. With a busy practice, find a tool or technique that fits your limited time between clients. For example:

- *Meditation.* I like to do a short 3-5-minute meditation before the client arrives.

- *Walking.* Take a short walk (5 minutes) to move your body and get some fresh air.

- *Mindfulness.* Use a mindfulness technique that focuses on what you can see, feel, hear, taste and smell, or try engaging with some breathwork just for a few minutes.

- *Affirmation.* Repeat an affirmation or mantra for a few minutes. There is one from the Havening Techniques® which is "I am safe, peaceful, calm and relaxed."

- *Journalling.* This can help you download all the 'distractions' in your head so you can be sure to leave the cat outside the door!

Use the techniques you have learned. As a Havening Techniques® practitioner, I use Havening Touch® for a few minutes whilst doing meditation. This is a self-soothing touch where you cross your arms and lift your hands up to the shoulders. Then brush down to the elbows in a stroking move, that is slow and gentle. It is like you are giving yourself a huge hug. Tiny receptors in our skin transmit information from the touch to our brains, and one of the things it signals is to lower the cortisol.

This gentle rhythmic touch also helps us shift into a delta wave brain state which promotes a sense of relaxation and safety.

COACHING REIMAGINED Expanding Human Potential

Personal development. Bessel Van Der Kolk's book *The Body Keeps the Score* explores how the unpleasant experiences we have had can affect the brain, body, and mind. I believe that when you do your own personal development, especially in relation to your childhood and any unpleasant experiences you may have had, you have an opportunity to release any unresolved emotions from your body. Having less trauma in the body means you will be more still within yourself.

Just Coach. As a new coach I didn't know how to be present with my client. Nor did I recognise the power of being present and how transformational it could be. So, I would highly recommend that you just coach. Coach and practise being present with each client and deepen your understanding of what that means to you. If you are unsure, set up some practise sessions with another coach and get feedback.

Ask yourself:
- What can I do to ensure that I am present with the client?
- What tools or techniques do I know that can help support the client in being present?

Client's Presence

Our clients show up in various emotional states depending on the issue that they have come to you for support. How they show up will determine what they might need from you to help them be present in the session. Some of the ways in which you could provide support to your client are:

Get Curious and ask questions. Where is the client at this moment? What is going on for them that might be distracting them from being present in the session? Do they need to sit in a particular chair that you have, or in a certain position? Do they need the door open or closed (either can help the client feel safer)? Do they need to see out of the window (if you have one)? What is it that they need to feel safe in that moment? What do they need to know or have answered before you begin?

I once had a client who had booked a Havening session. Before we began, I asked them what they needed for the session to begin. They said that they wanted to know how Havening worked. I spent the next 45 minutes answering questions. Once the client was happy with the neuroscience behind the technique, they relaxed and became fully present in the session, which I am pleased to say, had an amazing outcome.

Help them emotionally regulate. Sometimes a client shows up in a disturbed emotional state. Taking the client through some breathwork or mindfulness practices could help them to connect with their body and be more present. I personally invite the client to engage with Havening Touch® as it helps regulate the nervous system, and as explained earlier, helps them feel calmer. Sometimes I use Tapping (EFT) to help the client release emotions and thoughts from the day-to-day stress bucket. When the client has been acknowledged and validated, they have more capacity to be present.

Give Acknowledgment. It's okay if the client is distracted or not present. Acknowledge and validate this with them. They need to be who they are and where they are at that moment. This validation can help a client feel safer in the session. When they feel safe, they are more likely to be present even if it is not for the whole session or even that particular session.

Build Rapport. There is no need to rush into the client's presenting issue. Dedicate sufficient time, even an entire session, if necessary, to establishing rapport with the client. Rapport is about creating a connection with the other person. Connection can be achieved by demonstrating empathy, authenticity, and sharing relevant stories and experiences when appropriate.

Other ways in which you can build rapport could be through eye contact (again where appropriate and culturally safe), mirroring their body language, and by using their words and their language with them. You could also match the client's speech such as their tone, tempo, and volume. When you have rapport with your client, it will help promote trust between you and they will be more likely to be present.

When working with your client it is always useful to remember that coaching sessions are client led, and permission based. This means that the client is in control of where the session goes, and they lead the way. As the coach, seeking a client's permission to work with a certain model or a tool or technique helps build rapport and trust, which in turn helps the client feel safe and relaxed. A win-win for everyone.

Ask yourself:
- How can I help the client be present during the session?
- What do they need at this moment to feel safe and supported?

Environmental Presence

Physical space. Coaches use a variety of spaces within which to coach, including outside in nature, in workplaces, or in a designated coaching space either in-person or online. All are valid places, and I personally think that if you are truly present, then you can coach in any environment.

However, for me, as I work more in the 'trauma space', it is important for me to have a space where the client feels safe, comfortable, is private and ideally quiet. In addition to the space, where possible, it is good to have chairs that are appropriate for your type of coaching work. As a Havening Practitioner, because I use Havening Touch®, I don't have chairs with arms as that can interfere with my ability to provide Havening Touch® to the client. Stefa Jerma, a Registered Psychologist in Melbourne, told me that she uses sensory items like textured cushions. This is because when a client is not emotionally regulated or feeling grounded, they can use the cushion to self-sooth. As the client gets familiar with the therapeutic process, they become less dependent on the sensory item over time enabling the client to be more present with her.

If you have a coaching space, ensure the space is clean and uncluttered and has items in it that are appropriate to the work that you are doing. Take time to look around your space and notice what is pleasing to the eye or what might actually be triggering for a client. Ideally a coaching space should be distraction-free, well-lit and at a comfortable temperature and be easily accessible.

Ask yourself:
- How can I create an environment that feels inviting, safe, nurturing, and comfortable for the client?
- When online, what can the client do to remove distractions, so the cat doesn't get to play?

There is Power in Presence

Coaching is a 'we' process and not an 'I' one. As a coach, be mindful of your impact on clients. When you are truly present with the client, your presence can be a catalyst for change and transformation. Being present can give you an insight into the client and what is happening for them. Remember, with presence you see under the presenting issue. You hear the thoughts, feel the emotions, and see the behaviours. When you are aware of this, you can support the client to connect with their own inner knowledge and wisdom.

This is the Power of Presence.
Be courageous and do things your own way.
Trust your wisdom, your knowing.
Be an Isumataq.
Be Present.

Contact me:

Linktree: https://linktr.ee/franceslamb

CHAPTER 2
Mycelial Healing: Reconnecting the Fragmented Self
By Sarah Carruthers

The Body Remembers, Even When Medicine Forgets

For centuries, Western medicine has operated on Descartes' separation of mind and body, treating them as distinct entities. This approach has shaped healthcare into specialised silos skilled at treating separate parts—heart troubles go to cardiologists, stomach issues to gastroenterologists, anxious thoughts to therapists—while neglecting the whole person.

Yet, biology tells a different story.

Neuroscientist Dr. Peter J. Armour found that nearly 80% of neural signals travel from the body to the brain (afferent), rather than the other way around. The gut's enteric nervous system operates independently, the heart's electromagnetic fields influence brain function, and the immune system learns and adapts like a second intelligence, that rivals our cognitive processes. The body is not a passive vessel—it actively shapes our mental and emotional well-being.

Despite breathtaking medical advancements (conquering deadly diseases, transplanting organs, mapping genomes, observing the brain in real-time) suffering has morphed rather than vanished. Anxiety now grips one-fifth of adults in developed nations. Depression ranks as the world's leading cause of disability.

Despite significant medical advancements—such as conquering deadly diseases, transplanting organs, mapping genomes, and observing the brain in real-time—suffering has evolved rather than diminished. Anxiety now affects approximately 20% of adults in developed nations (ADAA.) Depression has become the world's leading cause of disability (WHO.) Autoimmune conditions and stress-related illnesses surge like an unstoppable tide.

We treat what bleeds and breaks, yet suffering rises beyond our capabilities and specialties.

Our sophisticated ability to treat symptoms has far outpaced our understanding of the deep, systemic roots of suffering—the interconnected web of biological, psychological, social, and spiritual factors that shape our wellbeing.

The Roots of Suffering

Our most persistent struggles—disconnection, trauma, addiction, fear, control—aren't random afflictions but echoes of early experiences, temperament, and attachment patterns. The landmark Adverse Childhood Experiences (ACE) study confirms what many intuitively know: unresolved trauma leaves lasting imprints. Individuals with four or more adverse childhood experiences face dramatically higher risks of depression, heart disease, and cancer—evidence that the body keeps the score, carrying imprints of what the conscious mind forgets.

Yet trauma isn't just about dramatic events. It also includes the quieter wounds—emotional disconnection, unmet needs, the loss of attuned relationships etc. When our feelings were ignored, our authenticity dismissed, our sense of belonging disrupted, our nervous system adapted, shaping core fears and coping strategies that continue to influence us throughout life.

"Trauma is not what happened to you, but what happens inside you as a result of what happened to you."

-Gabor Mate

Neuroscience reveals how these experiences hardwire neural pathways, stress responses, and relational patterns. The approval-seeking child becomes the adult who cannot feel worthy without external validation. The hyper-vigilant child grows into an adult whose body remains on high alert, even in safety. Whether through striving, withdrawing, or seeking intensity, these adaptations silently shape our choices and relationships.

"Where attention goes, neural firing flows and neural connection grows."

-Daniel Siegel

What once kept us safe can later keep us stuck. Survival strategies designed to secure love and protection become invisible prisons—limiting connection, dampening joy, and distancing us from our inner wisdom. Yet through the lens of Polyvagal Theory, these responses aren't flaws but brilliant adaptations. They were the nervous system's way of ensuring we remained seen, soothed, and safe when our very existence depended on it.

The Journey Home to Ourselves

The good news is that these patterns are not permanent. Our remarkable neuroplasticity—the same mechanism that created these adaptations—offers pathways to transformation. Through embodied presence, self-regulation, self-compassion and supportive relationships, we can rewire our neural pathways, expanding our capacity for choice, flexibility, and authentic expression.

Traditional coaching often targets symptoms: CBT for anxiety, NLP for limiting beliefs, solution-focused strategies for performance blocks. While useful, these approaches rarely address the underlying nervous system dysregulation that sustains these struggles. As Pat Ogden notes: *"The thinking brain is necessary but not sufficient for healing trauma. Healing happens in the body."*

Lasting change requires an integrated approach—where thoughts, emotions, and somatic wisdom move in harmony. We cannot 'think' our way out of patterns that were never created through thought.

The Mycelial Path: A New Vision for Healing

The mycelial web offers a profound metaphor for human healing. Beneath every thriving forest lies an invisible network of fungal threads connecting tree to tree in an intricate web of communication and support. Through this "Wood Wide Web," trees share nutrients with struggling neighbours, warn of incoming threats, and "mother trees" recognise and nourish their offspring through preferential carbon sharing.

> *"Trees talk to each other, even form alliances with other trees. Some are vulnerable, some are supportive, some are bullies, some are loners, but they all communicate through the network. And they communicate in a way that changes behaviors."*
>
> -Suzanne Simard

This underground intelligence reveals nature's fundamental truth: nothing heals in isolation. Douglas fir trees send carbon to birch trees when birch loses its leaves in winter; birch returns the favour when fir stands in shade. Wounded trees receive healing compounds through fungal connections. Older trees recognise kin and prioritise their seedlings through underground channels. Shaded seedlings receive vital nutrients through the community network, boosting survival rates by 400% compared to isolated trees (Simard et al., 2012).

Just as forests thrive through these mycelial networks, humans flourish through deep, interconnected healing. Our emotional, physical, and spiritual well-being depends not on fixing isolated symptoms but on restoring vital connections within our internal and external ecosystem. It's time to move beyond isolated symptom management toward an approach that honours the wisdom of wholeness—where healing and growth emerges naturally, when all parts of the self-communicate in harmony.

The Coach as Mycologist

In this paradigm, coaches function as skilled mycologists—attuning to energy's flow and blockages, guiding clients toward wholeness through connection rather than correction.

We don't impose solutions; trusting that given the right conditions, healing emerges through its own perfect intelligence if we can get out of its way. The focus shifts dramatically:

- From "fixing problems" to amplifying where healthy energy is already flowing.
- From "knowing what's best" to trusting innate wisdom.
- From isolated interventions to systemic reconnection.

This approach demands our expansion and trust—growing taller for perspective and deeper for resilience. As we honour the interconnectedness of all aspects of human experience, we cultivate coaching relationships that mirror the forest's wisdom—resilient, adaptive, and pulsing with living intelligence. This integration weaves together ancient Indigenous wisdom with contemporary research from diverse areas including interpersonal neurobiology, Polyvagal Theory, Internal Family Systems, conscious breathing, somatic practices, microbiome research and psychedelic-assisted therapy.

Reconnecting Through the Mycelial Lens

Just as a forest's health depends on the vitality of its underground mycelial network, the effectiveness of coaching depends on the coach's own internal and external ecosystem. We must first tend our own soil before guiding others—addressing personal trauma, cultivating self-compassion, and establishing coherence within our nervous systems. Like trees that grow both upward toward light and downward into soil, we develop multiple dimensional awareness: mental, emotional, spiritual, embodied, relational, and energetic. Our rootedness determines our reach.

When we've done this inner work, we become like nurse logs—fallen trees that cradle new life, offering nutrients, shelter, and stability to countless seedlings. We serve as compassionate witnesses, creating environments where clients feel deeply seen, physiologically safe, and reconnected to their inherent wisdom. Our coaching relationships become resilient, adaptive, and alive with the recognition that transformation flows naturally when fragmented parts of the human ecosystem reconnect—just as a forest regenerates through the invisible connections beneath its surface.

Toward Integration and Wholeness

The power of nature's collaborative intelligence was showcased when scientists removed all the needles from Douglas fir seedlings. The trees swiftly sent distress signals through their underground networks, prompting even unrelated neighbours to mobilise resources and deliver defensive compounds to their aid (Simard et al., 2012).

Daniel Siegel's concept of "Me + We = MWe" captures this dynamic perfectly—our well-being arises from integration, both within ourselves and within the larger web of connections around us. In this flowing state, the artificial boundaries between mind and body, self and other, dissolve into a cohesive wholeness. We no longer experience ourselves as isolated fragments, but as unique expressions within a vast, interconnected tapestry.

The result isn't merely symptom reduction but a profound homecoming—a return to our essential selves. Not fixed or finished, but continually becoming. Not perfect, but radically whole.

> *"The wound is the place where the light enters you."*
>
> -Rumi

Metaphor as Medicine: Forest Wisdom in Practice

When a client of mine arrived carrying profound grief, our journey extended beyond traditional coaching. After exploring her loss through Interactive Drawing Therapy and nervous system regulation, I offered the ancient medicine of metaphor—not as technique but as an invitation to connect with her body's innate wisdom.

Why metaphor? Because it bypasses the analytical gatekeeper, speaking directly to the body's constellation of intelligences in their native tongues: energy, symbol, imagery, sensation, wordless knowing… Like mycelium carrying messages between trees, metaphor creates neural pathways between disconnected parts of self.

When I speak of forests regenerating after fire or rivers finding their way to sea, I'm not merely creating pleasant imagery—I'm activating the same pattern-recognition systems that helped our ancestors read the natural world—where the client's inherent healing intelligence can flourish without being directed or managed.

The meditation that follows demonstrates this approach—an invitation to trust the body's implicit knowing. Just as a fallen log knows precisely how to transform into fertile soil without instruction,
your clients carry wisdom that needs not correction, but reconnection.

For the audio version: **https://www.theluminosityproject.nz/**

The Forest of Becoming

Find a comfortable place to sit where you will not be disturbed… allowing your body to settle into support, as if cradled by the earth itself.

As your eyes close... notice your breathing finding its natural rhythm.
Gently, without forcing it, inhale through your nose for a count of four. Exhale through your mouth for a count of eight. Let your exhale become twice as long as your inhale, whatever count feels right for you—like a sacred conversation between your human form and the eternal mystery that breathed you into being.
And you might not yet realise how your jaw can soften... your tongue can relax... that subtle gateway where human language constructs its walls... creating a spaciousness... allowing fewer signals to your left hemisphere... as deeper currents of wisdom emerge.

As your jaw softens, you can let your eyes rest beneath closed lids now. Let your breath become a gentle tide of grace.

Let your whole energy be one of allowing—like opening a sacred pipeline between conscious awareness and the ancient intelligence residing within and beyond you. Easily. Softly. Surrendering to a wisdom greater than yourself.

As you breathe, perhaps you can sense the divine spark within you—the luminous thread of consciousness that connects you to all of creation.
You are both the drop and the ocean.
Both the individual expression and part of the infinite source.

You may begin to notice the muscles under your eyes relaxing now... parts of your body you haven't yet been aware of loosening... as you continue breathing deeply... exhaling twice as long as you inhale... and you might be surprised how your body softens with that longer exhale, easily and naturally... helping you connect more fully to the present.

And as you breathe... you might sense yourself breathing through your heart... becoming aware of your heartbeat... not just a mechanical pump... but a symphony of electromagnetic intelligence... a drum beating in perfect rhythm with the universe. Feel it. Sense it. Hear it. Let it spread out beyond you—in rhythm with those around you.

Expanding now into the vast inner landscape of your body... spaciousness radiating through shoulders... arms... head... torso... down to the soles of your feet, right to your soul... wrapping wisdom and love around each cell.
Expanding.

You might wonder where do you feel tension?

COACHING REIMAGINED Expanding Human Potential

Where do you feel softness?
Where do you feel the touch of the infinite?

Your gut, your second brain, whispers ancient wisdom... Mastering your becoming, with purpose and meaning. This is your time.
Your skin forms a boundary that is also a bridge of sensation and connection.
Your nervous system connects you inside, outside and between.
Your breath a living river of transformation.

And as you let your breathing be slow and easy now.
Relaxing spaciousness. Inside and out. No longer just air moving in and out—but a living river.
A story of survival.
A song of resilience.
Expanding into a landscape of infinite possibility.

And perhaps now... or sometime soon... you might find yourself standing at the edge of a primeval forest—ancient, breathing, alive with potential. This isn't just any forest... this is the living map of your inner world... where every tree holds a story... every root a memory and lineage of wisdom, every leaf a possibility of transformation. The roots run deep, intertwining beneath the earth in a vast, intelligent network—a living mandala of interconnection.

The air here is luminous with possibility.
Mist curls between trunks that have witnessed centuries pass.
Sunlight filters through the canopy in shifting patterns of gold. Sparkling with the wisdom that has been passed down through generations.
And you might hear the forest breathing and see a gentle movement with every breath... moss whispering underfoot... ferns unfurling in slow meditation, fractal after fractal of new life emerging. And somewhere, water sings over stone as it flows naturally on its way into the unknown.

Perhaps you are aware now how the forest expands beyond the horizon that you can see and reveals itself in exquisite detail—the perfect spiral of a snail shell, the intricate veins of a single leaf, the complex society of a decaying log teeming with renewal. Vitality. Breathe.

Your body is not a battlefield of past wounds, but a sacred ecosystem of continuous renewal. Each cell carries wisdom refined through billions of years of evolution, whispering: "We are changing. We are always becoming."

The past does not define you—it illuminates you... teaching not who you are... but what you've overcome.
The future is a canvas of boundless beauty.
Honour every fallen leaf—each struggle and loss—now nurturing the soil where you stand. Feel how they transform into wisdom, feeding new growth that reaches toward light with ancestral confidence.

Within you flows the intelligence of rivers finding their way to the sea, the resilience of forests regenerating after fire, the patience of mountains shaped by wind and time.
Your body remembers how to heal—it orchestrates this miracle daily in ways both subtle and profound, transforming challenge into strength, wound into wisdom, ending into new beginnings.

Feel the ground beneath you. Alive with a vast network of interconnected intelligence—a dialogue of sensation, of wisdom passed through generations.
Your feet are not just standing.
They are listening, feeling, sensing.
Remembering.
Healing.
As you continue breathing...notice the spaces between your thoughts, your bones, your muscles, your cells.
You might become aware of how your breath carries stories—of survival, of adaptation, of resilience—and of the divine grace that moves through all things.
Slowly, becoming more aware of the invisible threads connecting everything around you. Like the mycelia beneath the forest floor, your experiences are not isolated moments but an intricate web of connection.
Mycelial whispers.
Threads of awareness weaving through your body—illuminating old patterns without judgment...honouring their brilliant survival strategies.
Every tension a story of protection...holding a moment of love turned inward
You never were broken.
You are a masterpiece still being painted.
All you are is changing.

COACHING REIMAGINED Expanding Human Potential

Evolving.

Breathe.
Loosen your jaw.
Swallow in the new knowing.

Where once there was fragmentation, there is integration now.
Where once there was separation, there is wholeness.
Where once there was doubt, there is grace and strength.

Your nervous system is a river of infinite adaptation... guided by wisdom beyond understanding. Some streams may have run dry, maybe just for a season... some may be blocked by stones of old hurts...and boulders of trauma... yet water always finds its way... Let it flow.

As you send compassion now.
Understanding.
Radical acceptance.
As this journey reaches its tender conclusion for now, remember healing is not a destination... It is a continuous, flowing conversation with your most authentic self.

Your body remembers... your body knows.
You are whole... you are becoming... you are sacred... you are infinite possibility.
And when you're ready... allowing your eyes to open... carrying the forest's wisdom within you... and the light that shines from within.

Welcome home.

Towards a New Paradigm of Coaching and Healing

As we stand at this threshold, we face a profound invitation: to evolve our approach to human suffering not through more sophisticated symptom management, but through ecological restoration of the whole being.

The forest has always known what medicine is just beginning to remember—true healing emerges from connection, not correction.

COACHING REIMAGINED Expanding Human Potential

Resilience flows from relationship. The path forward isn't about fixing what's broken but nurturing what longs to become whole.

Our calling as coaches is to embody this ancient wisdom—cultivating our own inner ecosystem so we might serve as fertile ground for others. To trust the innate intelligence flowing through every living system, recognising and respecting the interconnectedness of each part. To recognise that transformation isn't something we do to clients, but rather something we midwife by creating conditions where they can remember and reclaim their inherent wholeness.

The mycelial path asks us to surrender the expert stance and embrace the humility of the forest floor—receiving, connecting, nurturing without directing. To listen with all our senses to communication beneath the surface, to wisdom speaking through body and breath, energy and emotion.

This isn't a new technique but a "self-remembering" of what it means to be human—not isolated parts to be fixed, but interconnected
systems longing for integration.

The future of coaching lies in deepening our capacity to witness, to attune, to create sacred space where fragmented aspects of self-find their way home to one another. In doing so, we don't just heal individuals—we participate in healing our collective ecosystem, one relationship at a time.

The forest is calling us home. Are you ready to answer?

Illuminating the Path to Wholeness

At The Luminosity Project, we serve as mycologists of the human spirit—creating conditions where your inner ecosystem can regenerate naturally. Like the forest floor that nurtures everything from mighty oaks to delicate mushrooms, we provide fertile ground for your authentic self to flourish.

Just as bioluminescent fungi glow in forest darkness—visible only when we

COACHING REIMAGINED Expanding Human Potential

quiet ourselves enough to perceive them—your internal light remains present even in your darkest moments. This luminosity isn't something we create, but uncover, gently removing layers that may have dimmed your natural radiance.

Our offerings nurture your entire ecosystem:

- Integrated Somatic Coaching — Where fragmented parts reconnect through embodied awareness
- Trauma-Informed Healing — Transforming protective defences into pathways of strength
- Nervous System Attunement — Cultivating resilience in your internal environment
- Mycelial Connection Work — Rebuilding neural networks between disconnected aspects of self
- Professional Development — Training and supervision for coaches, therapists, and healers ready to embody new paradigms.

If you feel called to explore deeper layers of your becoming, to transform patterns that no longer serve you, and to remember your fundamental wholeness, we're here to walk beside you. Like trees in a forest, we grow stronger together.

Email: info@theluminosityproject.nz

Website: www.theluminosityproject.nz

COACHING REIMAGINED Expanding Human Potential

CHAPTER 3

Coaching wisdom within, without and between
By Dr Suzanne Henwood

They Asked her,
> "What is the key to saving the world?"

She answered,
> "You. You are the key. Heal Yourself, know Yourself, make yourself whole and free. Release all limits so that your love can flow unconditionally for yourself and the world, this will open the heaven of your heart completely and it will guide you without fail."

-Yung Pueblo

We are living in amazing and challenging times.

People are looking for answers and searching to understand issues such as:

- What does it mean to be human?

- What does it mean to be sentient?
- How have we become so disconnected from ourselves and others?
- Where do we belong?
- What are we doing to the planet?
- Can I truly heal from trauma?
- Am I safe?
- How do I find clarity in complexity and create calm in chaos?
- What is my purpose? Why am I here?
- What contribution am I making – do I make a difference – do I matter?
- Who can give me real, authentic approaches that offer depth and results in today's world?

Does this resonate?

Are you fed up:
- Playing at the edge of what is really going on?
- Being expected to fit in a box that is not YOU shaped?
- Being promised quick fixes and gimmicks?

I am on a mission to create a new form of coaching that says, "let's get real" and "love ourselves back to wholeness." A coaching approach that acknowledges the huge potential of what is possible – if we get out of our own way and recognises that we have to be active participants, making a conscious choice, and change our actions, to do life differently.

Coaching is ideally placed to contribute to individual and collective healing and growth; to equip people to create the change they want to see and be, and to lead the way in working deeply and systemically through accessing multiple sources of wisdom to enable us to live this one precious life.

And, to do this we need to step beyond coaching 'techniques' into a deeper way of being as coaches - one that empowers growth, fosters trust and invites lasting transformational change in the service of all. It will require some disruption to what is known and practiced, and it requires clear intention that moves beyond outdated business models that are about self-gain, money, status, power trips and ego.

This is not for the faint hearted.

Not everyone is ready, or able, to step up to this level of calling. It takes courage and commitment. A deliberate intention to step forward, onto a path that isn't clearly visible or fully known in advance.

This level of coaching calls for the coach AND the client to be wayfinding together - stepping into a shared coaching waka (a Māori canoe), paddling together in sync and embracing true partnership. It's about moving with intention, while staying open to the wisdom that surrounds them, attuned to the currents that nudge us along. Trusting the flow. Honouring the collaborative, wise, intelligent system to which we all belong.

And there has never been a better time to be a coach and to be coached to change the trajectory of travel for humankind than right now.

Coaching Evolution

I have been coaching for over 30 years in many different forms. 'How' I coach has changed beyond recognition since those early days. Today, my clients often don't know exactly what they want from coaching when they first reach out and may enter into a longer term exploratory coaching relationship.

They may be stuck in a difficulty they can't find the exit from, telling themselves a story over and over not realising this is wiring the issues even deeper into their neurology.

They may not be able to imagine what is possible beyond the present discomfort or have contemplated 'what if?' and 'what else?'

For many their focus is on survival and getting through. Being able to take another breath, another step today.

COACHING REIMAGINED Expanding Human Potential

They come knowing they want ***something*** to change – they have reached the point where they know they do not want to go on as they have been.

Some clients arrive with a specific context in mind—workplace conflict, a missed promotion, the aftermath of trauma, or a significant health event. Yet, most haven't explored the underlying patterns driving their behaviour or imagined a future where these patterns might shift.

As a coach, this makes contracting around goals and outcomes complex. In my experience, goals are rarely static; they evolve as the journey unfolds, with new insights giving rise to fresh desires and directions.

It can feel unsettling—for both coach and client—not to know exactly where the path will lead. Our brains crave certainty, seeking the comfort of a clear plan and the illusion of control. But true transformation often begins when we step into the unknown, allowing discovery to guide the way.

There is a vulnerability saying, "I don't know."

There needs to be deep trust and safety to even begin to explore.

There is so much more. If we can step into what is not yet known, not in our consciousness, then we can truly create new paths. We can recognise there are no limits, beyond the ones we set ourselves inside our minds. We step beyond 'I', and 'now,' 'this place' – the 'known' – all of which is limiting us from seeing 'what else?'

To step into this style of coaching it is essential to learn to hold a safe and sacred space, grounded in trust and co-regulation, to step into the unknown together knowing you have the skills and experience to artfully guide the client, allowing the path to emerge as it is walked.

This new approach to coaching raises some interesting questions:
- What sort of coach am I?
- What do I call myself?

COACHING REIMAGINED Expanding Human Potential

- How do I incorporate wide and diverse skills and experience over time?
- What no longer serves me and my clients?
- How do I advertise my services?
- Where do I fit in terms of professional structures and accreditation?
- Where do I go to keep growing?
- What do I not know?
- How do I plan for what I need developmentally?
- Who is my tribe?
- What is my role?

After 30 years it would be easy to get used to the way things are: to what coaching is and has been – and what we have always been told it is and isn't. But the world is evolving fast, and so are the needs of those we coach.

To truly support transformation, we must resist the temptation to go with the flow. Like fish swimming in water, we can lose awareness of the environment we are in, and all the aspects that affect it, missing the opportunity to innovate, adapt, and create meaningful change. To remain effective, we must step outside of what we know and embrace new ways of thinking, feeling, doing and being, so we can better meet the challenges of today and tomorrow.

What if we had the courage to truly become aware – and disrupt what we think we know?

How often as coaches do we fail to include the environment, technology, cultural, spiritual, social connections, the body, energetic and quantum reality that we are all apart of? Focusing only on the fish and the challenges the fish is facing that day?

I know for myself, the more I learned, the more I realised I didn't know. And add to that the exponential rate at which knowledge is advancing, it can feel overwhelming – for us and our clients – to keep up.
So, coaching is a journey.

COACHING REIMAGINED Expanding Human Potential

The terrain is changing and still being laid down.

We need to explore how we keep ourselves and our clients safe; be clear on what preparation and training we require; and how we keep our map updated, open to new frontiers coming into view.

For me this has involved weaving together an amazingly diverse toolbox of modalities, approaches and philosophies of learning, coaching, counselling and therapy, and realising that I was creating the future of coaching as I was practising it – just like I was helping clients to step into their new ways of being and doing in our sessions together.

What an absolute joy and privilege.
What does this look like in practice?

Let me introduce you to Matt.

Matt* is 44 —a high achiever who once thrived on challenge and momentum but now finds himself feeling overwhelmed and stuck in a cycle of stagnation. Once at the top of his game professionally, he's lost his spark, his confidence eroding with each setback. "I don't know who I am anymore," he admits, his voice laced with frustration and fatigue and a loss of hope.

Despite his best efforts, nothing seems to click. His drive has dulled, his instincts feel off, and the energy that once fuelled his success has faded. He says he has lost any sense of joy or fun in life.

Beneath the surface, his nervous system is signalling distress—trapped in a state of disconnection, neither fully at rest nor ready to engage, some symptoms are beginning to materialise in his body.

While Matt came to me about his work situation, he also shared problems within his blended family. He spoke about increasing unrest and arguments in the home, with his partner and her children. And whereas they had always been a team, now he felt like they were pulling in different directions.

At both work and home, he was questioning the very things that he had taken for granted that had given him stability in the past. It was like his rock, his firm foundation, had crumbled beneath his feet. He was not clear what his desired outcomes from coaching were – but he knew he could not carry on as he was.

Helping Matt was not about pushing him to try harder—it was about guiding him to listen differently. Instead of forcing his way forward, we started by tuning into his nervous system, recognizing the signals beneath his frustration and exploring the patterns of behaviours that he had created to keep himself safe. After mapping his nervous system patterns, Matt recognised that he was stuck in a functional freeze state, still going about life, but disconnected from his natural drive. Occasionally he described being able to fight his way into taking action, but without any sense of intention or direction, which drained him of the little energy he still had.

Through working with the body, using polyvagal theory, breathwork, somatic awareness, bwise coaching, mBraining2.0, and mindful reflection, we created space for him to reconnect with his body's wisdom, before making any changes to his way forward.

Our work was dynamic, creative and evolving beyond the initial presentation of stress and anxiety coaching, into deeper existential questions and life transformation. We worked at a systems level, looking at higher order changes, exploring beyond what was currently in Matts awareness.

The approach involved psycho-education and equipping Matt to be able to take back control, through understanding concepts (for example using neuroplasticity and a deep understanding of neuro coaching) so he had a reason and commitment to implement them. Matt was actively committed and applied his learnings in and between sessions, accelerating his progress.

His journey back to wholeness wasn't just about performance; it was about rediscovering the wisdom within, the connection without, and the space between where real transformation happens. It is about deeply connecting and listening to himself and gently loving himself to bring his whole self into alignment and trust his inner wisdom.

A Radical Self Care Plan across five Pillars of Well Being (Physical, Mental, Emotional, Social and Spiritual) was one of the key frameworks to structure and plan his new actions and behaviours, along with creating an active, embodied Gratitude Practice.

By fostering safety, curiosity, and self-compassion, Matt began to shift— regaining his sense of agency, rediscovering his motivation, and rebuilding trust in himself. He explored how he felt, how he wanted to feel – and how he didn't want to feel, through the Emotional Culture Deck and he used tools from Acceptance and Commitment Therapy, like the choice point, to take responsibility for what he was doing that took him away from his values, as well as what he did to move towards his values.

When he struggled to express himself, we used Interactive Drawing therapy to explore concepts on 'The Page', giving access to his subconscious mind and bringing new insights into his conscious awareness.

He found that his mojo wasn't lost; it was waiting for him in the stillness, in the gentle rhythmic movement and in the space between what had been drawing his attention.

Throughout the process, new emergent outcomes opened up opportunities that he had not previously considered, and we navigated through obstacles that arose, that held their root causes in past traumas, limiting beliefs and unprocessed emotion, which desperately showed up to defend their position. Havening was a wonderful adjunct to the coaching process to resolve old traumas and insert new resilient mindsets moving forward.

Matt saw improvement in specific health issues, as well as regaining energy. His sleep improved, along with his focus and memory. At work he negotiated a new role which he was excited about that fed into his sense of meaning and purpose that had emerged through the coaching process and The Map of Meaning framework. And at home, he reported that his relationship with both his partner, and her children improved significantly – they became a team again.

The woven, dynamic, embodied and systemic use of multiple modalities opened up the opportunity for real transformational change at an ontological level. Matt found himself and gave himself permission to be all he could be. He found a reason to change and understood how to move forwards in a new way.

On Reflection

As you can see from Matts story, coaching today has moved on, and up and out – for those who choose to step into the new paradigm that is emerging. It is not an easy, quick fix approach, though we do see some significant focused changes along the way.

This new coaching approach requires the client to play an active part through real, sustained effort, commitment, and disciplined implementation with the support of a highly skilled multi-modality coach that considers wisdom within, without and between.

- Wisdom *within* inner intelligence across the multiple complex adaptive networks in the body – and between them encompassing one interrelated system.
- Wisdom *without* from the environment, society, spiritual, cultural, energetic and quantum fields.
- Wisdom *between* that as you explore inner wisdom and outer wisdom you become aware of the wisdom within the apparent space between.

What's truly remarkable is how the original problem often fades into the background, as the coaching shifts toward new ways of being and doing. It becomes less about solving and more about becoming—stepping into the unknown and shaping it in real-time. New layers of consciousness emerge, revealing a deep, inherent wisdom that was always there, just waiting to be rediscovered.

And for the coach? Contracting in this new model can feel like navigating uncharted territory. You can't predict every detail upfront; instead, it demands a process of continuous, evolving agreements—regularly revisiting consent as the journey unfolds. It calls for a grounded understanding of safety, clear scope of practice, and a deep commitment to ongoing learning and supervision. It requires the courage to sit with uncertainty, to co-create with clients in true partnership, to model the self-exploration you invite them into—and, above all, to master the art of finely-tuned calibration, both internally and externally, to facilitate each next step with precision and care.

Who am I becoming as a coach?

Today I call myself a neuroscience-based coach and I speak about my coaching being embodied, holistic, systemic, raising wisdom and consciousness through evidence-based practices. There are such a variety of role titles, it can be challenging to find one that encompasses all that you offer and mine changes over time and in different contexts.

I don't fit in most standard models of coaching, it is one reason why I do not align myself with **one** coaching body. Many coaches and trainers I know have had to hide aspects of their practice to fit accreditation criteria, which feels inauthentic to me.

Instead, I chose to belong to carefully chosen organisations and professional bodies that provide a Code of Conduct, a Complaints Procedure for clients, and access to insurance, while aligning to my values and practices. And I have been honoured to be recognised as a coach with multiple awards, so I must be doing something right!
I believe the boundaries between roles are blurring.

I have often heard it said that therapy focuses on the past, mental health concerns and underlying emotional issues. Whereas coaching is future orientated, focuses on setting goals and overcoming obstacles.

I don't believe this clear distinction exists or is as relevant today.

As a coach, I can't imagine ignoring the tapestry of a clients' past events, learnings, patterns, and trauma—each one a thread in the intricate fabric of our lives—when working from a systemic and embodied approach. It's like navigating a vast, interconnected forest where every tree and trail contributes to the overall landscape – visible and below ground.

Nor can I overlook the essential aspects of emotional health and wellbeing in my work; each feeling serves as a signpost along our journey, a communication that is too important to ignore. Must we confine ourselves to only one camp when the terrain of human experience is so richly diverse? In the current epidemic of stress, anxiety and burnout, I believe we have an opportunity to open up this dialogue and embrace suitably qualified coaches to work in this arena. Right now, a reliance on psychotherapists and psychologists means that many people are going unsupported or are waiting up to 18 months to get appointments. It is clear from my experience that coaches could help to alleviate this suffering.

Are we brave enough to disrupt the status quo and find new and safe ways to move forwards?

The reality is that coaching remains largely unregulated, which offers both freedom and challenges. Clients often struggle to determine who is a "good" coach and worth investing in and are confused about the roles of coaches, counsellors, therapists, psychotherapists and psychologists. Is it time to support the evolving, integrative and systemic approach many of us practice today? To create a place for all in modern health and wellbeing?

The Future of Coaching

I believe coaching is evolving beyond a linear, goal-driven model. It is becoming about: deeper connections (within, without and between); wisdom; systemic awareness; and the integration of multiple modalities, with a desire to impact individuals, communities and the world – one person at a time.

As coaches, we hold sacred space for clients to discover new ways of being and doing – of becoming. New levels of consciousness emerge, opening wisdom that was always present but previously unseen – unknown.

I believe we are moving toward a coaching future that embraces depth, integration, and transformational change—for both our clients and ourselves - in these fast-changing, complex and uncertain times.

Just as our brains continuously rewire themselves through neuroplasticity, our approach to coaching must evolve to meet these new challenges.

> *"Integration is the key to healing, growth, and transformation—it's how we connect all aspects of our being to navigate life's complexities with resilience and grace."*
>
> -Dan Siegel

My work is built on neuroscience, holistic principles, and deep systemic awareness. I walk beside my clients as they rewrite their own narratives, and their neural maps—guiding them like a seasoned navigator, or tour guide, charting a course through uncharted waters, helping them break free from the limits they once believed were fixed, and loving themselves back to wholeness. At its heart, transformation isn't about discovering a single, static answer—it's about learning to dance with the ever-changing rhythms of life with wisdom, coherence, confidence, courage, connection curiosity and compassion.

If you are interested in exploring the emerging coaching evolution – As a client – or as an experienced coach – I would love to support you through the **bwise Coaching Academy,** launching in 2025. We work in partnership with the world leading psychometric tool (**wise**), which offers the only valid and reliable way to determine which intelligence you are using in decision making.

The **bwise Coaching Academy** trains coaches to offer excellence in this new style of coaching service provision, and links suitably qualified coaches to clients, who are ready to get real about change.

If you are an existing coach, or if you are new to coaching and want to develop the skills to work at this level, reach out and ask about our courses at the **bwise Coaching Academy**.

It would be my pleasure to support you.

https://linktr.ee/drsuzannehenwood

*Matt represents a composite of many clients I have coached in recent years.

CHAPTER 4
Ceremonial Coaching
By Shelly Bean

Unlocking Deeper Transformation Through the Power of Ritual

Do you have a ritual so essential, so woven into your being, that skipping it feels unthinkable?

- Lighting a candle before taking a bath—because the spirits of relaxation deserve a proper welcome.
- Putting on that one outfit—the one that makes you feel like a rockstar—before a big client call.
- Whispering a prayer under your breath before checking your bank balance.
- That song you blast before stepping out into the world, like an

armour woven from bass and lyrics.
- Pressing a lipstick kiss onto the mirror before a date—sealing your own approval first.

Rituals are more than habits; they are everyday spells charged with intention that shape how we move through life. In my coaching, rituals become the keys to rewriting tired narratives, dissolving self-imposed limits, and embodying abundance as if it were your birthright (because it is).

Let me show you how.

How did we get here?

The technologies and techniques we broadly refer to as coaching have advanced significantly in a relatively short period. By observing how humans think, feel, and behave, as well as their hopes, dreams, and fears, we've identified methods for creating personal transformation, promoting healing, and achieving excellence.

In fact, humankind has always sought ways to develop and grow. So, what did we do before coaching? We used elaborate ceremonial rituals and supernatural metaphors to achieve these peak states. We have been searching for answers beyond what we can see and calling on higher powers to help us evolve and transform since the beginning of time.

In my practice, I work with clients who don't gel with—and don't need—the intellectual, goal-orientated process of traditional coaching or the relentless cheer of self-help culture. People often come to me burned out and turned off by toxic positivity, looking for something deeper and more meaningful than the pursuit of endless improvement.

I help clients sort out the sticky stuff that most people don't talk about- money, sex and sexuality, relationships that don't fit the 'marriage, mortgage, mortuary 'formula, and all the shame and guilt that go hand in hand with not fitting in. These individuals seek an intangible result, leaving me asking: "Is the SMART process fit for all seekers?"

By infusing my coaching with ceremonial elements, I accelerate my clients' transformation by providing profound emotional, mental, and spiritual benefits. This approach respects the non-physical body that holds their present state and desired, emergent outcomes. It creates an intentional space for individuals to clarify and focus their energy on their desired outcomes, making their dreams feel more tangible.

The engagement of the imagination, emotions, and senses, combined with symbolic elements, deepens the client's connection with their inner resources and universal forces, fostering meaningful engagement with the coaching process.

And yes, I recognise this may not be the typical coaching outline.

What I have found is that the symbolic actions, ingredients, and metaphors used in ceremonial rituals have a unique power to bypass the analytical mind and directly influence the subconscious, helping to release limiting beliefs and reprogram old habits.

What does it mean to work with rituals?

Being in a ritual space helps people to embody and embrace new identities, reinforce new ways of being, and create space and separation from their current reality for lasting change to take root.

Grounding practices cultivate presence, mindfulness, and connection with life, anchoring insights and wisdom. Symbolic acts, such as dressing in meaningful clothing or lighting a candle to connect with a spiritual realm, help clients channel a more resourceful version of themselves and give them answers they might not have found otherwise.

Aligning rituals with natural cycles, such as lunar phases or seasonal changes, invites in the 'co-creative force of the universe' - a term used to describe the power of collective intention and universal energy. This helps clients feel more connected to nature and the rhythms of life, fostering ease and reducing resistance to change.

Incorporating ritual and energetic consciousness into coaching helps clients engage their mind, body and spirit, creating a holistic transformation that feels sustainable and deeply grounded. By blending evidence-based coaching tools such as positive psychology interventions, NLP techniques and Ericksonian Hypnosis with spiritual practices, ritual magic provides a multidimensional approach to personal growth and healing, opening the door to profound and lasting transformation.

So, what is a ritual?

A ritual is a series of symbolic actions - such as breath, prayer, meditation, movement and visualisation - performed with a specific outcome in mind. Participants incorporate objects that have become personally significant or sacred, such as candles, water, crystals and smoke, to enhance the ritual's meaning and impact. In many cultural and spiritual contexts, certain rituals are believed to have the power to create tangible change within the individual and in their external world.

Ritual behaviour is with us from our first breath and stays with us until beyond our last. Throughout our lives, we are immersed in customs that shape our interactions with our families, friends, communities, and the world around us. We shake hands, exchange hugs, and offer lingering farewells—everyday actions rooted in ancient social norms and often performed unconsciously. These rituals may seem ordinary and unimportant, but they help us establish mutual understanding, foster a sense of belonging, and deepen relationships.

Throughout history and across many cultures, rituals have marked significant life transitions. The birth of a child is celebrated with welcoming and naming ceremonies, baptisms, or other cultural rites. As children grow, we honour their passage into adulthood. Examples include Christian confirmation, Jewish bat or bar mitzvah, the Sikh tradition of receiving the turban, and the various indigenous coming-of-age rituals celebrated worldwide today.

As we move into adulthood, graduation ceremonies, complete with symbolic robes, hats and diplomas, marriage ceremonies, and baby showers, are ritualistic celebrations of personal milestones. Even death is met with rituals of comfort in grief and displays of solidarity and love.

Rituals have existed in diverse human societies throughout history, which suggests their essential role in providing meaning, shaping identity, and facilitating transformation. This primal, deeply human behaviour is relevant to coaching because it taps into the psychological, emotional, and spiritual elements that support growth and change. Rituals create a sense of sacred space and energetic possibility, allowing people to step out of ordinary consciousness, invite a sense of playfulness, and engage more thoroughly with their intentions.

Incorporating ritual elements into coaching can enhance the client's experience by giving them a tangible, physical component to their transformation - walking through a doorway to mark the transition from the old self to the new, for example - solidifying new behaviours and beliefs. The combination of intentional, symbolic actions and the supportive guidance of coaching can help even the most 'stuck 'clients move through life with greater purpose, clarity and empowerment.

How do you do it?

At the heart of ritual work is intention at its most raw and powerful. Intention is more than merely hoping or making wishes—setting an intention is to make a set of deliberate choices about how we will think, feel, and act. Unlike unconscious 'autopilot' behaviours, the elements and steps in a ritual are consciously chosen and enacted with purpose and the belief that they will create meaningful change. All religious, spiritual, and secular rituals require intentional energy alignment toward a specific outcome.

Unlike habits, for example, nail-biting, falling into social media scroll holes, which can be performed unconsciously and often develop accidentally to soothe or satisfy a need, rituals require presence and active engagement. The words, objects, symbols, and gestures that make up the ritual are carefully chosen to support the desired outcome, which makes rituals far more potent than passive routines.

The first step to creating a meaningful, effective ritual is to clarify the intention by asking both the thinking, head brain: what transformation or change do I want to make - and the feeling, values driven heart intelligence: what is my desired outcome? It could be to attract abundance, release limiting beliefs, or navigate a life transition, which is the ritual's anchor.

Once we have a clear intention, the next step is to choose elements that align with the desired outcome. Ritual work is powerful because it speaks in symbols, metaphors and sensory engagement - the narrative of the subconscious and the nervous system. Choosing meaningful and symbolic ingredients helps deepen the impact and personalise the ritual and makes it more likely the change will 'stick'. Incorporating meaningful objects - plants to symbolise growth, crystals for grounding, mirrors to symbolise self-reflection - or actions, such as lighting a candle or praying to connect with a higher power, brings a tangible element to the coaching session. These physical objects and actions bridge the client's current reality and their dream, helping anchor the change.

Like all good coaching sessions, a ritual is more effective with a clear beginning, middle and end. Opening the ritual might involve lighting a candle to signify the entrance into non-ordinary space, grounding techniques like coherent breathing or guided meditation to shift into a more focused state, and - depending on the client's beliefs - calling on guides, higher powers or ancestral energies to assist with the transformation. The heart of the ritual is symbolic action - performing specific movements like EFT tapping or shaking to release energy, writing down fears and releasing them by destroying the paper, or simply sitting in a power pose while meditating on the desired outcome.

The end of the ritual is equally important as it closes the energetic space, signifying to the participant's subconscious that 'it is done.' This usually involves expressing gratitude, sealing the intention with a gesture or specific word, and extinguishing the candle to mark completion.

Designing a physical space for ritual work enhances its transformation and impact. A carefully curated environment signals to the nervous system that something meaningful is happening and that it is safe to engage fully. This space doesn't need to be large or elaborate—a quiet corner decorated with meaningful objects and a comfortable chair is enough to prepare the mind and transform the atmosphere.

Aligning rituals with the natural rhythms of life and the planet can also influence their transformational power. Lunar cycles, seasonal changes, and personal milestones can set the scene and enhance the ritual's effectiveness. For example, a ritual for new beginnings may feel more potent when aligned with the new moon, while a release ritual is better aligned with the waning moon or the end of the year.

Any ritual requires the presence and engagement of the participants. While routines and habits can be performed without attention, rituals require mindfulness and connection with the multiple intelligences of the client's heart and body. This conscious involvement allows ritual work to bypass surface-level thinking, reach deeper subconscious and energetic layers, and draw on connections and wisdom from beyond the individual.

Guiding clients through carefully crafted rituals offers them an opportunity to literally 'make 'change in their physical cells and neural pathways, and in a way that is both metaphorical and grounded in action. Rituals can transform intention into action and action into lasting transformation.

How is that useful in coaching?

As we have already explored, incorporating ritual elements into coaching is a dynamic way to strengthen intention, create a safe, energetic space, and facilitate profound change.

Rituals help clients embody their transformation by taking abstract intentions and giving them deliberate, purposeful actions. Rituals are physical manifestations of intent, bridging the gap between thought and behaviour, internal desires and external realities. Using rituals in coaching helps clients access inner resources, navigate transitions, and deepen the coach-client relationship.

Intentionally stepping out of ordinary reality and into the framework of ritual channels energy and attention toward a specific outcome. For example, a client struggling with self-doubt might engage in a ritual where they smash a symbolic object to symbolise breaking free from old patterns – a meaningful action that not only symbolises letting go but also uses metaphor to embed the intention into their subconscious and nervous system.

Rituals also facilitate a shift into a non-ordinary state of consciousness or self-awareness, where clients can access insights, inner and outer wisdom and creativity that are often inaccessible from their everyday way of being. These altered states can be achieved through techniques like hypnosis, guided visualisations, somatic movements or breathwork, helping the client to 'get out of their head', hear their body's intelligence and access wisdom beyond themselves. In this expansive, playful state, clients can find solutions, process emotions and envision possibilities without getting stuck in the limiting patterns of how they usually think and behave.

Most importantly, rituals in coaching cultivate a stronger connection between coach and client, fostering a sense of community and deepening trust. The coach becomes more than a facilitator—they become a trusted collaborator and privileged witness to their client's transformation.

The relational dynamic is the 'secret sauce' in any partnership, and the shared experience of crafting and performing rituals together enhances the client's sense of being seen, supported and understood by their coach. Being actively involved in designing the ritual gives the client an even greater sense of safety and choice, reminding them they have the resources and power to change their situation. In group settings, adding ritual or ceremonial elements amplifies this effect by tapping into collective energy, shared purpose and belonging, which allows the group to process emotions together, access collective wisdom and connect with a supportive community.

Intentional rituals help clients access and anchor new identities and behaviours. Like how athletes mentally rehearse their win before it happens, coaching rituals help clients embody their desired identity. For instance, a client ending a toxic relationship may perform a ritual where they cut a cord while affirming, "I release this attachment," and then use the energy created by the ritual to visualise or mentally rehearse their newfound freedom and independence. This symbolic, embodied and future-focused act reinforces the emotional shift, making the new identity more accessible and real.

By blending the principles of intentionality, playfulness, symbolism, and deliberate action, rituals help align a client's inner world with their outer goals in a way that bypasses the gatekeeping of the conscious mind. They bring a tangible, tactile element to what is often a change that clients need to 'wait and see.' Rituals empower clients by physically engaging them in holistic, transformative change and providing tools they can use beyond the coaching session and into their daily lives.

How I use ritual in my coaching practice

Energetic consciousness is the foundation of my coaching practice and is intentionally woven into every stage of the client journey.

Rituals allow me to create a grounded and energetically aligned environment where clients can fully engage in their personal growth. Of course, this approach is always implemented with the client's full permission and guided by their spiritual beliefs – or lack thereof. It makes no difference whether clients come to me with specific spiritual beliefs or prefer a secular approach; as a coach and spiritual practitioner, I honour and adapt to their uniqueness, ensuring that ceremonial or ritual use feels authentic and right for them.

The coaching relationship is a ritual in itself, as it is an intentional, co-created transformational space. We begin with an opening ceremony to mark the start of our work together and energetically step into the space for connection, trust and vulnerability. Breath-work, guided visualisation or hypnosis, expressing intentions for our time together, and energetically charging a symbolic object, which I encourage my clients to keep as an anchor for their transformation.

Doing this allows the client to surrender to the coaching process and suspend any disbelief they may have in their ability to change, allowing them to step fully into the process. When the coaching relationship ends, I facilitate a closing ceremony to honour our time together and energetically seal the space. The most essential function of the closing ceremony is for the client to transfer power back to themselves - so they can see that they now have the resources and skills to create change by themselves. This also transmutes the coaching relationship into whatever form it naturally takes, whether that's a continued connection, a period of reflection or complete closure - whatever the client needs to support their integration and forward movement.

Because my coaching practices are 100% online, energy work and ritual allow me to bridge physical distance and create a powerful, shared, energetic space.

The virtual setting means I can design a physical environment that supports my presence and focus without having to 'tone it down' or risk making my clients uncomfortable with an atmosphere or decor that isn't to their taste. Likewise, clients can create an environment that works for them, with the bonus of being in their own homes - I'm convinced people can change more rapidly and thoroughly when sitting in their favourite chair. It is, however, essential to acknowledge that not every home is a safe space for transformation - some homes are filled with stress, distractions, or even triggers that make deep work more challenging.

In these instances, we explore ways to create a temporary sanctuary within their space—designating a specific corner or using noise-cancelling headphones to create a sense of separation. If that's not possible, they might benefit from attending sessions in an alternate environment where they feel safer and more at ease, such as a quiet park or a trusted friend's home. The key is creating conditions that encourage profound shifts and lasting integration. When the session ends, the client can linger and let the changes integrate rather than getting into a car and unravelling their relaxation in traffic.

Each coaching session begins and ends in the same loosely structured way - it is structured to provide consistency and safety for the client's nervous system and is deliberately loose to allow for the natural wonkiness that comes with being human.

The beauty of coaching humans lies in the mystery of what may unfold. By embracing flexibility within the structure, we grant clients permission to be imperfect, to welcome the unexpected, and to find joy in surprise. In doing so, we send a powerful signal—to both mind and body—that they are held in a space of safety, support, and infinite possibility.

Incorporating ritual elements into coaching with mindfulness and consent allows me to create a dynamic and sacred space. This intentional approach helps clients feel safe and seen. It fosters a deeper connection between coach and client and encourages profound, energetically supported, practically grounded shifts.

In Conclusion

Incorporating rituals into coaching allows us to meet our clients at the intersection of their internal desires and external realities. Rituals empower clients to heal past hurts, connect with their most profound wisdom, and embrace new ways of being. These symbolic practices engage the mind, body, and spirit and, if the client chooses, connect with the broader universe. They create a holistic and sustainable transformation while establishing a safe space for vulnerability and reflection, allowing clients to navigate transitions with clarity and confidence.

In my coaching practice, rituals are essential to transcending traditional methods. They facilitate deep, energetic alignment and allow my client and me to bridge the gap of physical distance that comes with being an entirely online practice. By combining the symbolic richness of magic and ritual with evidence-based coaching modalities, I create a multidimensional approach that supports each client's beliefs and unique humanness. Clients feel supported, inspired to embrace lasting transformation, and empowered to create change for themselves long after the coaching relationship has ended.

Rituals are ancient whispers of transformation, echoing the very essence of modern coaching—our profound capacity for change. Growth isn't just a mental shift; it's an embodied journey, a dance between intention and action. When woven into coaching, rituals elevate the experience from a structured process to a sacred alchemy—empowering clients to rewrite their narratives, forge deeper connections with life, and step unapologetically into their most authentic selves.

Are You Ready to Transform?

Rituals have the power to unlock deep transformation, shifting not just what you do but who you *become*. If you feel called to a coaching experience that goes beyond logic and linear progress—one that taps into the unseen, the symbolic, and the sacred—let's connect.

I work with seekers, rebels, and visionaries who crave more than mindset shifts; they desire soul-level transformation. Through intentional ceremony, energy work, and subconscious rewiring, we dissolve what's holding you back and weave new possibilities into your reality.

This is not traditional coaching. It's ceremonial coaching—where transformation is not just discussed, but embodied.

If you're ready to break free from old patterns, claim your power, and create a life aligned with your deepest truth, let's talk.

COACHING REIMAGINED Expanding Human Potential

https://linktr.ee/Shellybean.co

CHAPTER 5
Loving Back to Wholeness
By Jean de Bruyne

From The Inside Out – Take 2

Alas, alack the clocks have moved forward, YET AGAIN!

A ticking and a tocking life moments away.

What will I be in this moment? My story or myself?

I'm lulled into nothingness between these two states by a soporific wave.

NOTHINGNESS – where all things come.

Today, my psyche, cajoles, call softly, urging the discovery of my YEARNINGS.

COACHING REIMAGINED Expanding Human Potential

I breathe deeply and plunge down into my depths, meeting parts of ME that I had ignored, tolerated, disliked even.

We begin the re-acquaintance like shy teenagers, each tentative about making the first move.

...One does, and the rest respond in this dance of connectivity.

Like jewels splashing forth, blessed are we all as we stand at the portal of this intra psychic transformation.

THE END

Jean de Bruyne
Auckland, New Zealand
Dec 2008

Getting Into It

Everyone who is interested in personal or professional growth, is typically filled with hope and aspiration, and also perhaps with some dread as to what can of worms they might be opening. Sometimes people put their heads in the sand in the hope that by not paying attention it will cause the situation giving them pain or a niggle to go away. Alas, this never happens, in my observation. The lessons merely repeat themselves and each time there is a re-presentation, the lesson intensifies, as if to say, "give close and thoughtful attention." Humans are self-patterning machines, and our psyche is conservation minded.

There is a level of intrigue in all questers and what we want is to be witnessed and validated on our journey. Whilst we are on that trajectory, to be offered pointers or new information that we can consider and then meld with what we already know, is a pathway that is wide open to invitation. This then allows us to continue navigating our chosen path with increased self-efficacy. In so doing, stormy choppy weather encountered at a futurist time becomes less fearful as we have already begun the learning process of captaining our own ship.

Coming from a mixed ethnic background and work experience in other cultures, has given me an insightful opportunity into how this perspective influences us, including myself, in a socio-cultural or organisational context. What I attempt to bring to a situation is a deeper and wider perspective to others' thoughts and emotions. It is an invitation in leading others to use their own knowing, experience and skill in how they view themselves, their world, the situation at hand and the outcome they are after. It is an inherent belief that we all have it, it's just that sometimes it's hard to hear/see/feel it, when the internal churn has the loudest and biggest claim on our attention.

There are 3 core ideas, presented in this chapter that underpin the way that I practice.

> 1) The psychic energy within all of us is transformable and cannot be destroyed.
> 2) Early life influences play an important part in who we are and who we want to be in the world.
> and
> 3) The cultural context that we grew up in exerts an indomitable force

When all three land on fertile ground for the conscious betterment of the individual, we have the first inklings of what Carl Jung, the famous Swiss psychiatrist, psychotherapist and psychologist, referred to as "giving birth to Self."

The Power of Our Psychic Energy

According to the various experts in the field of psychology, across the eons, there is much psychic energy within all of us. It is not something that we can make go away or destroy. What is key is how we align our internal selves to the external demands of our physical reality, because it is always the Internal Self that ultimately has the upper hand, no matter how polished the external veneer might look to others and even ourselves. As someone once said, "Our internal landscape determines how we experience the external world."

Too much of our old, or even current ways of thinking, convinced us that in order to achieve and be successful, even, if only to ourselves, we could learn new things, plan and control things. The reality is that we are always dealing with constantly moving, and in many cases, unpredictable, parts to the equation.

In many ways, it is how we become more conscious in the choices, not decisions, that we make, so that life "unfolds" for us, as oppose to "unravels." When we learn to discern the difference between making a choice versus making a decision, we begin navigating our world on the path to freedom.

Decisions are usually intellectual head brain activities allowing us to neatly map out the pros and cons of a situation, organising and structuring the information gathered in a rather logical, maybe even formulaic way that allows us to use our logic and analytical skills, eventually leading to an answer that "makes sense" to us. The rationalisation process is a key attribute that is called upon in decision making.

When a decision goes well for us, our chests puff out with pride because we made a clever decision that has paid off. If it does not fall to our favour, then we begin to distance ourselves citing all sorts of reasons why the decision did not deliver the anticipated outcome. Sometimes, our decision making is down to a level of deciding between two evils, adding to our already torturous dilemma. And instead of alleviating the pain and suffering it could potentially have added to it.

Because of the way we are built as humans, the level of predictability in our lives is something that we highly cherish. This makes decision making heavily reliant on our past, and our memories which tend to not always be as reliable nor consistent as we might like them to be. We are also known to recall our stories differently depending on who we are talking to and their own persuasions. This, known as "audience-turning effect," further confuses how we make decisions.

Choices on the other hand, do not demand this intellectual prowess. The individual chooses, because that is what they are drawn to. It is an inner prompting, most likely driven by a set of beliefs that drive our values which then causes us to act in a certain way. This pats the individual to move in a specific direction, even when there is no logical reason or outcome that can be easily articulated.

In this situation, the individual is expressing free choice and as such has no one or no external situation to blame if something does not transpire according to plan. If the choice pans out, then they have equal claim to be the hero to their own story.

So, in many ways, making a choice is more of a heart driven activity allowing the unique expression of Self and in so doing, it takes away the blame mentality that we can all have when something does not go our way.

We Do What We Know - Early Life Influences

If we reflect on the short creative writing piece that opened this chapter, we can intuitively see that who we think we are, has generally been shaped when we were very young. As part of our growing up, we adopted certain roles and strategies in order to survive, even in the most "perfect" of all families. This writing was done when I gained my own insight after delving deeper into myself.

This observation was made by Virginia Satir, the well-known 20th century psychotherapist who is often referred to as the pioneer of family therapy. She coined the phrase "The family is the 'factory' where people are made."

This pattern continues repeating into adulthood and it is thus no surprise to see this play out in organisational life, even when people claim, till they are blue in face, that who and what they are at home is definitely left at home when they turn up for work. Our unconscious mind is always at work. The invitation to all of us to grow the conscious part of our psyche, and to live a life that is more purposeful.

The question then becomes, "How do I navigate all this? How do I ride the wave, know which one to catch, when to get off and catch the next one? or just STOP for a period of reflection, recalibration and realignment!"

The answer to this is "congruency" but to get there requires much intrepid journeying, heading butting, meeting and slaying our demons or in some cases co-existing with them, whilst we hold ourselves in loving grace believing in our capability of rising each time we are tripped up by our shadow.

Our Cultural Framework

The first and prime psychological need we all have is to "belong." When we know our tribe and where we fit in, then only can we attempt the journey of getting ahead and finally making sense of the world.

The connection between societal culture and personal culture is also crucial. Each of us is shaped by the society we belong to, yet we also carry with us the nuances of our personal upbringing and experiences. When we become aware of both influences, it can help us navigate the tensions between individual desires and collective expectations. In this way, we may be able to make more authentic choices—moving through life with a sense of purpose and awareness, without feeling constrained by rigid societal norms or the pressures of constant striving.

Most of us reading this chapter have attained knowledge - learnt and regurgitated at the appropriate times to ultimately have the label of some degree of competence given to us. The level of what we know and our ability to predict gives us a degree of comfort, even if, at times, it could be misguided. This, however, bolsters a perceived level of confidence enabling us to do something.

COACHING REIMAGINED Expanding Human Potential

Cultures across the global have an infinite wisdom that cuts across space and time. Many of us have forgotten this and insist on adopting what is currently the most fashionable model, usually external to us, as opposed to going in to conquer this last frontier of humankind – going inwards.

It's a truly daunting thought to consider that we might discover even better answers by setting aside everything we currently know and stepping into the unknown. The very structures we build for self-protection, which are meant to keep us safe, often end up blocking the path to our own transformation. We become so attached to our familiar ways of thinking and living that we can inadvertently keep ourselves from growing. However, the deeper understanding we're gaining is that healing, especially on a psychological level, requires us to let go of our tight grip on certainty and take on the role of captain in navigating the uncertain and sometimes treacherous waters of life. This journey asks us to embrace vulnerability and the unknown, rather than shying away from it.

The Sufis have a beautiful way of describing this process. They refer to these moments as "states of grace," which they view as distinct from the awareness we normally acquire through conscious effort in our day-to-day lives. States of grace, in this sense, are fleeting and often intangible, yet they hold tremendous value. What disappears may hold just as much significance as what remains because it can open us to entirely new perspectives or loosen the knots we've tied ourselves into in the present moment. This shift in perspective is what allows us to expand our capacity for growth and understanding.

The teachings of the Sufis encourage us to embrace life with a spirit of "Curiosity & Wonder – The Wisdom in Not Knowing." Rather than focusing on gathering more facts or information to solve our problems, they invite us to look inward and deepen our understanding of ourselves on a profound level. This introspective journey is not about finding neat, packaged answers, but about developing the wisdom to make choices rooted in inner knowing, rather than reacting out of habit or relying on outdated patterns. By aligning with this approach, we open ourselves to making more intentional, growth-oriented decisions, rather than seeking temporary relief or sticking to old strategies. The Sufi path shows us that by being open to the unknown, we unlock an entirely different, more expansive way of living.

The Maori, in New Zealand have a heart-warming and profound concept. The phrase "Mā te wā e whakakite ngā hua o āu mahi nunui. "Te wā " captures the idea that time is cyclical and everything has its season. It's not just a reflection of natural seasons, but also a guiding principle for personal growth, change, and understanding. The notion that "time will reveal the fruits of your many deeds" is a reminder of the long-term impact of our actions and encourages patience and perseverance.

Incorporating such wisdom into practice, especially in a culture with a strong connection to its history and ancestral teachings, offers a meaningful perspective. The renaissance of Māori culture and the renewed emphasis on Te Tiriti o Waitangi have made these traditional concepts more accessible, not just to Māori but to everyone in Aotearoa New Zealand, helping to bridge understanding and respect across communities.

"Wei wu wei" is another fascinating and profound concept that touches on the balance between action and non-action. It calls for an openness to what comes next, rather than a rigid focus on pre-determined outcomes – a strategy that many of us have been schooled in and have kept. It invites us to consider that some of life's most valuable outcomes, like happiness or love, often arise when we stop forcing them and instead allow them to unfold naturally. This philosophy suggests that sometimes the best way to "achieve" something is not through direct, forceful effort, but by aligning with the flow of life, allowing things to emerge without excessive interference.

The use of parables and stories also speaks to us in such a symbolic way that it has direct connection with our psyche, minimising the influence of language and its ability to be twisted to fit our current narration of our situation.

In summary, we all play and juggle multiple roles in our lives. Not all are complementary, some could be in conflict. Let us recognise this and bring our differing parts to a collective whole which then allows us our unique expression of self.

"A Journey of A 1000 Steps Begins with The First One."

In a quiet moment pick a few of these introspective and reflective pointers below. These pointers could be helpful for gaining insight into your thoughts and feelings about your life dynamics and expectation. Irrespective of whether you take on a solely career focus or a broader life perspective, what it invites you to do is to open yourself and enter deep conversation.

1. **Feelings about your job expectations**: This question aims to help you explore whether your expectations are realistic, and how they align with your current emotional state. It can uncover any feelings of stress, satisfaction, frustration, or motivation.

2. **Unit members' well-being**: Listening to your unit can give you valuable insights into their moods, concerns, and energy, and in turn tell you something about yourself. This question encourages empathy and awareness, helping you understand what might be going on with them, beyond just what they say.

3. **Relationships within the unit**: Looking at interpersonal dynamics allows you to gauge how well members are getting along and if there are any underlying tensions, conflicts, or synergies that need attention.

4. **Making sense of observed behaviours**: This is about interpreting both verbal and non-verbal cues to better understand the meaning behind what you've seen or heard. It's about gathering context and ensuring accurate perception. Perception is our reality

5. **Interpreting a unit member's words**: Sometimes the way someone speaks can carry deeper meaning. This question asks you to look beyond surface-level communication and think about the motives, emotions, or concerns driving those words.

6. **Letting go of expectations**: It encourages introspection about

whether you're holding on to something that no longer serves you, and whether you're open to change.

7. **The role of expectations in your work/life**: This asks you to assess how your expectations impact your actions, attitude, and decisions in the workplace. It can help identify if your expectations are fuelling progress or creating frustration.

8. **Benefit of expectations**: What does holding onto these expectations bring to you, in terms of your own growth, success, or sense of fulfilment?

9. **Hope for something different**: What change are you hoping to see in the future? This taps into aspirations and the desire for improvement, whether it's for yourself or the unit as a whole.

10. **Unit member's unmet needs**: Understanding what someone else might have hoped for, and didn't get, can foster empathy and help you improve communication and support.

11. **Deep desire or core need**: This is about what you fundamentally want—whether it's recognition, growth, respect, or balance. It's a clarifying question that distils the essence of your goals or values.

12. **Work relationship desires**: What specific outcomes do you want from your interactions with colleagues? This question

    examines how you define success in work relationships.

13. **Cost of your expectations**: What are the sacrifices or downsides associated with your current expectations? Are they manageable, or are they hindering your growth or well-being?

14. **Changes for fulfilment**: This is about identifying the specific changes you need to make, either personally or within the unit, to achieve the outcomes you truly desire.

Final Words

"In life, we have no control but we have CHOICE about the interpretations that we give to what happens to us and who we want to be in the world. When we know this, we have FREEDOM."

and

"Of course I talk to myself. At times I need EXPERT ADVICE."

Practising as a Registered Psychologist in the Industrial/Organisational scope, I was conferred Fellow status by my professional society for my advanced knowledge and contribution to this field for organising and developing the work of others in New Zealand.

My eclectic style is uniquely shaped by my exposure to many different societies and sectors within each.

Connect with me via my email or website

Email: jean@qedservices.co.nz

Website: www.qedservices.co.nz

CHAPTER 6
The Transformative power to being wholeheartedly yourself
By Angèle Te Baerts – Fleurkens

"It's not about feeling better, it's about getting better at feeling."

- Dr. Gabor Maté

Have you ever felt lost, even in a familiar place?

Imagine playing in a sun-drenched cornfield maze, trying to find the others and for a way out. Growing up in a rural setting, this was a very familiar playfield to me. But also often I felt lost, searching for connection and only finding the isolating rustle of towering stalks. My normal childhood masked the inner turmoil of a highly sensitive person yearning for harmony.

In environments where emotions and feelings were often unspoken and hierarchical structures dominated, I adapted by prioritizing others' needs above my own, striving to please, and setting high standards. This constant shape-shifting distanced me from my authentic self.

Years later, my journey of personal development has been about reclaiming that lost sense of self, learning to feel—truly feel—without judgment or fear. Alexia Chellun's "Allowing me to be me" beautifully captures this path.

It's tough to be authentic when the world keeps telling you to conform. I know, I've been there. Yet, through these challenges, I've learned that the real magic happens when you embrace who you truly are. Wholehearted living is about having the courage to be vulnerable, standing strong in your values, and expressing your unique self.

The Transformative Power of Authenticity: Unveiling Your True Self

In today's fast-paced world, sometimes described as BANI (brutal, anxious, non-linear, and incomprehensible), where change is constant, it's easy to lose touch with who we truly are. Bombarded by societal expectations and unpredictable challenges, we often build protective layers around our core identity, obscuring our essence.

But what does it mean to be our "true self?" This question has intrigued thinkers, spiritual leaders, and psychologists for ages. Rather than a fixed state, authenticity is a fluid, evolving journey. The belief in a singular, unchangeable identity can actually hold us back. Instead, embracing our dynamic nature allows us to grow, integrate new experiences, and adapt to life's challenges.

A powerful metaphor for this journey is the story of the golden Buddha. In 13th-century Thailand, a massive clay Buddha was found to conceal a solid gold core beneath its protective layer. This golden Buddha had been hidden for centuries to protect it from invading armies. Similarly, our authentic selves often become buried beneath societal conditioning, fears, and learned behaviours. Over time, these layers obscure our inner brilliance, but they never erase it.

The process of revealing our true self isn't about uncovering a static identity—it's about peeling back these layers with awareness, curiosity, and courage. As we reconnect with our true essence, we become more resilient, make choices aligned with our values, and foster deeper connections. This journey is not about finding something lost; it is about revealing the potential that has always been within us.

Embodied Wisdom and the Golden Buddha Heart: A Journey to Wholehearted Living

In our quest for authenticity, we often seek answers externally or get lost in overthinking, chasing validation instead of true self-discovery. Yet, one of the most profound sources of wisdom lies within our own bodies. This concept, known as embodied wisdom, recognizes the deep connection between mind and body. Our physical state shapes our thoughts and emotions, just as our thoughts influence our physical well-being.

Embodied coaching recognizes and embraces this inter-connectedness, integrating mind, body, and spirit to foster self-awareness, personal growth, and authentic living. By tuning into the body's signals, we access a source of insight essential for transformation and overall well-being.

In practice, embodied coaching involves tapping into our innate intelligence by paying attention to our body's signals, sensations, emotions, and intuition. This might include somatic awareness exercises, guided movement or breath work. Embodied wisdom manifests as the whisper of your gut instinct, the flutter in your chest when you're on the right path, the tension in your shoulders when you're not living your truth. It's a symphony of sensations, emotions, and intuitions that have been playing in the background of your life, waiting for you to listen.

Embodied coaching in personal development has emerged as a powerful approach to uncovering our authentic selves. This method recognizes that wisdom resides not just in our minds, but in the entirety of our being. It views our true self not as a fixed entity to find, but as a dynamic and evolving essence, ready to be embraced.

The Golden Heart: Our core essence

As we delve deeper into embodied wisdom, we encounter the concept of the "golden heart" or "quantum heart" – a center of wisdom and authenticity within us. Throughout history, cultures have recognized the heart as more than just a physical organ. The ancient Greeks spoke of 'kardia,' the Sufis of 'qalb,' and Latin traditions of 'cor'—all referring to the heart not just as a biological pump, but as the seat of the soul, divine wisdom, and the center of feelings and intellect. Today, we find ourselves revisiting these ancient wisdoms through the lens of quantum science, speaking of the 'quantum heart,' 'cosmic heart,' 'golden heart' or 'golden essence.' And which I will refer to as 'golden (Buddha) heart' or 'golden essence.'

The concept of the golden heart aligns beautifully with the story of the golden Buddha, whose true nature was hidden beneath layers of protective clay. Similarly, our own golden essence often lies concealed beneath layers of conditioning, fear, and societal expectations.

The heart can be viewed as our radiant core, a gateway to our intrinsic wisdom and golden essence. It's the seat of our intuition, a wellspring of compassion. And the heart also functions as a powerhouse, emitting an electromagnetic field that extends far beyond our physical form. Research from the HeartMath Institute has revealed that this field is approximately 60 times stronger in amplitude than that of the brain, radiating outwards, and interacting with the world around us.

More fascinatingly, it's believed to transmit emotional and intuitive information, creating a more coherent field when we experience positive emotions. Some researchers even propose that through these fields, our hearts can communicate with each other and with the Earth's magnetic field, suggesting a profound interconnectedness.

Embodied wisdom is the intuitive knowledge that resides in every cell of our being, with the heart acting as an important interpreter. This wisdom manifests as intuition, emotional intelligence, coherence (the alignment of our physical, mental, and emotional systems), and resilience. In embodied coaching, we learn to listen to and trust these bodily signals.

Each day presents new opportunities to listen more deeply, act more authentically, and fully embody one's true self. By embracing the quantum nature of our heart and its embodied wisdom, we can experience a life of authenticity, deep connection, expressing our unique abilities, and finding greater purpose and fulfilment in life.

Your 'Golden Buddha' within, is always present, waiting to shine forth in all its radiance. As we continue to explore and apply these concepts, we unlock the potential for a more vibrant, authentic, and wholehearted way of living.

Navigating the shadows: Obstacles on the Path to Wholehearted Living

As we embark on the journey of embodied living and embracing our authentic selves, we inevitably encounter obstacles that challenge our progress. These barriers, often deeply ingrained in our psyche and behaviour patterns, can make it challenging to fully express our true nature. There are numerous and varied obstacles, which may include:

Limiting beliefs

Like the clay-covered Buddha, we all have a core of pure, authentic brilliance within us. However, over time, we accumulate layers that obscure our true essence.

As we journey through life, we collect a myriad of experiences that shape our beliefs, habits, and defence mechanisms. These layers form a complex tapestry of identity, influenced by childhood experiences, family dynamics, societal expectations, cultural norms, traumatic events, and our educational and professional environments. These layers become our limiting beliefs – the silent whispers that tell us we're not good enough, smart enough, not deserving happiness, or telling us we are not worthy enough to pursue our dreams or express our genuine selves. Each of these factors contributes to the persona we present to the world, often obscuring what we might consider our authentic nature.

Inner Attitude & Saboteurs

Our inner attitude plays a crucial role in reinforcing or challenging limitations. Shaped by our experiences, it forms our worldview, perception of others, and self-image. If early experiences led to the belief that the world is dangerous, people are untrustworthy, or we are unworthy, these impressions solidify into a fixed inner narrative: *The world is unsafe. People are threatening. I am not valuable.*

This mindset influences how we perceive, behave, and interact with the world. A rigid belief in unchangeable abilities creates invisible barriers, hindering risk-taking, growth, and self-discovery. Shifting this perspective is key to unlocking our true potential.

Our inner saboteurs are perhaps the most insidious of all – those critical voices in our heads that undermine our efforts and sow seeds of doubt. These saboteurs come in many forms: the Judge who constantly criticizes, the Perfectionist who paralyzes us with unrealistic standards, the Victim who convinces us we're powerless, the Pleaser who prioritizes others' approval over our own needs and desires or the Hyper-achiever who equates self-worth with achievement. Each saboteur serves as a guardian of our comfort zone, keeping us safely tucked away from the vulnerability and potential disappointment that we fear can come with authentic self-expression.

Other factors

External factors also contribute to the layers obscuring our golden Buddha. Societal norms, cultural expectations, and even well-meaning advice from loved ones can all influence how we perceive ourselves and our place in the world. We may find ourselves living according to others' scripts, rather than authoring our own stories.

The fear of judgment and rejection often keeps us from revealing our true selves. We create personas – carefully curated versions of ourselves that we believe will be more acceptable to others. In doing so, we unknowingly distance ourselves from our authentic core, trading genuine connection for the illusion of approval.

Recognizing these obstacles is the first step in moving beyond them. Through embodied practices, we can begin to release these limitations, allowing our 'golden heart' to guide us towards more authentic, more wholehearted living. We allow our inner light to shine, illuminating not only our own lives but also inspiring others to embark on their own journey of self-discovery and authentic expression.

Discovering Your Golden Buddha Within

The path to wholehearted living, to embracing your true self, is a process of uncovering the radiant Buddha hidden within – your inner embodied wisdom, your golden essence. This isn't about flexing your mental muscles or deep philosophical thinking; it's about *feeling* your way through life, connecting with the innate knowledge and wisdom within you. It's about **DISCOVERing** who you truly are.

So, how do we peel back those layers of clay obscuring our golden Buddha nature? How do we move beyond the obstacles that keep us from shining our brightest? The answer lies in embracing a path of self-discovery guided by embodied wisdom.

This journey begins with cultivating awareness, turning your attention inward, and becoming attuned to the subtle sensations, tensions, and energies within your body. Think of it as learning a new language – the language of your heart and of your whole being. Through practices like mindfulness meditation, body scanning, mindful listening, or somatic experiencing we can start listening to and decipher these messages.

As you develop this inward bodily awareness, patterns will emerge. A tightness in your chest may signal that you're not being true to yourself, while an expansive feeling in your abdomen may indicate alignment with your core values. These physical cues act as a compass, guiding you toward wise choices and modes of self-expression.

On the path of discovering, you will take many steps, encountering various experiences that lead you to your radiant, true self. Consider it a journey of stepping stones – each one revealing a new layer of discovery.

The steps of DISCOVERing

- **D**elving (or **D**etecting) and **D**iscomfort: Acknowledge any discomfort and resistance within; transformation begins where we are most uneasy. Where do you feel fear? That feeling of discomfort may indicate or reveal where you are resisting showing your true essence.
- **I**nward Attuning: Turning your awareness within to listen mindfully. Close your eyes, take a few slow breaths, and listen and feel into your body.
- **S**omatic Sensations: Attending to the subtle signals of your body – a tightness in your shoulders, a churning in your stomach, dis-ease in your chest – as a roadmap to your inner truth.
- **C**ompassion & **C**ourage: Approaching yourself and your journey with bravery and unwavering kindness, especially when facing shadows or finding parts of yourself that you have previously rejected. Show yourself the love you would show a dear friend.
- **O**bserving without Judgment: Witnessing your feelings, emotions, thoughts and patterns with detached curiosity, as if you were an objective observer. Allow them to simply be, without labelling them as "good" or "bad."
- **V**alidating & **V**aluing your Experience: Acknowledging the truth and worth of your unique journey, emotions, and perspective. Your experiences, even the painful ones, have shaped you into the person you are today.
- **E**valuate & **E**volve: Reflecting on the lessons you've learned from your experiences and consciously choose to evolve beyond limiting beliefs and behaviours. What can you release? What new patterns can you create?

- **R**elease & **R**adiate: Letting go of what no longer serves you – old stories, toxic relationships, self-limiting beliefs. Releasing the clay and allowing your golden essence to shine forth into the world.

Uncovering your radiant Buddha requires courage to confront and question limiting factors, gradually chipping away at the layers of clay hiding your true nature. As you peel back these layers, you may discover aspects of yourself that surprise you – both light and shadow. Embracing your whole self means acknowledging and integrating all of these parts, rather than selectively hiding those you deem unacceptable. It's about recognizing and embracing the dynamic nature of your being. It's about developing the capacity to be present with your experiences and observing your thoughts and emotions without total identification.

This journey, though sometimes challenging, is deeply rewarding. It's a path toward self-acceptance, authenticity, and the full expression of your unique, golden self. You'll find yourself more present in your body, more connected to your deepest values, and more capable of expressing your authentic self in the world. This is the essence of wholehearted living – being fully embodied, heart-centered, and true to who you really are.

Embodied Wisdom – exercises

Below are my favourite practices, including:
- coherent breathing
- exploring the gremlins of your inner attitude
- and a meditation

Each is designed to encourage introspection and to help you learn and understand more about your patterns and the possibilities for letting your inner light shine.

Coherent Breathing: Harmonizing Heart and Mind

Coherent breathing is a powerful technique that synchronizes breath with heart rate, promoting physiological coherence throughout the body and overall well-being. A steady pace of about six breaths per minute (5 seconds in, 5 seconds out) helps to align heart, mind and emotions.

Coherent breathing regulates heart rate variability, calms the nervous system, and enhances emotional resilience.

Moreover, when combined with positive emotions like gratitude and love, coherent breathing amplifies the heart's electromagnetic field, which extends several feet beyond the body. This expanded field positively influences both personal health and interactions with others.

Regular practice of coherent breathing can help create alignment of mind, body, emotions and spirit through the power of the heart. It can lead to improved stress management, overall emotional resilience, and a heightened sense of well-being. Heart coherence can enhance compassion, intentions and actions, making a daily practice of coherent breathing a wise investment of time.

Exercise: Following are steps in coherent breathing to stimulate positive emotions and heart connection. (For a guided recorded version, scan the QR code.)

Practice coherent breathing at least once a day, for 8-12 minutes. For optimal benefits, you can incorporate it into your routine 2-3 times a day. Consistency is key to experiencing the full benefits of this practice.

- ♥ Sit comfortably in a quiet environment and focus on your breathing. Begin breathing in for 5 seconds and then exhaling for 5 seconds. Maintain this rhythm of breathing consistently…

- ♥ Bring then your focused attention to your heart. You can also place your hand(s) over it for a physical connection.

- ♥ Bring something to mind that evokes feelings of love or gratitude. You can think of something or somebody you feel grateful for or imagine scenarios such as spending time with a loved one, feeling the sun on your face, feeling grateful.

- ♥ Focus on the feelings and amplify the positive emotions you experience. These can be experienced as images, colours, inspiration, sensations, allowing yourself to feel an inner smile.

- ♥ Visualize filling your body fully with these positive feelings, sensations, colours of love and/or gratitude. Expand the feeling to every cell of your being. Giving yourself, your whole being love and gratitude.

- ♥ Then expand this feeling, colour, sensation outward, expanding to your environment, expanding to the world, your extended field of awareness.

Inner attitude / critical mind: Mindful gym

Maybe you're familiar with your critical mind - like a gremlin that pops up at the worst times. It might appear after a chaotic morning: spilling coffee at breakfast, rushing to drive your child to school after they miss the train or bus, arriving late at work, dealing with a crashed computer during an important presentation, or facing a difficult customer.

In these moments, your inner saboteurs take over, feeling frustrations, negative self-talk, anxiety, and stress.

You can reset by doing the following:

- Notice your pattern, your saboteur and say STOP
- Shift your attention with a mindful exercise; take a deep breath; notice the room around you, and become aware of where you're sitting or standing. Then slowly scan the space,
- And while breathing slowly, bring your attention to an object you become aware of. This can be a certain colour, something on the wall or something else, and focus on one aspect of this object. Keep focusing for about 15 seconds.

COACHING REIMAGINED Expanding Human Potential

- Then shift your attention to another object and gaze again for about 15 seconds, and then shift your attention to a third object, gazing for about 15 seconds – noticing what you can notice about each.
- Then, if you like, close your eyes, focus on your slow steady breathing, noticing sensations in your body, drop into your heart, being present in the now and ask your wise heart: what is important now

Limiting beliefs: an exercise

Seeking a deeper connection with your inner wisdom? I have a guided meditation, an invitation for you to step into a transformative journey. You'll be guided through grounding practices, a journey of release, and a sacred space exploration, to gently release what no longer serves you and connect with the wisdom within.

Ready to connect with your true self?
Just scan the QR code and dedicate 15-20 minutes to yourself. Your heart is calling.

The Journey Continues

The journey of self-discovery is about recognizing and embracing the dynamic nature of your being. It's about developing the capacity to be present with your experiences and observing your thoughts and emotions without total identification.

Just as every being is unique, every heart is unique. Your golden Buddha heart holds the key to your individual gifts, purpose, and way of being in the world. Remember, integrating embodied wisdom and golden heart living is a journey, not a destination. Be patient and compassionate with yourself as you cultivate these practices. Each moment of heart-centered awareness is a step towards a more authentic, wholehearted life.

COACHING REIMAGINED Expanding Human Potential

As you continue on this path, you may find that your perception of self and the world around you begins to shift. You might experience a greater sense of interconnectedness, enhanced intuition, and a deeper alignment with your life's purpose. Trust in your inner wisdom and your golden heart, and allow it to guide you towards your highest expression of self.

Is your Golden Heart calling? - Connect with me:

Every heart is unique, a golden Buddha holding the key to *your* individual gifts and purpose.

If you're ready to go beyond coaching, reveal your golden essence, I invite you to connect through: **linktr.ee/angeletebaertsfleurkens**

As a neuro-transformative coach and trainer, specializing in mBIT/mBraining, NLP, and hypnotherapy, I guide you on a transformative journey toward your authentic self. My approach integrates neuroscience, embodied wisdom, multiple intelligences, and heart-centered practices, to break free from limitations, develop self-compassion, and unlock your full potential.

This is the essence of mBlooming: helping you shine your unique inner light, ignite your golden heart's wisdom and live a more authentic, wholehearted life.

Link in section connect with me:

Linktree: linktr.ee/angeletebaertsfleurkens

COACHING REIMAGINED Expanding Human Potential

CHAPTER 7
Coaching for the Soul: A Transpersonal Approach to Bring the Mystical into the Mainstream
By Henrietta Lait

Flag in the Sand

I'm not a one-size-fits-all, cookie-cutter coach. Far from it.

This chapter is an opportunity for me to 'come out of the shadows,' to share how I innately incorporate my version of the 'mystical' elements of energy, spirit, and ancient wisdom, beyond the process of traditional, linear coaching.

It's not fluffy or touchy-feely. I call it 'Pragmatic Woo-woo.' It is intuitively soul-led, flexible and practical.

This wasn't something that happened overnight, it's taken time. This is my personal perspective of coaching, garnered since I began working in the coaching space in 2000.

What I share may seem controversial and *not coaching*. It may challenge your beliefs as a coach. And I'm OK with that. If it sparks conversations, great! There are no specific teachings or fancy models. My aim is to expand your awareness around what is possible for you as a coach and for your clients.

Some of the concepts I share may open doors of possibility for you that take you beyond your current thinking and experience.

I invite you to stay curious and open as you read on and to contemplate and reflect on some of the questions, along the way, in relation to your experience. Notice if, and how, the themes and ideas resonate with you.

Daring to be Different

A theme of my life. Maybe you feel, like I did, an observer of life, on the outside, looking in, figuring out who you are needing to be in any given context. And the sense of not fitting in or knowing where you really belong?

A chameleon who learnt to adapt and be flexible. For some this is innate. And others, it can be exhausting to maintain.

'Is this something you can relate to?'

I wonder, who you are as an individual? As a coach? Are they the same or different? Perhaps you're being who you think you should be to fit in or be accepted by others.

Learning to fully know and understand myself, at my purposeful core, is the difference that makes the difference of who I am today, and why I'm here. I can fully show up as my whole self and for others. In embodying this knowledge, I can support others with their self-exploration and discovery.

COACHING REIMAGINED Expanding Human Potential

'What would it be like to really know who you are, confident in your sense of self and future possibilities?'

My Story

I wear many different hats. Fitting into a box isn't my thing. It never has been. I colour between and beyond any lines.

As an Executive Coach and NLP (neuro linguistic programming) Trainer, there is a specific criteria, framework, syllabus and standard to teach students for certified accreditation.

I'm passionate about teaching and developing coaches when they are starting their journey. My overarching outcome is to inspire and encourage them to become the coach they're meant to be. To intentionally, apply the knowledge I share and embody their learnings. And, with regular reflective practice, to trust themselves and the process.

My Applied Coaching Master of Arts dissertation explored "The Use and Integrative Application of Mind, Body, Spiritual and Energetic Principles and Psychologies to Support Coaches and Enhance Best Practice in Contemporary Coaching." What tools do coaches incorporate that support themselves and their clients?

The way I work in the coaching space has evolved over time.

I've developed and become an embodied coach, from curiosity, life learning, and the breadth and depth of my experience. My authenticity guides my work and purpose.

I continue to learn for myself, from clients and students, supervision and ongoing investment in my continuing personal and professional development. Just because you've been on a coaching course doesn't make you a coach. That's when the journey really begins.

What's your story?

COACHING REIMAGINED Expanding Human Potential

Our own story can have many common or universal themes, and it is totally unique to us. We don't have to be defined by it, unless we choose to be. Neither do we have to be stuck or immobilised by it. From past events or experiences to possible challenges in the 'now' and the unknown and uncertainty of your potential future, your life, as with coaching, is a journey. You are where you are. And that is where I meet you, in our work together. Working with what shows up.

"Yesterday is history. Tomorrow is a mystery. Today is a gift. That's why we call it The Present."

Eleanor Roosevelt

In appreciating the present, we can learn from the past, plan for the future, and in being fully present, heal the wounds of yesterday and lay the foundations for future possibilities.

Your story is a valuable roadmap, a record of your lived experiences. It shows your themes, and patterns as well as highlighting your gifts and talents if you pay attention.

I invite you to consider your story for a moment. 'What are you aware of, or drawn to?'

A New Chapter?

'Who are you, deep down in your soul?'

What would it be like to have clarity around who you truly are? To feel inspired and gain insights regarding your potential purpose? Gain answers to some of the bi 'life' questions you may be pondering. To understand, with a deeper sense of self-knowingness. To Feel acknowledged, validated, seen and heard in a way that enables you to really embody your natural essence and sense of self.

'What difference would it make to have that level of knowing?'

And sometimes, exploration, and the possibility of the unknown, can be scary but also exciting. The potential for discovery… We can explore this together, you don't have to do it on your own or feel alone.

How did I get to where I am today?

It wasn't a straight line!

I comfortably work in the transformational and transpersonal coaching space and beyond, combining various modalities tailored to client outcomes. I combine a multitude of evidence-based coaching modalities, with integrative therapies and ancient wisdom.

My kaleidoscopic wisdom transcends traditional coaching. Wisdom gained over years of experience working in a variety of roles and fast-paced careers, including nursing, psychotherapy, hospitality and international business. I became adept at learning and processing quickly, having the flexibility and interpersonal skills to fit into each organisation. I was an ambitious multi-potentialite, determined to succeed, gain appropriate qualifications and seek opportunities as they arose. When it was time to change and move on, I knew. I trusted my intuition.

I question things, I'm curious, a seeker and a life-long learner having qualified in various coaching and therapeutic modalities. Through experiences and synchronicities, I have become the coach I am today.

My learning has been intentional. Exciting and revelatory. Discovering and connecting inter-relational threads and concepts to create a unique tapestry of knowledge and information. Being open and aware, knowing and sensing what's possible, and welcoming opportunities as they arise.
Sometimes things don't work, go according to plan, or there are lessons to learn. Some of my biggest personal aha's have been when I've got out my own way, trusting and allowing the process. I can pinpoint times when I had real embodied shifts in my ongoing development. These have informed my work.

Opening to Possibilities

COACHING REIMAGINED Expanding Human Potential

Since I was a child I have been fascinated by the cosmos, leading to my interests in astronomy, and astrology. I loved the fact that there is ancient wisdom in the sky.

From early adulthood I've practised different forms of yoga, enjoying the time and space it afforded me to connect with my body and experience the serenity of my practice. And I enjoy spending time in nature.

All my life I have been fascinated by the human condition. 'What makes people tick?' Why do they do what they do, when, how and where? As a nurse, that led me to want to learn more about the mind-body connection and the relationship to health and well-being.

Attending talks at a local alternative health clinic introduced me to many different yet complementary healing disciplines. Linking what I learned to my medical background, it all made perfect sense. This new-found esoteric knowledge felt important and relevant in some way. I wanted to learn more.

The demands of business were stressful. To maintain balance and alignment in my body and reduce my mental activity, I started to learn how to manage my energy.

I received acupuncture, aromatherapy massages, and learned Transcendental Meditation for my well-being. And Tarot. Not random at all if you look at my bookshelves!! The first time I received Reiki; I had a seismic shift of embodied realisation. I physically felt the energy moving and was told it was 'part of the healing process.' That normalised the benefits of understanding energy.

Personally experiencing these initially 'mystical' ancient wisdom and esoteric practices, I felt more comfortable, lighter, and at peace within myself.

Shift Happens

In parallel, I felt my career had reached a plateau. Feeling unfulfilled and conflicted, it was uncomfortable. I had an itch that needed scratching. For once I didn't have a plan.

I started pondering the 'big' questions around life, purpose and contribution. Hoping for answers, I had astrology readings for guidance and learnt what was beyond my star sign and daily horoscope. I could start to focus on what might be possible.

Then the universe stepped in. I was unexpectedly made redundant. It was the worst and best thing that happened to me.

After running on the business treadmill for so long, I chose to stop, reflect and take stock. I hadn't realised how burned out I'd become. For the first time in my life I had space and time to contemplate my future. Uncertainty met the unknown. My innate wisdom and inner compass guided me.

What questions might you be asking yourself, regarding your 'What next?'

Realisation's and 'Aha's'

There were times in my life when I had the experience of not being seen or heard for who I was. My experience and endeavours were unacknowledged and taken at face value. It was disheartening. At times I was admonished for speaking up and learnt to 'bite my tongue' and shut up. It wasn't safe or appropriate to state my view.

'Is this something that's familiar to you?'

Becoming an observer, I paid attention, watching scenarios play out, and witnessing relational dynamics from afar. I became adept at noticing often hidden patterns and could 'join up dots.' Aware of the emergent shifts, the potential impact or likely consequences affecting individuals or situations.

I could feel, sense and know the structure and history of the pattern including the possibilities going forwards. This gift has enabled me to carve out my own path in life. I wasn't going to be shoehorned to follow or live up to other's expectations.

COACHING REIMAGINED Expanding Human Potential

'Finding' Coaching

I didn't set out to be a coach, a trainer or a therapist. I 'stumbled' across a magazine article. I realised I was already doing what was described as coaching, in some shape or form in my various careers and throughout my life.

This 'aha' changed the direction of my life and introduced me to a whole new world. A world in which I learnt to fully understand myself as a 'work in progress' and also my ability to support and facilitate others to deeply appreciate who they are, and to be 'perfect in their imperfections.'

'What would it be like to really know who you are, confident in your sense of self and the possibilities of life, going forward?'

Spiritual Development

I met my first spiritual teacher at a Coaching Circle and never looked back.

My 'weird and wonderful Woo-woo' journey had really begun in earnest. Knowing I could trust, rather than question my experience, I continued to be guided by my intuition. I became a crystal and reiki healer, studied Energetic NLP (neuro-linguistic programming) and other spiritual and psychic modalities, finding those that resonate with me.

I've had many teachers since, who have nurtured and supported my ongoing energetic, spiritual and psychic development.

And I found my tribe. A disparate group of seekers who fully support one another in our new found learning, evolution and awakening. I am seen and accepted for who I am. I belong, I fit in. There are no expectations, or judgements, just a mutual trust.

Client Collaboration

COACHING REIMAGINED Expanding Human Potential

Many clients come to me by word of mouth on the suggestion of 'needing some of Henrietta's magic'. I'm known for facilitating them in practical and grounded ways to help them discover their own solutions and navigate their future. Our relationship is one of deep trust and collaboration. A partnership. Like a dance. There's an innate musicality. Our moves comfortably shift and change, with the rhythm. It flows.

You may be familiar with the widely touted concept 'the coachee has all the answers.' They may do, and my response to that is yes, no, and also 'it depends.' Sometimes they 'don't know' and that's Ok too.

Often clients are dealing with multiple, seemingly unsurmountable issues. They are also seekers of inner truth, wanting to know who they are, in an ever-changing and uncertain world. They want to feel re-energised and inspired and are curious to learn about the extraordinary, as well as the ordinary concepts of life. My clients inform my approach which supports the direction of my work.

A Safe Pair of Hands

I'm known for creating an inclusive, non-judgemental space. Clients often report how calm and grounded I am, which enables them to relax and experience peace, and ease, during and after sessions. This enables them to bring whatever they want to a session, knowing they will be seen and heard, acknowledged and validated. Feeling lighter is a regular comment after a session. Shifts are palpable, often bringing a sense of relief and a release that accompanies a different level of 'knowing.'

If you're drawn to work with me, we don't sit on the side with our toes in the water, nor do we paddle in the shallows and stay on the surface. We dive, we go deep, we safely go beyond and re-emerge at a different point. My role is to be a Catalyst for Transformation in whatever way that naturally transpires for each client.

Coaching In the Moment

Sharing my experience and journey reflects the ethos of my purpose and

gives you a sense of what's possible beyond traditional coaching.
I intuitively guide your physical, mental, emotional, energetic and spiritual systems. It's a non-prescriptive, free-flowing, generative collaboration. Outcomes are held lightly, as they can, and do, change. Intangible wants and needs often require exploration before a level of clarity is gained for tangibility.

I've had clients not sure what they wanted to cover in a session that's (successfully) ended with a "Wow! I hadn't expected to go there today!" No subject is off limits. Removing expectations frees you to fully engage in your emergent process. This gives a greater sense of knowing and realisation that is ecological and aligned, and it's life-affirming.

The Difference That Makes the Difference

Incorporating the 'The Woo-woo' with coaching and integrative therapies. I am able to read people's energy or emotional state, like a sort of Cosmic jigsaw puzzle. Using my extrasensory gifts I work deeply with clients, by invitation, to be a 'way-shower,' when it's
appropriate and agreed.

I am deeply connected to and understand the cycles of life, especially significant transitions. I can identify things out of their awareness and reflect back their experience in a way that makes sense to them and their inner knowing and understanding. This creates natural shifts and healing for body, mind and soul alignment.

Having an awareness of what's possible, and future potential, I support clients to fully explore their internal and external landscapes to plan ahead. In gaining more understanding about their place in the world and who they want to be, our facilitative work allows them to navigate their path with clarity and resilience.

Acknowledging a client's emotional and material resources, I intuitively know how much I can ask of them, how broad or deep they are ready and willing to work, using a tailored approach whilst respecting their choices. I teach them to embrace their intuitive capacities, whilst honing their abilities, resilience and courage to face life's challenges. And to nurture and realise their many hopes and dreams.

Holding intrinsic curiosity about inner truths and the unknown can lead to breakthroughs and new understandings, fostering growth and evolution for themselves and others. The journey is about harnessing these energies to realise their fullest potential.

I incorporate the ancient wisdom of Astrology, Numerology, Gene Keys, Human Design and Soul Blueprint Readings as divination tools. These succinctly highlight the gifts talents, and purpose for individuals, across contexts of personal, business, health and relationships. I combine the information to help clients understand themselves at a deeper level, realise their innate qualities, giving a purposeful directionality which has so far been elusive.

Working at this level, I value my own self-care and energy management highly. I also teach other highly sensitive people and empaths to do this for themselves in sessions and as part of my Spiritual Development courses and workshops.

On Purpose

Recognising and combining my ongoing passion and interest in the (energetic and spiritual) psychic realm, positively influences my eclectic coaching style and approach. Learning to trust my intuition reconnects me to my inner wisdom and soul spirit. It was the missing piece and peace. I had come home to myself.

In Closing...

I believe that all human beings are spiritual in their nature. How much they access in this lifetime can depend on many things. And in most cases, it is a choice.

After hiding in the 'spiritual closet' for most of my life, I can now authentically own and appreciate my extrasensory gifts. and talents as

COACHING REIMAGINED Expanding Human Potential

'Pragmatic Woo-woo.' The appropriate utilisation of mystical and ancient wisdom, continues to prove to be practical and invaluable for myself and my clients, personally and professionally.

Who are you not to show up and be the coach you're meant to be?

I invite you to embrace who you really are, your true authentic self. Step into your sovereignty. Be seen, be heard. Find your tribe. Have the courage of your convictions to follow your passions and incorporate them into your own work. And share your unique contributions to enhance the evolution of coaching, from what it has been, to help shape what it is becoming.

> *I have sent you my invitation,*
> *the note inscribed on the palm of my hand by the fire of living.*
> *Don't jump up and shout, "Yes, this is what I want! Let's do it!"*
> *Just stand up quietly and dance with me.*
> *Excerpt from The Dance by Oria Mountain Dreamer*

Contact: https://linktr.ee/henriettalaitt

CHAPTER 8
Turning life's hard hits into wins
By Tiffanee Cook

'DING, DING, DING...'

No turning back now. Hands encased in leather, mouthguard in. The world and everyone in it faded into the background. Sights, sounds, thoughts, stories... gone. Only the truth remained: blows, danger, failure, courage... standing toe to toe baring a soul not yet seen.

8pm October 27, 2012. Was this the first time she had truly 'let go,' 29 years in?

A single round where time stood still and yet stretched into an eternity. Fear, courage, isolation, trust, visibility and uncertainty collided. Yet ironically, a certainty she had never-before experienced.

'Letting go' wasn't the neat surrender she'd imagined. It was messy, raw, and liberating. Her body was drained yet electrified by the adrenaline still surging through it. She could feel everything and yet nothing all at once. The referee clutched that now-free left hand and raised it high above her head; a stance that changed her forever. Emerging from that ring with both hands free to grab hold of a whole new reality. The underdog *can* come out on top, they don't even need to know the rules. Perhaps she wasn't truly born in May 1983, but rather in that boxing ring in October 2012.

One crazy 'just say yes' moment had become a night that redefined a lifetime. In that ring, with fear and adrenaline coursing through my veins, I met myself for the very first time. I experienced the power of letting go. Letting go of fear. Letting go of self-doubt. Letting go of every story I'd ever told myself about who I was and what I was capable of.

That night in the ring wasn't just a fight; it was a reckoning. A literal and metaphorical punch in the face that cracked open a whole new reality. Boxing became my mentor, my mirror, and an unshakable metaphor for my life. A space where courage, resilience, and vulnerability took centre stage, and where nothing existed but the raw, undeniable truth.

But the fight wasn't over; it had only just begun.

Turns out, this wasn't just a wild decision - it was a catalyst. Looking back, I can see how every lesson in that ring shaped the way I now coach, but at the time, all I knew was that something inside me had shifted forever.

It seems like an odd place to start, hey? Getting punched in the face and calling it my mentor…

"Tiff, isn't this a book about 'coaching'?"
I hear you, but when I look back at the wild old ride that is my life, it's this particular moment that forever holds the greatest significance around understanding who I am and how I am. And those lessons - unexpected, messy, and profound - now fuel the work I do as The Mind PT, guiding others through their own metaphorical fight camp.

COACHING REIMAGINED Expanding Human Potential

When I discovered the personal growth, healing, and wisdom hidden within my newfound passion for boxing, it felt like unlocking solutions to struggles I hadn't even realised were holding me back.

That's the thing about somatic experiences - those that are felt in the body, not just thought in the mind. There is a wisdom we can tap into that our minds may have been rejecting. Before I stepped into the ring, I wasn't accessing that deeper layer of knowing. Boxing cracked open doors in my mind and body that had long been bolted shut. It invited me into a world of truth, beauty, and possibility beyond my wildest dreams.

I said yes.

Looking back, I truly believe that no traditional coaching could have led me here. Before this, those doors simply weren't open, and I wasn't knocking. In fact, I'm not even sure I knew they existed.

The ring doesn't lie

> *"The fight is won or lost far away from witnesses - behind the lines, in the gym, and out there on the road, long before I dance under those lights."*
>
> – Muhammad Ali

What we love and how we connect with it reveals a lot about who we are. In the ring, there is no dodging the truth. Boxing has a way of peeling back the armour we build around ourselves - the stories, the reasons, the masks. Boxing sure doesn't give a toss about the comforting tales my mind rattles off, or the meaning it attempts to create. The only reality in that moment is me, my opponent, and the truth of who I really am beneath it all. It's raw. It's humbling. It's
brutally honest.

Boxing has been my most influential teacher and ally. It grabbed me by the hand, commanded my attention, and held up a mirror to my soul. It drew answers from me for questions I'd have undoubtedly rejected should any human have dared to ask.

COACHING REIMAGINED Expanding Human Potential

"Hey Tiff, why aren't you scared of getting punched in the face? Doesn't it hurt?"

Proudly I'd scoffed at this question time after time, until eventually boxing leaned in whispering in my ear "they're onto something you know; what are you scared of, if not getting punched in the face?" Indeed an odd place to feel *at home*, I'd had to admit. Roped off in that tiny 'square circle,' standing toe to toe with someone who wants more than anything in the world at that moment to knock your head clean off your shoulders.

The answer to that very question eventually emerged from somewhere in the pit of my stomach and punched me in the chest. Vulnerability. Connection. Visibility. - *really* being seen. Those things seemed to evoke a visceral kind of unrest within me. As for my body? Feeling its sensations, connecting with it, understanding it, loving it, and trusting it to keep me safe. These things I had long since disconnected from were stirring beneath the surface.

Weird as it sounds, entering that ring felt like speaking fluently a language I'd never even come across before. Technical skills are definitely not what I'm referring to here. I'd be more closely compared to a newborn foal taking her first steps, from that perspective. The magic, however, was in the meeting myself, raw, real, and untethered for the very first time. Every round, a reflection of who I really was beneath the facade. My fear, my courage, my grit, my vulnerability - they all showed up in ways I couldn't control or deny. Boxing taught me that life, too, is about showing up unmasked, even when it's uncomfortable or downright terrifying.

I was confronted by the reality that I couldn't merely decide on how I would react and respond when getting landed with those unexpected punches under the primitive influence of adrenaline. That opportunity to reflect was only offered after the fact, when my mind caught up with where my instincts took me. From there, my power lay in the ability to train - again and again - until my primitive instincts were rewired for a better outcome. This is neuroplasticity at its most raw; the brain and nervous system changing and adapting to a new experience, a new set of challenges. In simple terms, surrendering to (and accepting) who I was in that moment, and then taking the personal responsibility to change it was probably the biggest gift I had ever given myself.

The parallels between boxing and life were striking (pardon the pun). Every jab, hook, slip and weave, were a reflection of the challenges we face outside the ring. Sometimes you're mastering the ring, moving forward, and creating opportunities. Other times, you're on the back foot, weathering blows and looking desperately for the space to counter. There are moments of triumph, where the stars align, and your hard work and preparation pays off. And then there are moments of failure, when you're knocked to the canvas and faced with the decision of whether to stay down or get the hell back up and stay in the fight.

Boxing became my greatest teacher and my guru, because it didn't just ask for my strength; it demanded my honesty. It forced me to confront my fears, embrace my vulnerability, and rise above the stories that no longer serve me. And in doing so, it showed me how to live - not just when and how to fight, but also when and how to surrender.

The body keeps the score… and fights back

It is important to realise that the body remembers everything, even the stuff the mind forgets.

Those butterflies before a fight… they weren't just nerves; they were echoes of every moment I had felt unprepared, unsafe, or unseen. They spoke of vulnerability, danger, and the fear of failure. But instead of silencing them, boxing invited me to lean in. To feel them fully. Slowly I began to trust my body again, to understand its language and recognise that it wasn't my enemy; it was my greatest ally.

Inevitably, two years into boxing and I catapulted myself from that comfortable swivelling chair in the corporate office straight onto the gym floor in the world of personal training. A seemingly natural unfolding of circumstances that felt somewhat accidental at a glance, like I'd unknowingly followed the bouncing ball to where I have landed today. Without a shadow of a doubt, where I am meant to be. Understanding where you've been and why, allows you to connect the dots and take with you the crucial aspects from one chapter and experience to the next.

Let me hit pause here and share with you another moment when I saw firsthand how boxing can help the body release stored tension and heal in ways the mind alone can't. This process I now know is called somatic healing. It is a therapeutic approach that focuses on the mind-body connection, using physical sensations, movement, and awareness to release stored trauma, stress, or emotional blockages. Unlike traditional talk therapy, which primarily engages the mind, somatic healing works with the body's innate intelligence to process and heal unresolved experiences.

In 2017 I was appointed coach and facilitator for a Government Funded Women's Empowerment Program. A pilot program for female participants, referred through clinical support services, who had experienced family violence and/or abuse. A cohort of incredible women coming together in what could only have been an extremely daunting new experience, to learn boxing for the first time in their lives. Their goal was to battle their demons and learn how to turn life's hard blows into their own wins.

We laughed, we learned, and all the while we all knew that beneath the surface, everyone in that room had some version of significant and somewhat relatable trauma to one another. The magic unfolded, fists landed on bags, emotions whirred, and tensions unravelled. 12 weeks, one session per week.

By this stage I'd been training almost every day for the last five years, so the idea of such significant shifts from one 60-minute session once per week felt a bit unrealistic. Imagine my surprise when after only four weeks one of our gorgeous participants in her 60's bounced through the door one day and said "Tiff, I haven't had a single panic attack for two whole weeks." For a number of years she had been grappling with them daily.

This was coaching somatically in a whole new way.

Sometime after this program I found myself training a good friend, who happened to be a Clinical Psychologist and thus knew a thing or two about trauma. We'd train weekly, I'd teach her the graceful art of boxing, and she'd be in awe of how intricate and technical it is. One particular day I finished our session with one of my favourite high-intensity rounds. Me holding the round punch shield as she pummelled that bad boy with everything she had, for 60 seconds straight.

Talk about a liberating experience. How often do women allow themselves to truly let go and express their power? To channel force and strength through their own bodies? To assert both physical and emotional boundaries? To surrender and let their bodies speak and express without restraint?

The bell signalled the end of the 60 seconds. Her hands fell to her sides, and a wave of emotion surged up, spilling out through her tears. I held space, and after some moments, she filled me in on the psychological definition of what she had just experienced. Something she was well versed in understanding, yet her typical professional practice lacked the somatic nature to enable her own clients to access such release. She moved from knowing with her head, to knowing with her whole being.

Back then I didn't understand the psychology behind it all, but each experience like this (and there were many) sent me on a quest for deeper understanding.

The lies we live by

Ah that glorious human mind of ours. It does not give up without a fight. It is a masterful storyteller, and it commands our attention. Weaving its elaborate tales from threads of fear, doubt, and past experiences. Taking our fleeting thoughts and turning them into unwavering limiting beliefs we'll go on to live our lives by, should we not think to question them.

For three decades, I let those stories define my reality. They were just what they were, but I softened their impact by wrapping them in my own version of a comforting 'truth'- a story that made them easier to live with.

Tiff Cook - she's fierce, independent, decisive and courageous as f#%$. Ha! That's what I believed and thus portrayed like the lead actor in my own Hollywood film.

Enter boxing. She's not fierce, she's reactive. She's not independent, she's incapable of boundaries so avoids real connection. She's not decisive, she's terrified of uncertainty and her ability to make good choices. She's not courageous, she believes courage is facing other people's fears.

Uh oh, the reality stick took to me good and proper at this point. That mask I'd worn my whole life slipped right off and hit the canvas. Beneath it, the face of a girl I wasn't all too familiar with at all and I knew needed to connect with.

How you do one thing is how you do everything.

We've all heard this bandied around before, right? Well, I know I've lost count of the number of times I've been smacked in the face (metaphorically, this time) with a pattern or a response I see in myself in the boxing ring that directly reflects other areas of my life. Not just in boxing, but in any activity where I simply let go and find myself in some fully immersed state of focus and presence.

I recall spending significant time drawing and thus observing curious patterns in thoughts and behaviours that echoed a truth in other areas. For example, the first time I picked up a pencil and sketch book whilst in Melbourne's infamous, and seemingly endless, lockdown in 2020 amidst the pandemic. As my first sketch started to take shape and really resemble the reference photo, I found an almost silent voice in my head wooing me into leaving it unfinished and starting something new… for if I fail by the choice to not continue it's not really failure, right? And that's a hell of a lot easier to digest than screwing it up on those final strokes of graphite.

In that moment right there every chance I'd ever taken and every choice I'd ever made flashed through my mind. I recognised every successful venture I'd nailed right off the bat but regardless, abandoned and found something new to kick off. That's one way to avoid failure, huh. I finished that sketch, and I finished every sketch I started from that moment. Because… that's right, how you do one thing is how you do everything.

When I get in the boxing ring, I am there 'til the final bell.

Recognising the stories is one thing; breaking free from them is another. In boxing, I learned that change doesn't happen in a single epiphany - it happens through repetition, consistency and practice. Just as I trained my body to move instinctively, I began to train my mind to question its dialogue. When the thought *You're going to fail* crept in, I responded with, *Oh, that's interesting!* The ring became my training ground for rewriting the script, replacing fear-driven stories with ones rooted in agency, courage and possibility. There's a space between stories and truth. In that space is wisdom.

In the ring, there's a split second where time seems to slow down. You feel as though you see the punch coming and you make a choice in that moment. But the truth is, the choice was made long before you stepped into the ring. Your body was already in motion, reacting to instincts and training before your mind caught up to register the punch heading your way. In boxing, waiting until you see the punch is too late; the response must already be in motion. Similarly, in life, there's a space between the stories we tell ourselves and the reality we live. The key is to find that space and learn to exist within it.

Finding my voice, one round at a time

Now I am sure you have your own 2020 story. What you were doing. What you had to give up. And maybe what you gained. We all have a 2020 story. The world descended into turmoil overnight with the introduction of Covid19 and all the new rules and regulations around a worldwide pandemic.

Maybe I am a bit different, but I've always functioned extremely well in unexpected collective chaos. It made me curious, and rightly so, as it most definitely resembles a level of familiarity with that infamous fight or flight reaction us humans have to danger. For some of us, that feels like home (bit like that boxing ring did for me).

Long story short, I adapted like a boss to life in lockdown, despite having my fledgling fitness studio business shut down and my livelihood threatened. Pages in this book don't permit me to elaborate on the many insights and lessons that bad boy dished up, but let's explore the value of diving headfirst (perhaps a little naively) into the uncharted world of podcasting. Another in-the-moment radical decision that became one of the most valuable resources for my development as a coach and mentor.

Firstly, when I started my podcast, I didn't realise it would become an extension of my time in the boxing ring - a space where I would face myself, not with gloves but with words. Each episode became a round in my emotional boxing match, a place where I grappled with vulnerability, visibility, and authenticity. It was terrifying and exhilarating all at once. Just like stepping into the ring, podcasting demanded that I show up - publicly, fully, and honestly - in ways I never had before. I remember noticing how naturally it happened, yet I had never put myself out there like this, offering and inviting the kind of vulnerability that this space required.

Over 880+ conversations later, the *Roll with The Punches* podcast has been one hell of a teacher, refuge, and a university of life. Speaking with some of the world's most respected researchers, psychologists, neuroscientists, thought-leaders, academics, and survivors, opened doors to perspectives I hadn't even known existed.

Amidst a series of 60ish minute conversational moments of viewing life through the lens and experience of others across the globe wasn't just education, it was an invitation to expand my thinking, deepen my empathy, and embrace endless curiosity.

"The more I read, the more I acquire, the more certain I am that I know nothing."

– Voltaire

I believe the greatest lesson I learned through these conversations is the true value of critical thinking and curiosity. The willingness to challenge my own ideas and assumptions, to ask stupid questions, to admit my own ignorance, to ask uncomfortable questions, and to lean into the perspectives of others transformed not just how I understood the world but how I understood myself. It gave me a deeper respect for the complexity of the human experience.

Eight billion versions of you and I roam this planet. Carrying different stories, different genetics, different beliefs, different biology, different values and different hopes and dreams. I believe (with all my own bias, conditioning and current beliefs, of course) that great coaches hold space for *'I don't know'* and *'maybe.'*

I've learned from some of the top-dogs in their respective fields, and I've breathed a sigh of relief to hear them say these phrases to my curious questions.

The power of critical thinking and curiosity seems at times profoundly undervalued.

The fight that set me free

Fighting to surrender sounds like a contradiction, but it's actually one of the biggest battles we face - both in and out of the ring. It's that internal war between control and letting go, between force and flow, between gripping tightly and trusting deeply.

It's the part of us that's been conditioned to believe that strength is about pushing harder, never backing down, always fighting through. That surrender is weakness, giving up, losing, quitting.

But real surrender? Well, that's next-level strength.

It's standing in the fire of discomfort without needing to control the flames. It's releasing the need to force an outcome and stepping into trust instead.

It's knowing when the fight isn't about swinging harder, but about exhaling, and rolling with (not against) the punches.

Fighting to surrender means unlearning the belief that success equals force and finding the courage to let go when holding on is what's really holding you back. It's the ultimate paradox: sometimes, the biggest fight is the one where you choose to stop fighting.

> *"A teacher is never a giver of truth; he is a guide, a pointer to the truth that each student must find for himself."*
>
> – Bruce Lee

As it stands now, it makes perfect sense to me to realise that the greatest part of my development as a coach came not from the classroom where I learned the traditional guidelines to become a coach, but from the sweet science of boxing preceding that. We are most valuable when we deeply connect with that which opens the door to our own personal self-discovery and beyond.

I needed to embrace the fight to understand the power of surrender.

Guiding and influencing another human in shaping their own life is a profound responsibility - one that demands both knowledge and nuance. It calls for a blend of education, psychology, and science, but equally, empathy, intuition, interpersonal skill, and perspective. We must facilitate in a way that sparks curiosity and possibility, guiding others toward answers beyond any model or structure.

The number of therapies, coaching experiences, workshops, and mentors that have shaped me is too vast to list - probably even to fully recall. And without a doubt, far too many to fit into a single chapter of a book like this. What I hope is that this fleeting snapshot of my own experience may just crack open a door that you might not have yet realised was even there for you.

I wish you all the best in your own *fight to surrender*, may you find your own version of the boxing ring.

"It isn't the mountains ahead to climb that wear you out; it's the pebble in your shoe."

Muhammad Ali

Let's connect:

www.tiffcook.com

linktr.ee/rollwiththepunches

CHAPTER 9
What's Next?
By Andrew Mills

What's next for life coaching, counselling and personal development? Advanced mastery or something else? Whether you're a coach, a leader, or simply someone curious about unlocking more of your potential, this chapter will introduce a unique approach to deepening awareness. It's not about throwing out everything you already know it's about expanding it.

Imagine we fused together a mix of personal growth and self-improvement methods to get people to the metaphorical airport. Let's call this blend "X" for now, a unique mix that could be the start of a new modality, like assembling a car. You wouldn't need to know how each part works, only how to drive it. Would such a creation be overwhelming, illogical or logical?

Before exploring whether this fusion makes sense, let's define living.

COACHING REIMAGINED Expanding Human Potential

What is our human experience? Neuroscientists have found our brains are processing 400 billion bits of data per second, yet we're aware of only 2,000 - a mere 0.000005% of what we're processing. What does this mean? Imagine trying to understand Earth by only examining a small area of land like Hertfordshire in the UK. Would this snapshot capture Earth's diversity, including oceans, deserts, jungles, mountains, and icecaps? Clearly, it wouldn't be a fair representation of the Earth.

Consider how life would change if we could see, hear, and smell beyond our current sensory limits. And if our perception sharpened, how would we feel? Our human experience could be vastly different.

Since we're only aware of 0.000005% of what our brains are processing, do we really need more information? Or should we focus on understanding what we are already processing?

The big question is: how can we boost our level of neurological awareness, i.e. consciousness? First, let's break down what we mean by "illogical" and "logical." At first glance, you might think this is obvious. "Illogical" means lacking clear reasoning, while "logical" is defined as sound reasoning. But is it that simple?

Imagine we travel back to a Medieval English tavern. Over a drink, we discuss how the Earth is round and orbits the sun at 66,600 mph. How would our fellow drinkers react? They'd likely find our ideas far-fetched! But how does something once considered crazy become more generally accepted? Take the Earth's shape: most people believed it was flat until new information emerged. Similarly, with greater awareness, what seems logical today could one day seem illogical, and vice versa.

This back-and-forth between what's illogical and logical is what I call "illogical/logical". This reminds me of a quote by Grant Soosalu, co-creator of a coaching modality called mBraining: *"True Wisdom is the Ability to Comprehend Multiple Perspectives."*

Let's test this. Write the number 6 on a piece of paper. Turn it 180 degrees, it looks like a 9. Turn it 90 degrees clockwise; it resembles a snail! What does this teach us? True wisdom isn't about clinging to one viewpoint. It's about being open-minded, flexible, and compassionate in understanding why others see things differently.

Life is uncertain, and resistance to change often creates conflict. But by approaching situations with patience and a genuine willingness to understand others' perspectives, we can grow together in wisdom. Some call this evolution. One perspective focuses on force and resistance, the other on openness, compassion, and understanding.

How can we speed up the journey from illogical to logical? By staying open to exploring ideas that seem illogical. What we dismiss as wrong or fake today might be seen as right or true tomorrow. Since we are only aware of 0.000005% of the data available to us, isn't it likely that our current view is incomplete?

So, what's the other way to accelerate evolution? Progressing through "X."

Think about Medieval England's understanding of the Earth; if we could have shown them its true form, they'd have understood much faster. Similarly, instead of merely describing "X," it's best to experience it through a 45-minute exercise. This exercise is a mix of the illogical and logical, triggering greater awareness.

Getting Ready for the Weekend Morning Exercise

This exercise is best performed first thing in the morning during the weekend when your mind is open and receptive before distractions arise and you are still half asleep. Keep this book at the side of the bed, and work through the following after waking and before any food. Sit in a quiet, comfortable spot where you can relax for about 45 minutes without distractions. If you can't do this right now, BOOKMARK THIS SECTION AND RETURN to it when you can fully immerse yourself. Otherwise, this exercise will not work well.

Turn off any devices and take a moment to breathe steadily. Picture yourself on a warm beach with the sun on your skin, feeling a gentle breeze carrying the fresh smell of the ocean.

As you watch the waves rise and fall, match your gentle breathing to their rhythm: inhale as the waves rise and exhale as they flow back to the sea. Aim for a breath about every 10 seconds, focusing more on the rhythm than on the depth of each breath.

Let this calming energy wash over you. Read and go through each stage at a time while remaining in a relaxed state. Imagine yourself preparing to meditate and enjoy this peaceful moment.

Demonstrating "X" – Stage 1

Take a moment for yourself as you start this exercise. If you feel the urge to yawn, that's completely natural - it's just a way to release tension. Close your eyes for each phrase and tune into whatever feelings arise as you focus on each one in turn. Spend at least 30 seconds on each, fully embodying each phrase, top to toe, before moving on to the next. Keep breathing steadily in and out, and notice any thoughts or sensations that come up. Let's start with these guiding phrases:

- I am Love
- I am Compassion
- I am Joy
- I am Loving
- I am Being Loved
- I am Gratitude

Preparing to Ask Questions

You will be answering rhetorical questions in the following stages while focusing your full attention on different body parts. Yes, this is one of those illogical/logical things.

Before asking yourself each question, keep your key feelings from Stage 1 in mind and rub the palms of your hands together to generate warmth each time, then place one hand gently on your:

- **Forehead:** when asked, calmly ask your forehead the question

while focusing on your forehead.
- **Heart**: when asked, really focus on the beating of your heart, sensing and appreciating it for enabling your life. Wait until you feel a full sense of loving and gratitude for your heart, and then calmly ask your heart the question.
- **Belly button**: when asked, focus on your stomach, noticing any sensations, gurgling, warmth and appreciate it for fuelling your body. While tuning into your belly button area, direct the question to it.

Demonstrating "X" – Stage 2

Forehead: Ask it, *"How happy am I, on a scale of 1 to 10?"* where 1 is terrible and 10 is fantastic. Take note of the first number that comes to mind without questioning it.

Demonstrating "X" – Stage 3

Heart: Ask your Heart, *"How happy am I, on a scale of 1 to 10?"* 1 being terrible, 10 being fantastic. Again, mentally note the score that arises without questioning it.

Demonstrating "X" – Stage 4

Belly button: Ask it, *"How happy am I, on a scale of 1 to 10?"* 1 being terrible, 10 being fantastic. Note the score that comes up naturally.

Demonstrating "X" – Initial Review

Now, take a moment to review the answers from stage 2 to 4. Did all three scores match? Interesting, isn't it? It's almost as if you were accessing different information from each part of yourself. Let's dive a little deeper.

Demonstrating "X" – Stage 5

Forehead: Ask it, *"On a happiness scale of 1 to 10, what would it take me to be a 10?"* Mentally note the answer without questioning it. Then, ask yourself, *"What baby steps can I start taking today to move* towards a 10?"

Demonstrating "X" – Stage 6

Heart: Ask your Heart, "On a happiness scale of 1 to 10, *what would it take me to be a 10?*" Again, mentally note the answer that comes up naturally. Then ask yourself, *"What baby steps can I start taking today to move towards a 10?"*

Demonstrating "X" – Stage 7

Belly button: Ask it, *"On a happiness scale of 1 to 10, what would it take me to be a 10?"* Just note the answer mentally. Then, ask yourself, *"What baby steps can I start taking today to move towards a 10?"*

Assessing the Unknown

Our brains process an incredible 400 billion bits of data every second, suggesting we might have more capacity to assess the unknown than we realise. Let's explore more of this idea.

By now, you've gathered that 'X' is a new modality available for purchase. Here's arguably one of the most illogical sales pitches but bear with me; it is meant to engage your intuitive, embodied intelligence rather than just your logical mind. The key facts to consider are:

- It is not a Master Course.
- It's incomplete and will never be complete.
- One size fits all.
- It connects you to your inner wisdom
- It provides only 2% of the information.
- There is no accredited qualification.
- The price, at the time of writing, is unknown.

Demonstrating "X" – Stage 8

Reconnect with your key feelings from Stage 1. If necessary, repeat Stage

1 to bring yourself back into a calm and clear state.

- **Forehead:** ask it, *"On a scale of 1 to 10, should I buy this course?"* (1 being an absolute "*No*" and 10 being an absolute "*Yes*.") Mentally note the score that comes to mind without questioning it.

Demonstrating "X" – Stage 9

- **Heart**: Really focus on your heart's loving, and ask it, *"On a scale of 1 to 10, should I buy this course?"* (1 being an absolute "*No*" and 10 being an absolute "*Yes*."). Mentally note the score that arises.

Demonstrating "X" – Stage 10

- **Belly button:** ask the belly button, *"On a scale of 1 to 10, should I buy this course?"* (1 being an absolute "*No*" and 10 being an absolute "*Yes*."). Mentally note the score you receive.

Assessing the Unknown – Review

Compare the scores you noted. Were they all the same, or did each area give a different response?

Typically, the forehead presents a logical answer, while the belly button gives an instinctive answer, both aiming to keep us safe. But the Heart? It often knows what we truly need before we do. The answers it provides may not always seem rational at first, yet they hold the kind of wisdom that aligns us with our deepest truth.

That's why I call it 'illogical/logical' because sometimes, the most profound insights don't make sense until they do.

What's Next?

Since you're reading this book, you're already on the path and

likely at Level 4 of consciousness, according to the Barrett Values assessment framework. This level emphasises personal growth, self-awareness, and letting go of old habits. People at this stage are often seeking to transform their lives by facing their fears and limitations head-on.

Now that you have the neurological ignition keys, you have a choice about your next step. Here are three paths forward:

1. **Go it alone:** Embrace the learning and skills you've gained from this (abridged) neurological driving lesson. Continue using the techniques you've discovered and applying multiple perspectives to make wiser life decisions, helping you tackle life's challenges independently.

2. **Seek support along the way:** Continue using your multiple brains (yes, your heart and gut are brains also) perspectives, and turn to life coaches or counsellors when you need guidance or support.

3. **Explore "X":** Use your new neurological skills and follow the path of "X," known as "I Am Toot™", an online self-coaching course designed to help you find answers while expanding your neurological awareness. How? By asking you rhetorical questions that unlock new perspectives in a non-critical process. This is the "illogical/logical" option. At the time of writing, I Am Toot™ is in development, but by the time you read this, you may be able to explore it further online.

At this stage, convention would suggest I tell you about the personal transformation that lies ahead, but the truth is, it's highly likely you would not believe me. If someone had told me what my life would be like now, 30 years ago, I wouldn't have believed them either.

You have the ignition keys, and you've learned to drive your neurological vehicle. The question is: where will you choose to go? Perhaps the real question is, what else might you discover along the way?

Think of life as a kind of university where each of us chooses our courses. It makes sense we would take on challenges, believing we can handle them. For a long time, I saw my life struggles as obstacles, but when I plotted them on a timeline, I had an epiphany: each challenge had prepared me for the next, much like in school, where we build on foundational lessons before advancing.

Some people are just starting out, while others are further along their journeys, facing more complex lessons. This is where I Am Toot™ helps. It raises our neurological level of awareness, making it easier for us to navigate life's challenges. Our brains are already processing vast amounts of information; we just need the right questions to bring this into our conscious awareness.

Understanding Our Neurological Vehicle

Let's take a closer look at I Am Toot™ and some of its multiple modalities fused together:

- **mBraining:** combines science and ancient wisdom to harness the power of our multiple brains.
- **Barratt Values:** provides values-based tools and assessments for individuals, teams, and organisations, helping them identify core values that drive behaviours and shape culture.
- **TetraMap:** uses four basic elements of nature (Earth, Air, Water, Fire) as metaphors to understand human behaviour and communication styles, enhancing interpersonal understanding and team cohesion.
- **Heart Rate Variability (HRV):** reflects changes in heart rate over time and its connection to breathing. Higher HRV is associated with better well-being, while lower HRV can indicate stress or anxiety.
- **Psychology:** the study of the mind and behaviour. Psychology explores conscious and unconscious processes to understand thoughts, feelings, and motivations.
- **Neurolinguistic Programming (NLP):** often viewed as pseudoscientific, NLP explores how thoughts, language, and behaviours are linked. It focuses on changing unhelpful habits to help people achieve positive life goals.
- **Dowsing:** body dowsing is an alternative practice claiming to reveal psychological insights through muscle responses, though it is generally viewed by scientists as unproven.

- **Spirituality:** is a personal quest for meaning and connection. While it can contrast with science, emerging parallels, especially in quantum physics, highlight interconnectedness.

The observer effect in quantum mechanics raises intriguing questions about consciousness and reality. Both quantum physics and spirituality suggest an interconnected universe, hinting they might be different expressions of the same principles. Scientific thinkers like David Bohm and Amit Goswami have studied these overlaps. As quantum science advances, it may reveal more about the nature of reality and our place within it.

Let's dig a bit deeper. I have likened our human experience to driving a car, and each modality represents a key role in making our life journey smooth and fulfilling:

- **mBraining** – *The Ignition Key*: Without it, the car won't start.
- **Barratt Values** – *The Diagnostic Machine*: Just as a mechanic diagnoses issues, Barratt Values helps identify what may be off in our inner world.
- **TetraMap** – *Driver Behaviour Training*: Learning to recognise the road and others' behaviours, adjusting our own responses accordingly.
- **Calibration** – *Dashboard Indicators*: These show fuel levels, engine temperature, and speed, keeping us attuned to our inner state.
- **HRV** – *A Smooth-Running Engine*: If HRV is erratic, the drive (life) becomes challenging.
- **Psychology** – *The Electrical Circuits*: Ensures all parts are communicating effectively, creating harmony within.
- **NLP** – *The Fuel Additive*: Helps the engine run cleaner and more efficiently.
- **Dowsing** – *The Satnav*: Guides us from point A to B in the best possible way.
- **Spirituality** – *The Road Itself*: Filled with challenges and

learning opportunities, giving purpose to our journey.

What if the key to unlocking your full potential has been within you all along, just waiting for you to notice?

Back Story and About the Author

Driven by a deep sense, there must be more to life than this; I have been passionately engaged in personal development for over 30 years. My quest for continuous self-improvement began two decades ago when I started to notice connections among various modalities. At first, these approaches felt unrelated, but gradually, the pieces began to fit together.

The breakthrough came when I discovered mBraining. This approach intrigued me with its focus on three brains, contrasting with Tetramap's four natural elements. Despite the apparent disconnect between the three and the four, I instinctively knew these modalities would align in a meaningful way.

A pivotal moment in my journey occurred during a challenging period in my life when my expanding internal guidance played a crucial role. It helped steer me through a near-fatal car crash and supported me through dark moments when I contemplated ending my earthly existence.

As I continued my introspective journey, I began experiencing lucid dreams, where I was aware of my dreaming state and could often control the scenarios. In one vivid dream, I was shown how to connect with an ultra-intelligence. I forced myself awake - it was 5:00 a.m., an unusual time for me, and I sat up and repeated the exercise. To my utter amazement, it worked! In an instant, I was connected to an incredible super-intelligence. The consciousness seemed to hold answers to everything. The magnitude of what I'd done dawned on me, and I wondered, had I connected to God?

With fear and a hint of apprehension, I asked, "Are you God?" The answer came back gently, "No". Phew, I thought, that was close. I felt a wave of relief. Then, I began to think, if you are not God, who the heck are you? After what felt like ages of questioning and sensing a patient amusement, I finally asked, "Are you my Higher Self?" The answer was "Yes." This profound encounter revealed a new part of my mind, linking beautifully with the fourth element in Tetramap.

What began as an exploration of a purely scientific coaching modality morphed into a fusion of science and what is considered esoteric. By expanding my neurological awareness, I am discovering profound insights and new levels of understanding.

This journeying is transforming my view of human experience and abilities. I have found my purpose: to help others reach that metaphorical airport, the starting point for their inner journeys, expanding their neurological level of awareness and enhancing their understanding of life on Earth.

Biography

Andrew Mills is a carpenter/joiner by trade, a chartered valuation surveyor by profession, and a life coach by choice, specialising in practical neuroscience-based coaching. His approach integrates the functions of our multiple brains for personal and professional growth.

With a passion for emerging sciences and ancient wisdom, he's always had an affinity for finding correlations between seemingly unrelated elements. This skill has served him well in pioneering valuation formulas in surveying and evolving neuroscience-based coaching practices. He operates under the belief that:

> *"True Wisdom is the Ability to Comprehend Multiple Perspectives."*
>
> -Grant Soosalu.

www.IAmToot.com

CHAPTER 10
How you are designed for purpose and meaning
By Fay Millington

It is never too late to be what you might have been - George Eliot
(Mary Ann Evans 1819-1880, English novelist, poet, journalist, translator and one of the leading writers in the Victorian era)

What if there was a surprisingly precise way to understand yourself more deeply?

An approach that honours your uniqueness and the way you interact in and experience the world.

One that guides the way to recognise who you could be, in your highest expression.

One that describes how you operate in your work, your optimum decision-making strategy, purpose, and so much more.

COACHING REIMAGINED Expanding Human Potential

The usual approaches to finding purpose

Many coaches, consultants, and authors take a structured approach to purpose discovery. This often begins with a series of written exercises followed by a process of elimination, ultimately leading to a chosen purpose. From there, an action plan is created to guide the coaching process.

These written exercises encourage reflection on past work roles, life experiences, strengths, talents, passions, and values—essentially prompting us to explore what Simon Sinek refers to as our 'why'.

Another common method is guided meditation or creative visualisation, where individuals imagine an ideal future or workday, later translating those insights into concrete goals.

While these methods can be useful, relying on them exclusively has its drawbacks. The process of analysing experiences and clarifying values can sometimes lead to overthinking, self-doubt, and decision paralysis.

Without a simple action plan, inertia can set in. Seeking advice from friends or loved ones—though well-intentioned—can introduce external biases, steering clients toward choices based on expectations rather than authentic desires.

So, is there a more effective way to uncover one's true purpose? Absolutely.

In my experience, two approaches—rooted in both ancient wisdom and modern science—have transformed the way I help clients find clarity and direction.

Your purpose is in your unique Human Design

Have you ever wondered why you think, feel, and act the way you do? Human Design is a system that helps you understand yourself deeply—

how you are naturally built to interact with the world, make decisions, and live a life that feels right for you.

The Human Design System combines ancient wisdom with modern science to give you a unique map of you and your life purpose. Human Design is the science of differentiation, spotlighting your uniqueness.

It combines ideas from Astrology, the Chinese I'Ching, the Chakra system, and the Kabbalah with sciences like Quantum Mechanics, Astronomy, Genetics, and Biochemistry. The founder of the Human Design System, Ru Ara Hu encourages you to test it for yourself and see what fits.

> *Human Design does not ask you to believe anything. It merely offers you the opportunity to explore and experiment with the mechanics of your nature, and your evolving consciousness, in order to find out for yourself exactly what works for you.*

When I first learned about my own Human Design, it helped me understand myself in a way I never had before. I had so many 'Aha!' moments. Moments that made me realise why I think and act the way I do.

By following my unique design, I feel more in tune with who I really am, what I am here to do and how to do it.

I found it an enlightening experience and felt it raised my consciousness.

Human Design doesn't put you in a box. Instead, it helps you understand yourself so you can make choices that feel right. It encourages you to stop comparing yourself to others and start embracing your unique way of being. Your 'Human Design Chart'—also called the 'Bodygraph'—is a special map of how your energy works. It shows how you interact with the world. Number columns appear on each chart side. The right column represents the parts of yourself that you are aware of, while the left column represents deeper traits that shape you but might not always be obvious. Each number connects to a 'gate', and there are 64 gates in total. These gates describe unique traits or qualities that make up who you are; the specific energies that make up your strengths and challenges.

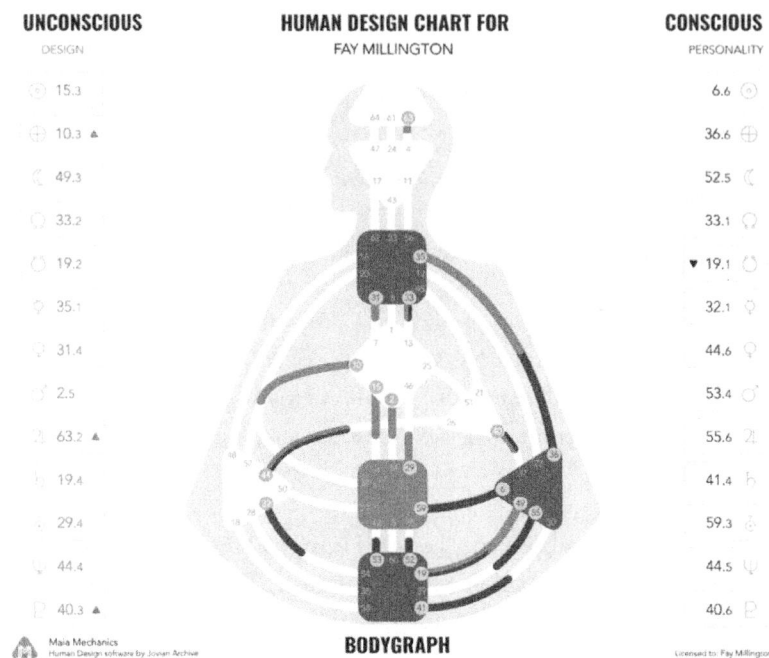

One of the most powerful aspects of Human Design is how it helps you discover your purpose.

Your 'Type' is a key part of this because it shows how your energy works best. Each Type—Manifestor, Generator, Manifesting Generator, Projector, and Reflector—has its own way of engaging with life and decision-making strategy.

Let's take a quick look at each Type from a work role perspective. I'm using language translated from the original source.

Manifestors are the initiators who bring originality and inspiration into something new. They are not here to be guided, asked or told. Manifestors make up about 9% of the population.

Generators are the builders who are designed to do work they love through a step-by-step process, bringing inspiration into reality. If they don't love the work, it drains their energy. Generators and Manifesting Generators make up about 70% of the population.

Manifesting Generator is a subtype of Generator. The difference is they do work they love in a quick and efficient way. Sometimes they do the work so quickly they have to go back and make changes later.

Projectors guide and advise the Generators, rather than do all the work. Projectors make up about 20% of the population.

Reflectors are the evaluators who reflect to others how they are going, giving a unique perspective and objective assessment of people, communities and businesses. Reflectors make up only about 1% of the population.

Did you find you intuitively resonated with one of the Types?

When you follow the natural flow of your Type, life feels easier, and things seem to fall into place. If you go against it, you might feel stuck, drained, or unsure of what you're supposed to do.

Your 'Profile' gives you a deeper look at how you express yourself and interact with others. It helps explain why you think the way you do, how you build relationships, and the challenges you might face. It also reveals how others see you, sometimes in ways that may surprise you.

Understanding your Profile helps you understand how you are meant to show up in the world, in your highest expression.

There are 12 main Profiles, and they have two numbers from 1 to 6. The first number is the dominant Line number. The secondary line number is shown after.

Let's take a quick look at the line number roles that make up a Profile. Again, I'm using language interpreted from the original source and the focus is work role. Consider which phrases or key words resonate with you the most.

Line 1 is the Authority; known for seeking details and investigation, laying a solid foundation based on information, introspection, being a chameleon and having empathy. Modest, creative and seeks security. The Profiles starting with Line 1 are 1/3 and 1 / 4.

Line 2 is the Natural; Natural potential talent, likes being alone, absorbed in own process, democratic and discerning. Likes harmony, things to come easy and simple or won't be interested. The Profiles starting with Line 2 are 2/4 and 2/5.

Line 3 is the Pioneer; Trial and Error/Evolution, discovers what doesn't work, adapts and needs experience to understand. Stands up for principles, learning through failure, resilient determination, bringing new solutions and revolutionary change. The Profiles starting with Line 3 are 3/5 and 3/6.

Line 4 is the Influencer; Influential Networker, externalises wisdom, great influence on others and has innate friendliness and warmth. Creates close networks, opportunities through others, comradery, can suffer people fatigue and need time alone. The Profiles starting with Line 4 are 4/1 and 4/6.

Line 5 is the Leader; Practical marketer/messenger, universalises something new, provides practical solutions, seen as a General or Saviour, a Natural Leader. Likes to fix and solve problems – step in–fix–step out, has 'outside the box' answers, naturally attracts attention and reputation is important. The Profiles starting with Line 5 are 5/1 and 5/2.

Line 6 is the Role Model; Living example, objective leader, a natural authority, observer, has mature wisdom and is naturally trusted. Authentic, optimistic, aloof, influential and gives advice and guidance.

There are three stages of a 6th Line: challenges and learning from the School of Hard Knocks (up to around age 30), Introspection and recovery during the middle years (between approximately 30-50) and the Wisdom of an Objective Leader, influencing others (after 50). The Profiles starting with Line 6 are 6/2 and 6/3.

How did you go – did one or more Lines particularly resonate with you?

Knowing your Type and Profile gives you insights into how you can go about your life's work. But what is it according to your Human Design?

Your 'Incarnation Cross' is one of the most important keys to discovering your purpose. It represents the deeper themes and life lessons that shape your journey. It is based on the top four gates in your chart and provides insight into the impact you are meant to have in the world.

There are 192 basic Incarnation Crosses which are then modified for each Type, resulting in a total of 768 specific Incarnation Crosses. Far too many to go into detail here. But for your purpose to fully emerge, you need to live in alignment with your Type.

If life feels off-track or confusing, it may be a sign that you're not following your natural energy flow. By understanding your Incarnation Cross and embracing your Type, you can step more confidently into the work and life path that is truly meant for you.

Living in Alignment with your Human Design

When you explore your Human Design, it's like unlocking a map to understanding yourself. Things that once felt confusing—like why certain situations energize you while others exhaust you—make sense. You see why some things feel easy, while others feel forced. You stop fighting against what isn't meant for you and start allowing what is.

Being in alignment with your Human Design is also called being in your 'Highest Expression.'

COACHING REIMAGINED Expanding Human Potential

Why is this valuable? Many of us move through life trying to be what we think we 'should' be—pushing against resistance, struggling with decision-making, or feeling disconnected from our true selves.

Human Design helps remove that resistance by showing you how you are naturally wired to thrive.

Understanding your Human Design helps you make better decisions, feel more ease in your relationships, both personal and professional, less frustration and self-doubt and to trust your intuition.

Most importantly, it gives you a way to align with your true purpose and live a life that feels meaningful and fulfilling.

Your journey with Human Design is personal. Chart exploration yields self-understanding and purpose clarity. The insights you discover will help you live more authentically and step into your highest potential.

So why not start now? Begin exploring your Human Design and uncover what truly makes you 'you.'

Your next steps

If you're curious about what your Human Design reveals, getting a personalised report is a great way to start.

This invitation encourages self-discovery, helping you connect with your authentic self, unburdened by conditioning. Are you ready to discover your unique design?

So, you have explored the relevant information for your unique Human Design to understand yourself better, experienced the 'Aha!' moments of insight and realised what is possible for you.

You are excited and bursting with ideas, however, you may not have clarity on the direction or best options for your future just yet.

You might be stuck in overthinking or second guessing yourself on how best to apply this information to your life. Now what?

I'll let you in on a secret. There is a way to gain clarity through whole body integrated decisions. How, you ask?

Accessing your body's multiple intelligences for wiser decisions and action planning

So, you now have ideas or a plan of how you might step into your purpose. And I am curious, are you someone who thinks things through in detail or do you make decisions based on how you feel about it?

Some people prioritise logic, others emotion, and some take gutsy action then reflect.

Knowing your own preference is key to putting your Human Design Plan into action.

Neuroscience has confirmed the understanding held by ancient Chinese Taoist, Sufi and other ancient wisdom philosophy of there being three minds, intelligences or energy centres within the body.

It isn't all in our head.

Our body is an astonishingly complex dynamic system with deeply interconnected components and a coaching technique I have learned, called multiple Brain Integration Techniques (mBIT) explores the way you are using your multiple brains.

mBIT is a range of practical techniques for communicating with, aligning and harnessing the intelligence of your multiple brains.

And yes, I do mean brains.

Based on evidence and how scientific literature defines them, each 'brain' has its own complex, adaptive, neural network, which has its own Prime

COACHING REIMAGINED Expanding Human Potential

Functions and its own Higher Expression.

Understanding the optimal function of each, enables you to deliberately change your approach to meet your desired outcomes and access your own inner wisdom.

The prime functions for the head brain are cognitive perception, thinking, and logic and making meaning. The head brain's highest expression is creativity.

The prime functions of the heart brain are the process of emoting/feeling, values and what is important to you, and relational affect and connecting with others. The heart brain's highest expression is compassion.

The prime functions of the gut brain are personal identity, self-preservation/safety, and mobilisation, motivation and the courage to act. The gut brain's highest expression is courage.

Advanced training goes beyond the original scope of the three brains in mBraining; by extending to knowledge of the Autonomic Nervous System (ANS) and the pelvic region. Of relevance here is a linkage to exploring shared purpose through co-creativity with others.

Our ANS is a part of our nervous system, which is usually outside of our conscious awareness and manages system stability and safety. Learning to balance the two arms of the ANS: the sympathetic nervous system and the parasympathetic nervous system, through a balanced breathing protocol, we can learn to recognize when we are off balance and find our way back through to a calm, alert state using a range of tools and techniques.

Working wisely across all intelligences, we can manage and moderate our state in response to events around us, so that we are more likely to excel; find meaning, purpose, happiness and satisfaction, as well as impacting on our health and well-being.

My own experiences of mBIT have shown me it is an effective means to achieve wiser integrated decisions and problem solving. It brings to the surface wisdom beyond our head brain's awareness, opening up what coaching is and can be in practice.

Did you ever decide firmly on change, then see nothing happen? Is it possible that your head brain decided, but your heart didn't truly desire it, or your gut didn't feel safe, so it didn't mobilise you to act? Do you check in with all your intelligence centres when making decisions?

Many people don't realise it, but their body is listening in on their thoughts and words.

Exploring what the multiple brains can contribute to the discovery, decision making and actions for your desired outcomes hugely enhances the effectiveness of the coaching process.

If we look at the synergies between Human Design and mBIT (mBraining), they include:
- both are built on a synthesis of ancient wisdom and modern science.
- each has an emphasis on the aim to function at our highest expression.
- each plays a role in helping us to understand ourselves better and to support decision making.

To me, there is an obvious fit for combining these systems into my coaching method to help people understand themselves better, make wiser decisions and create wiser action plans to implement so they experience more meaning and purpose.

It is my pleasure to guide you to access the embodied wisdom of your multiple brains, to receive their individual and unique feedback in response to the information, insights, proposed direction, and options.

And to weave that into your own unique Human Design.

This opens a new process of integrated decision making that can take place, with aligned action steps agreed across the multiple brains.

The agreed desired outcomes and action steps will provide you with an embodied wisdom plan of action that relates back to your Human Design, that you will have no resistance to.

Would you love to have a more integrated wise approach that sets you up for success?

Let's be real. Implementing a plan isn't always easy. Competing priorities can delay or derail you from achieving your outcomes. Circumstances change, and as time progresses, a changed approach is often required.

That's when having a coach and mentor to provide guidance and help keep you on track is beneficial. Especially a coach and mentor who understands your unique Human Design, includes your multiple intelligences, and reminds you who you are BEING at your highest expression.

It would be my pleasure to support you to understand when you are operating in alignment with your Human Design and when you are not.

To work with your multiple intelligences to ensure you are operating in alignment, so that everything will flow easier, and your purpose will seem like it is coming to you.

Connect with me...

I am passionate about helping midlife and older women to create more meaning and purpose in their lives, experience fulfillment and become who they are meant to be.

I am also an ageism activist who has joined the fight to end ageism and its negative and life shortening impact on us all.

It would be my pleasure to support you.

COACHING REIMAGINED Expanding Human Potential

The Linktree link below offers a range of ways to connect to me, learn more and how to create your unique Human Design Chart.

Fay Millington (6/3 Manifesting Generator)
Precision Coaching by Design
Master mBIT (multiple Brain Integration Techniques) Coach
Master Practitioner of NLP (Neuro-Linguistics Programming)
Master Conscious Hypnotist, Consultant and Writer.

Linktree: www.linktr.ee/faymillington
Scan the QR Code:

Notes:
Ra Uru Hu (born Robert Allan Krakower), who co-authored the book, *The Definitive Book of Human Design–The Science of Differentiation*, Lynda Bunnell & Ra Uru Hu, published in 2011 founded the Human Design System in 1987.

mBIT was created by Grant Soosalu and Marvin Oka, who wrote the book *mBraining, using your multiple brains to do cool stuff* published in 2012.

CHAPTER 11
Creating the future: unlocking neurocreative leadership
By Rory Lemon

Shifting the fomo to 'flowmo'—harnessing neurodiverse creativity for sustainable success

*[If you struggle with reading, concentration, or other types of language processing, feel free to **access the video version of this article** via the QR code at the end of this chapter.]*

Introduction: embracing a new era in coaching

In a world that often prizes uniformity, creativity can struggle to find its voice and permission to thrive. As an artist and passionate advocate for neurodiversity, I have witnessed the incredible power unleashed when unique creative abilities are recognised and nurtured.

NeuroCreative Leadership offers more than just strategies—it is **an invitation to translate innate heart-driven potential into purpose-driven reality**.

Perhaps you know what it's like when your best ideas constantly slip away from being realised, or feel your creativity is a hindrance rather than a help?

These doubts can deceive us, but creativity is not the adversary; it is an untapped resource waiting to elevate every aspect of life.

This chapter delves into the future of coaching and leadership through the lens of neurodiversity, showcasing how compassionate NeuroCreative Leaders are breaking free from outdated paradigms.

By embracing a holistic approach that **intertwines creativity, health, and leadership,** neurodivergent (ND) creatives are opening up brand new possibilities by honouring their unique strengths and mental landscapes.

While generating groundbreaking ideas, neurodiverse individuals may also face disabling challenges like **procrastination, perfectionism, self-doubt, and self-sabotage**. Traditional coaching often emphasises rigid performance strategies. However, the future necessitates guidance attuned to heart-centred intuitive creatives—entrepreneurs, artists, performers and innovators—crafting in their distinct ways.

Here's what we'll explore in this chapter:

- **The Problem:** How creativity can work against us.

- **The Shift:** Viewing creativity as a far-reaching optimisable skill.

- **The New Focus:** Through the science of commitment, we can engineer powerful creative cycles and unfurling structured brilliance.

COACHING REIMAGINED Expanding Human Potential

- **The Transformation:** Journeying to become visionary creatives with unstoppable energy and influence.

- **A New Era of Creative Mastery:** Embracing NeuroCreative Leadership—for the collective benefit.

> *"Because I mainly just loved watching Sesame Street and Jim Henson films as a child from the age of 2-6, does that now make me a Muppet?"*
>
> (Rory Lemon, 2025)

- **The Problem:** The Pain and Promise of Neurodivergence

For many neurodivergent (ND) creatives, **heightened sensitivity, divergent thinking, and vibrant imagination** are both powerful assets and sources of immense challenge. These attributes can lead to debilitating cycles of overwhelm, procrastination, and compulsive behaviours, yet these hurdles are not insurmountable.

Through a lot of personal encounters and in-depth research, I've observed that:

- Juggling a myriad of ideas often results in **mental scatter and distraction**.

- **Perfectionism fuels indecision**, leading to frustration.

- **Inadequate support structures** stifle innovation, progress, and potential.

Such struggles, however, frequently misunderstood, are very common among visionary minds, consistently balancing their brilliance with deep struggles and disappointment. Yet, here's the empowering truth: **with appropriate insights and tailored support, these challenges can transform into gateways for expansive growth.**

COACHING REIMAGINED Expanding Human Potential

Redefining Potential

Neurodivergence isn't a condition to be cured, but a prism revealing a spectrum of captivating innovations. This is where coaching resonates—**harmonising with unique neural pathways to facilitate equilibrium and creativity.**

After overcoming my own struggles—culminating in a deep immobilising period of psychosis—through natural methods, I realised that **so many elements of our minds and bodies are not fixed**. This insight fuels my commitment to assist ND creatives in refining their health, wealth, mindset, and career development.

Over the years, I've crafted an approach that transcends diagnostic labels, blending coaching, holistic health, and personal development. It's about transforming emotional roadblocks into strengths and **using these rooted challenges as fuel for professional development and collaborative visionary projects,** promoting inclusivity and sustainability.

My mission is driven by connecting with those who share this vision. Together, we're not just navigating personal struggles—we're co-creating a future where creativity empowers flourishing productivity.

"Do something useful with the human mind ... before it does you!"

(Rory Lemon, 2025)

The Shift: Creativity as a Non-Stop Structured Symphony

Automated self-judgement, blame, and victimisation have been passed down for generations, clouding the real true discernment and perception of ourselves and others, **intensified by our powerful imagination and ability to create what we choose.**

Creativity and imagination should not be seen as fleeting gifts fraught with challenges, but rather as a structured symphony where its harmony can transform struggles into growth.

Navigating the Pathways of "The 4 Types of Creativity"

For neurodivergent creatives, recognising four fluid types of creativity helps align innovative potential and productivity:

💥 **Disruptive Creativity:** Here, creativity turns inward, amplifying procrastination, confusion and unhealthy compulsive behaviours.

💡 Recognising these patterns enables the choice to channel energy constructively.

💥 **Aimless Creativity:** Although intertwined with possibility, this creativity lacks a focal point. Overwhelm, boredom, or self-doubt overtake commitment, leading to distractions like Netflix or social media.

💡 Prioritising intention helps harness energy more effectively.

💥 **Functional Creativity:** Structured creativity in temporary bursts—yet without translating work into inspiration. This type awaits purpose and vision.

💡 Reigniting deeper meaning fuels impactful work.

💥 **Visionary Creativity:** Full energetic alignment turns creativity into an effortless expression. Resonating across personal and collaborative frontiers.

💡 It's **the realisation of "FlowMo," (prolonged activated flow-states)**—where ideas are transformed into momentum and success.

These four types are not fixed entities but fluid experiences that shift throughout days and even moments. Hence, a visionary artist may still have an addiction, or a graphic designer may have aspirations and healthy routines, yet feel apathetic at work.

The goal is to spend more time in visionary states, where **creativity fuels action, health, fulfilment, and productive impact.**

Recognising The Signs of Creative Challenges

ND individuals often endure challenges such as immobilising emotional reactivity and heightened discrimination due to consistent **"automated personalization."**

Without embodying practiced methods for mentally and emotionally detached focus and processing, many face burnout from:

⚡ **Doing without saying:** Creating bottled emotions and a lack of external support, feedback, and collaboration.

⚡ **Saying without doing:** Succumbing to fears, procrastination, and wishful thinking.

⚡ **Doing without resting:** Hyper-fixation causing a neglect of self-care and rest.

Harnessing Potential Through Neurodivergent Coaching

Focusing on embracing inherent strengths while developing self-trust along the way, integrated coaching facilitates:

🌱 **Inner-Work:** Developing self-trust and emotional regulation through vision-mapping and planning.

🌱 **Creative Cycle Engineering:** Mastering flow states for maximising well-being.

🌱 **Inspirational Action:** Using "Wiction" (Wisdom in Action) to turn ideas into reality through the science of commitment.

🚀 **Chaos to Brilliance:** Through focus and tailored support, turning challenges into groundbreaking innovations.

This engaging, dynamic approach nurtures a **learning—creative flow cycle** that transcends fear-based thought loops.

By **tapping into conscious proactive divergent thinking, pattern recognition, and hyper-focus**, neurodivergent individuals can surpass cognitive barriers and embrace improved productivity.

Fostering **"FlowMo" (self-perpetuating learning—creative flow cycles),** involves working with effective:

🚀 **Mind management**

🚀 **Energy management**

🚀 **Productivity management**

In this revolutionary coaching perspective, neurodivergent minds lead the way to future success, harnessing creativity's full power. 🚀

"Awesomeness eventually finds awesomeness."

(Rory Lemon, 2024)

💡 The New Focus: NeuroCreative Leadership Frameworks

Introducing NeuroCreative Leadership: A Catalyst for Change

Central to personal transformation, NeuroCreative Leadership (NCL) empowers neurodivergent individuals by **interweaving neurodiversity, neuroplasticity, bioplasticity, and holistic growth**.

COACHING REIMAGINED Expanding Human Potential

The following core concepts support wellbeing across all life areas—**from health and career to personal projects and relationships**—by fostering self-leadership and mastery over internal landscapes for sustainable practice and defining true success.

1. Holistic Fitness: The Basis for Sustainable NCL

NCL is fuelled on the grounds of **"Holistic Fitness"**—recognising that **mental, emotional, physical and vocational health are interconnected**.

These principles establish a resilient foundation for creative flow and adaptability by addressing each individual's whole circumstance, including the environments necessary to thrive.

2. Plasticity Power: Embracing Adaptability

The next key to NCL is understanding "Plasticity Power"—the brain and body's ability to rewire, regenerate, and evolve.

Embracing this concept allows individuals to engage a growth mindset, **blending strategic challenges and necessary active recovery to maintain resilience and adaptability.**

3. Convergent and Divergent Thinking: Engines of Innovation

Appropriating divergent (idea generation) and convergent (idea execution) thinking is vital in the NCL framework.

This approach **optimises creativity and holistic decision-making,** by mastering when to expand possibilities versus refining ideas, ensuring best possible personal and collaborative successes.

4. Forgiftance: Bridging Self and Collective Growth

NCL leaders cultivate personal and community advancement by **embodying qualities of unparalleled empathy, curiosity, and**

visionary thinking.

Leaders foster a culture of inclusivity and collaboration through strategies of non-attachment, generosity, forgiveness, and **"Forgiftance"— providing unconditional encouragement for progress**.

5. Harnessing "Personality Power"

Personality traits formed during early life stages influence how we engage with the world. NCL looks to reframe these traits as strengths to empower personal and team dynamics.

Beyond acquired traits, unique combinations of intrinsic personality tendencies further shape how neurodivergent individuals engage with the world. These include:

- **Supportive (Empathy & Nurturing):** Builds deep, meaningful connections but may lead to over-giving and burnout if not tempered with healthy boundaries.

- **Analytical (Logic & Precision):** Provides insight and rigorous structure yet potentially fosters perfectionism and avoidance when unchecked.

- **Promotional (Vision & Influence):** Fuels creativity and inspiration but can spiral into impulsivity and overcommitment without guidance.

- **Controlling (Decisiveness & Leadership):** Drives direct action and explicit focus; however, it risks becoming rigid and defensively controlling without flexibility.

When neurodivergent minds lack purposeful engagement, they **risk defaulting to cognitive overload, self-doubt, and stress-induced behaviours**, which intensify challenges with focus and communication.

COACHING REIMAGINED Expanding Human Potential

Effective coaching reframes these patterns from points of shame into ND strengths, encouraging:

Divergent Thinking & Innovation: Uncovering solutions overlooked by others.

Creativity & Hyper-focus: Generating unique ideas and executing them with unmatched intensity.

Pattern Recognition & Detail Orientation: Connecting the dots across disciplines, fostering interdisciplinary innovation.

Resilience & Passion: Navigating adversity while sustaining meaningful and impactful endeavours.

Overall, by realising a flow of empathy, logic, vision, and leadership, neurodivergent individuals can flourish.

6. The MIND Model: A Holistic Approach to Insight

The **'Multi-Intellectual Neuro-Divulgence' (MIND)** model helps understand the intricate links between cognitive processes with somatic awareness by integrating intuition and wisdom across various areas of intelligent processing:

Head - Encompassing logical analysis and reasoning.

Heart - Empathy-driven intuition.

Gut - Natural instinct decision-making such as proactive spontaneity in play and dance.

Pelvis - Sensing longer-term connections and healing intuition.

Fascia - Deep-body wisdom and environmental awareness.

By also taking into account how each of these also interrelates with the **conscious, subconscious, and superconscious mind**, this multi-faceted approach further enriches holistic decision-making, providing a comprehensive lens through which to view individual and environmental interactions.

7. Uncovering Your Unique Learning Ability (ULA)

Understanding our ULA sparks innovative ND potential.

Being 'visionary' is not tied to purely mentally viewing things as pictures or imagery. By uncovering an individual's **intuitive processing style— be it more linguistic, sensual, or visual**—coaching enhances self-awareness and creativity, fostering impactful collaboration and growth.

8. The Source of Happiness: Accessing Heart-Driven Enrolment Energy

Central to the NCL approach, the idea that true satisfaction and creative fulfilment stem from **a harmonised flow between input, action, and expression.**

This balanced process, visualised as a triangular ecosystem, is powered by **information, inspiration, and meaningful action.** *(See diagram 1)*

☑ **In -** Growth begins with the inputs—by **what we choose to connect with physically, mentally, and emotionally**.

💡 Filtering consumption and embracing feedback fuels motivation and purpose.

☑ **Do -** Sustainable fulfilment involves conscious engagement with this information through deliberate self-practice—**using deep awareness, self-appreciation, and creativity.**

COACHING REIMAGINED Expanding Human Potential

- Prioritising mental fitness, learning, self-care, and renewal.

☑ **Out -** Outcomes manifest through filtering our **expression, communication, and collaborative endeavours.**

- Reinforcing growth and shared inspiration through intentional outward presentation.

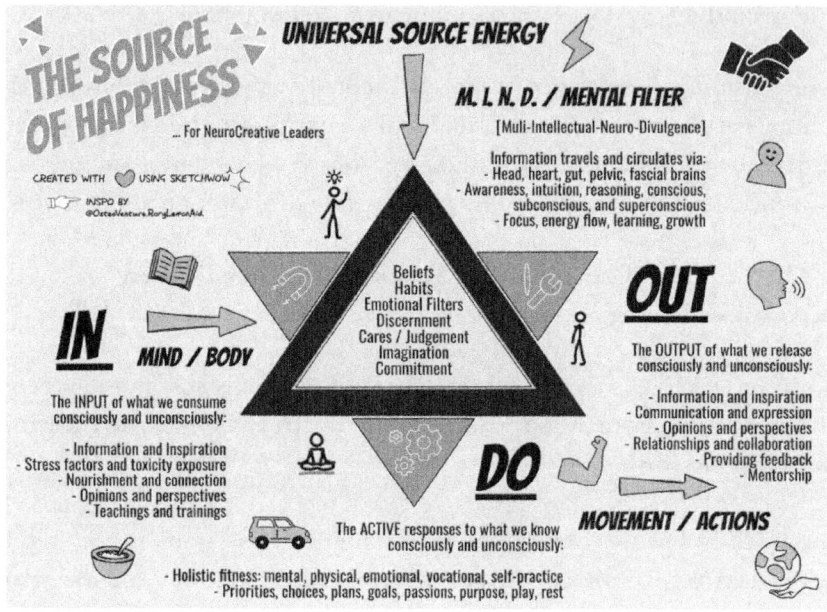

(Diagram 1 - "The Source of Happiness")

- Maintaining this equilibrium involves **mental fitness training and emotional regulation,** vital for preventing burnout.

Mindfully managing these elements allows NeuroCreative leaders to cultivate lasting happiness, self-trust, and impactful presence in both personal and professional realms.

9. Navigating Decisions with Inspirational Clarity (The 4Rs Framework)

Decision-making, though complex due to diverse emotions and sensitivities, becomes especially empowered through the 4Rs Framework:

Recognise: Identify and observe limiting patterns without judgment.

Refresh: Clear cognition with integrative tools for new perspectives.

Rehearse: Use imaginative intention to embody heart-centred desired realities.

Result: Translate visions into tangible actions with **"Wictions" (Wisdom in Action)**.

With this highly dynamic neuro-integrative framework, ND individuals navigate challenges creatively and confidently, facilitating **real-time inspired decision-making, emotional regulation, and reflective daily planning practice** for long-term transformational growth.

"Go define "useful" and fill your day with it."

(Rory Lemon, 2025)

The Transformation: Holistic Fitness for Creative Mastery

Harnessing Creative Flow and Prosperity

Transforming scattered ideas into powerful creations requires more than generic productivity hacks; it necessitates **deep alignment with individual rhythms to fuel health, wealth, and sustained creative flow**.

The journey of **Holistic Fitness Creative Mastery is powered by three key accelerators**:

Flow Habit Stacking: Develop daily rituals of impactful habits to nurture creativity across all of life's dimensions.

COACHING REIMAGINED Expanding Human Potential

🚀 **Energy Mastery Flow-Mapping:** Align personal energy rhythms with optimal work practices to enhance productivity.

🚀 **Accountability and Creative Sprints:** Establish foundational structure and support to shift delaying and realise creative projects efficiently.

The Triad of "Flourishment": Integrating Health, Wealth, and "Stealth"

Holistic Fitness is built on decades of research in holistic health, peak performance, and creative entrepreneurship, offering a spectrum of self-tested tools designed to align with unique neurodivergent strengths and drive sustainable success.

1. Holistic Health: Foundation for Sustainable Success

True creative freedom begins with a commitment to holistic health—incorporating the unique interplay between physical, emotional, and mental well-being.

"Holistic Health Hygiene" *(see diagram 2)* supports this through crafting personalised routines encompassing daily habits like movement, breathing, nutrition, and mental fitness, all aiming to minimise offering a blueprint for a purpose-driven life.

COACHING REIMAGINED Expanding Human Potential

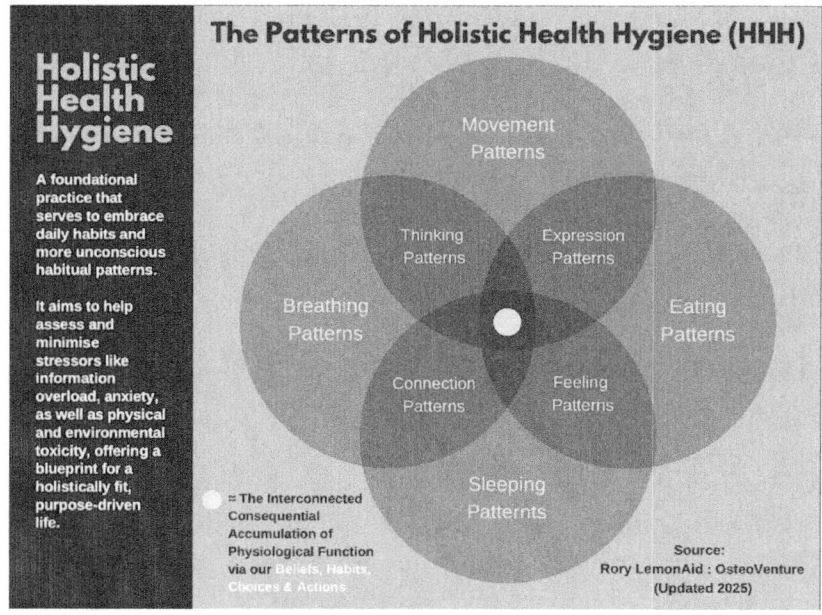

(Diagram 2 - Holistic Health Hygiene - HHH)
Although too extensive for including in this chapter, complementary Holistic Fitness systems like the 5BS™ Energy & Emotion Regulation and the 7Ms of Habit Formation™ provide further well-structured, tailored approaches to managing healthy resilience.

2. Wealth: Redefining Value and Richness

Beyond accruing financial gain, holistic wealth-care involves **defining values, cultivating meaningful relationships, and optimal environments** that enable creativity to thrive. Designing adaptive income streams aligned with personal strengths supports fulfilling ND careers.

Individuals can build fulfilling lives through **People, Places, and Power,** by fostering strategic partnerships, productive work spaces, and exercising the power to make confident, aligned choices.

3. Stealth: Mastering Focus, Structure, and Peak Performance

Stealth translates health and wealth using effective implementation. Core practices include:

- **"Wictions" (Wisdom in Action)** - Bridging vision, action, and the science of commitment.

- **The Art of Inspired Decision-Making** - Utilising deep awareness, The MIND Model & The 4xR Framework

- **Flow-State Engineering** - Mastering sustained creative cycles (FlowMo).

These practical strategies for daily productivity ensure self-trust and sustainable inspiration, especially encouraged through the power of **strategic communication, mentorship, and supportive feedback.**

Here, other stealth-care components to bear in mind are:

- Maintaining focus through **subtle awareness adjustments.**

- Aligning emotions **using sound and rhythm techniques.**

- **Creating adaptable and tailored routines** that suit individual needs.

- **Blending self-care with productivity via flow-mapping** to ensure sustained motivation and energy.

The Daily 5Ds™ System: Empowering Consistent Creative Flow and Success

Lastly, **"The Daily 5Ds™" System** is a cornerstone of stealth-care, promoting holistic self-directed productivity and engagement:

- **Dream – "Imaginate" & Envision:** Consulting multi-brain intelligence (MIND Model) for clear decision-making in desires and true values.

⚡ **Drop – Relax & Release:** Clear mental clutter, reset systems, and prioritise recovery with strategic activities and delegation.

⚡ **Draw – Design & Develop:** Reflect and journal to focus ideas, turning vision-mapping into tangible outcomes through daily planning.

⚡ **Drive – Activate & Embody:** Mental rehearsal techniques to focus commitment and reinforce pathways, ensuring consistency and follow-through via **"Wiction"** (Wisdom in Action).

⚡ **Dance – Flow & Celebrate:** Integrate flow mastery in work and play, enhancing performance and joy while reinforcing motivation through celebration and sharing.

💡 **Key Learnings in Holistic Fitness:** Integrating strategic insights with committed action transforms vision into tangible accomplishments. Aligning health, wealth, and stealth-care practices creates a synergistic framework where neurodivergent creatives thrive with finesse, turning potential into impactful reality.

"Words have no meaning in the compassionate chambers of the heart."

(Rory Lemon, 2024)

💡 A New Era of Creative Mastery: Bringing It All Together

The Vision-Mission of NeuroCreative Leadership

Throughout my life, I have guided individuals through profound transitions, helping them reshape perceptions of what is possible, especially in health. Whether through my hands, words, or guidance, I remain driven by deep intuition and a desire to explore beyond conventional boundaries.

COACHING REIMAGINED Expanding Human Potential

Holistic Fitness for NeuroCreative Leaders is about **creating with ease, joy, and sustainable momentum**. When health, wealth, adaptability, and peak performance align with ND strengths, creative flow becomes a natural and repeatable process rather than an exhausting battle.

Our NCL mission envisions a world where 100 million neurodiverse creatives uncover and celebrate their unique talents, **fostering visionary projects that inspire inclusivity and mental sustainability.**

A world embracing Unique Learning Abilities, turning challenges into profound growth opportunities.

This Journey Begins Now

🔥 **Information & Knowledge** is the fuel for confidence → yet without focus, potential remains untapped.

🔥 **Confidence & Action-Taking** is the rocket fuel → converting ideas into opportunity, creating momentum.

🔥 **Mentorship & Consulting** is the fire starter → streamlining experiential knowledge into confident action steps.

🔥 **Commitment, Repetition & Celebration** is the flame-thrower → ensuring lasting wellbeing, success and joy.

🔥 **Coaching, Accountability & Feedback** is the map, car and safety belt → accelerating clarity and progress with purpose.

As heart-centred NeuroCreative Leaders, we aren't just shaping our own lives—we pioneer a future where creativity, personal growth, and well-being drive transformation. **By championing inspirational projects and coaching-based leadership, we accelerate this vision globally.**

Real change begins when we honour the diversity of our nervous systems, recognising that:

☑ **Each mind has unique requirements to thrive.**

☑ **Environments must be tailored to neurodivergent strengths.**

☑ **True success comes through collaboration marked by awareness, empathy, and self-acceptance.**

The Wisdom in Action

Imagine a world where distraction and doubt give way to focused, fulfilling creative flow. Where creativity, aligned with neurodivergent strengths, fuels leadership and innovation. **This isn't just a coaching revolution; it's redefining our engagement with creativity and impact.**

A Call to Action: From Insight to Activation

Are you ready to help heart-driven neurodiverse creatives thrive?

To join the revolution that transforms self-sabotage into visionary success. For years, I've seen potential slip away amidst burnout and unfulfilled dreams.

When I discovered the key to **'remembering to remember'** everything changed for me and my productivity, and supporting ND creatives going **from FOMO (fear of missing out) to FlowMo**—where scattered ideas transform into thriving projects—will change the world!

Discipline can seem difficult, yet the regret of unrealised potential is much harder to bear.

Let's not spend another 25 years figuring this out.

COACHING REIMAGINED Expanding Human Potential

☞ **Nor wait until we hit rock bottom to seek change.**

☞ **And let's not do it alone!**

Join us, engage in the dialogue, and embark on this journey.

Together, we can craft a thriving, inclusive future—starting now.

[Please use the QR code to connect further, watch the Video Article version, book a Creative Mastery exploration interview, or take the NCL Vision-Mission Survey.]

Rory (LemonAid) - lemonaid.xyz -

hello@uniquelearningability.com

"Life doesn't have to be beautiful, but it is."

(Rory Lemon, 2024)

CHAPTER 12
Reframing – The Art of Thinking Differently
By Wendy Shaw

My World is Not Your World

Imagine waking up in a place where everything feels just slightly... odd. The air smells dry, the day moves at an unfamiliar pace, and even the smallest interactions require a moment of translation. You think you know how things work—until suddenly, you don't.

When I moved from England to Dubai 25 years ago, I expected adventure, but I hadn't anticipated the full force of culture shock. The rules were different. The unspoken norms, the way people connected, the very meaning of time itself—it all operated on a wavelength I hadn't yet tuned into.

I had a choice: resist and struggle or adapt and expand. And that's when

I realized something powerful. If I wanted to be effective in this new world, I couldn't just see things through my own lens— I needed to explore different lenses and update my frames of reference.

Working as a hotel training manager in Dubai, my audience was suddenly much more diverse. Every interaction required curiosity. What shaped their world? What did we share? What was different? What did that mean here? And most importantly—How could I connect with my audience and be relatable – truly connect?

The truth is, we don't always see eye to eye. We all carry different perspectives, shaped by culture, experience, and deeply ingrained beliefs. But perspective isn't fixed—it's fluid. The moment we embrace the possibility of thinking differently, of seeing the world through fresh eyes, everything shifts.

Reframing isn't just about thinking differently—it's about realizing there's more than one way to think.

The Power of Reframing

I didn't always realise the power of reframing. As a child, my grandmother had little patience for my sharp humour. "Sarcasm is the lowest form of wit," she would scold, unimpressed by my clever remarks. I remember thinking at the time—well, I don't find that funny at all!

Fast-forward years later, and I discovered Neuro-Linguistic Programming (NLP), where I was introduced to the concept of reframing. Suddenly, everything clicked. Reframing is the art of shifting perspective—recognizing that meaning isn't fixed but fluid. A situation, a setback, even an offhand comment—it all depends on how you choose to see *it* and what you make *it* mean. Context, language, and interpretation can transform an experience from limiting to liberating.

Politicians and comedians have long mastered the art of reframing. And it turns out, so had I. That so-called "sarcasm" my grandmother once disapproved of? It was actually a gift—an ability to see multiple angles, to challenge assumptions and to rewrite narratives in real time.

I couldn't resist the moment I told her about my new title— "The Queen of Reframing." I expected a grand reaction, but she simply rolled her eyes. And that, I thought, was her way of saying, *Touché*.

In this chapter I want to share some of my favourite reframing tools and give examples of how I have used them in different ways with clients. And I invite you to try them on and see if they can be useful for you.

We Can Choose How We Respond

I was around 10 years old when I wrote two very different thank you letters on the same day. One was super positive; the other was negative. Yet I was unconsciously sharing what each of my grandmothers focused on. Mum's mum was always looking at the bright side and thought everything was a blessing. Whereas Dad's mum was a worrier and complainer. She had some health problems, regular doctor appointments, she always worried about things.

That day I consciously realised I had a choice. I could choose what to focus on. Perhaps this was the foundation for my reframing skills! I can't remember when I started being fascinated with people. I just remember growing up curious and knowing that everyone is different. A perfect platform to explore reframing.

Focus On What You Want

When we first meet a coaching client, gaining clarity of what they want from coaching is useful. Yet, sometimes, especially if they're in a disempowered state, clients can have a laundry list of *what they don't want*.

It's a common pattern. Think about it—after an unsuccessful personal relationship, it's easy to rattle off all the things we *don't want* in our next one. But here's the thing: *we get what we focus on*.

COACHING REIMAGINED Expanding Human Potential

Our brains are wired to bring attention to whatever we say, both out loud and in our thinking. The reticular activating system—a small but powerful part of our brain—acts like a radar, constantly scanning and highlighting everything that aligns with our words. We will make that our reality. So, when we focus on 'what we don't want,' that's exactly what we attract.

Reframing those 'don't wants' into clear, positive statements of *what we do want* is more than a mental exercise—it's a powerful shift that changes the course of our lives.

I'm deeply fascinated by linguistics and the profound impact of the words we choose. Our language shapes our reality. Knowing that every word we say sends a signal to our brain, and in turn, the world around us, makes me very conscious and deliberate with the words I choose.

One of my favorite reframes is the shift from **Crisis to Opportunity.**

How do you respond in a crisis? Does your heart race? Do your muscles tense up? Do you go on high alert, scanning for any signs of danger? Now, imagine living every single day with that same heightened sense of urgency, constantly bracing for the worst. It will take its toll on you.

Life's challenges come to us all—it's inevitable. But what if, instead of reacting with fear or panic, we begin to *seek* the opportunities hidden within those challenges? How would that shift in perspective change your responses—and ultimately, your life?

Let me give you an example. I put Crisis versus Opportunity to the test when leaving Las Vegas and my flight was delayed. Becoming aware of my 'crisis' reaction and choosing an 'opportunity' reframe.

> Crisis - will I make my connecting flight?
> Opportunity – have a coffee, open my laptop and get some work done.

We eventually take off two hours later.

> Crisis – I will miss my connecting flight.
>
> Opportunity – I may be spending some time in Los Angeles.

That's an unexpected adventure.

When I reach the lounge in LA and explained I had missed my connection due to the delay.

> Crisis – they are looking for alternative flights and their system is slow!
>
> Opportunity – I offer to wait in the lounge, and they offer free drinks!

Given a hotel voucher and told the next flight is at 6am, two stops and a total of 17 hours travel time.

> Crisis – I will get minimal sleep and have to be back at the airport early.
>
> Opportunity - I could request a later direct flight and have a whole day in LA.

Hotel shuttle bus to the hotel.

> Crisis - lots of upset passengers who have been delayed.
>
> Opportunity – it's a complimentary stay in a 5-star hotel and I have a dinner voucher!

Check in was busy and the receptionist is dealing with many frustrated guests.

> Opportunity – be friendly and nice and I get a room upgrade!

I had somehow created a day in Los Angeles, got to paddle for the first time in the Pacific Ocean at Manhattan Beach and got home one day later than expected. Imagine what the outcome may have been if I had stayed with the initial, and understandable, crisis reaction.

Consider how you can apply the crisis versus opportunity reframe the next time you face a challenge. Choosing to seek opportunities can positively impact your behaviors and attitude which ultimately leads you to more positive results.

Reframing Situations

Perceptual Positions is another of my favourite reframing techniques which is useful to navigate and explore conflict scenarios from different angles.

When was the last time you experienced a difference of opinion with another person? Did you argue and push your point of view? Were you able to see where they were coming from? Did you reach a resolution or leave it unresolved? Or perhaps you agreed to disagree?

As humans, we are wired to analyze, criticize, and judge—to make sense of the world around us. But how often do we allow ourselves to pause, be curious, and truly understand the meanings behind what others say or do? Instead, we're quick to judge, jumping to conclusions without ever considering different perspectives. And let's face it: we all see the world through unique filters. Some of us perceive things in black and white, while others see fifty shades of grey. Words themselves can carry vastly different meanings to different people, which can dramatically shift the way we interpret and respond to situations.

What Is the Perceptual Positions Technique?

Imagine two chairs facing each other, one chair represents you and the second chair represents the other person involved in the scenario.

Position 1: Sit in the first chair. Revisit your experience of the situation from your perspective. Seeing it through your own eyes, associated into your emotions.

Position 2: Sit in the opposite chair and associate into the other person, putting yourself in their shoes to look at the situation through their eyes and connect with their emotions. Recount the situation from their point of view.

Position 3: Step back and look at the two chairs as an observer - considering how they are each behaving, what beliefs and values are important to each of them? What is there for you to learn?

Finally, return to Position 1 – sitting in the first chair as you, re-associate and integrate your learnings and new understanding of position 2, and the insights as an observer from position 3. Reflect on how you might respond differently now.

Perceptual Positions in Action

Case study: Peter, an executive coaching client, was really frustrated. He'd just had a heated meeting with his Board of Directors. They were "idiots!" He had a solution, and they were blocking him. He was adamant he had to convince them and if needed he would go above their heads and complain directly to the company owner.

We used our coaching session to explore the situation by fully considering each person's perspective by associating into their reality.

1st position – associated as Peter, reviewing the situation through his own eyes, justifying his behaviors, feelings, logic and reasoning. He was right, they were wrong.

2nd position we used three times! – seeing it through the eyes of each director, using a different seat for each one. In each role he was asked to vocalise their behavior, their beliefs and values, allowing Peter to consider each of their points of view and their reasoning behind it.

3rd position – standing back as an observer looking at the situation from the outside. Peter turned to me with his realisation "You have saved my job! They can't support what I am pushing for because in their roles they see other impacts that I hadn't even considered."

Just like Peter, it's likely that you believe that you are 100% right in everything you think, everything you say, and everything you do. The challenge when you are facing a conflict or disagreement with someone, they are also 100% right according to them.

When you experience a disagreement with someone, stop for a moment and consider how their point of view maybe different. Step back as an observer and consider how the other person is feeling, behaving and relating. Switch on your curiosity... Are there different values and beliefs that are driving different behaviors to your own? Is this an opportunity to understand them better?

Using Perceptual Positions When the Client is Stressed

Case Study: Andrew loved his job at the nightclub and thrived on busy weekends with his large team and loyal customers. However, one Saturday night, his boss arrived and demanded immediate VIP service despite the club being full. Andrew tried to help but was met with an explosive outburst of swearing and insults.

Days later, Andrew looked visibly shaken and pale. After visiting a doctor, he was signed off work, feeling humiliated and emotionally shattered.

In our session, I guided Andrew to dissociate from his intense emotions by asking him to move seats, becoming an observer (position 3).

Instead of viewing the situation from each perspective, we used two imaginary chairs to gently examine the attitudes and beliefs of both himself and his boss.

Andrew identified that he had a choice: to leave or stay in his role. We discussed what conditions would allow him to stay.

By the end, Andrew felt calmer and more in control.

Guiding Andrew to step back into position 3 helped him dissociate from his highly emotional state into a calm safer space. He was able to view and explore position 1 and position 2 objectively, from a distance, leading him to clarity and identifying actionable steps.

COACHING REIMAGINED Expanding Human Potential

As a Coach, I can only work with clients when they are ready and willing. Let's face it, some people LIKE having problems!

For example, if you have health problems, you need to see a doctor who takes time to listen to your problems. That could be the highlight of the week. You can talk to your friends and family about your problem and gain sympathy.

I believe that a problem is only a problem when we decide it's a problem. Up until then, it's just information.

Using Perceptual Positions to Unpack a Behavioral Strategy

Case Study: A mother sought help for her 17-year-old son, Steven, who had a severe stutter. The mother initially stated that he wasn't able to call due to his stutter, but he did. Our long call marked the beginning of his journey toward overcoming this challenge, especially as he was preparing to study abroad.

Steven had stuttered for nearly a decade, impacting his education and family interactions. He received extra support at school, was often excused from activities, and spent time on hobbies like rap music and video games. With the upcoming transition to living independently, he felt motivated to overcome his stutter.

During our sessions, we explored his secondary gains from stuttering—how his mother's advocacy and the special treatment had shaped his experience. Once he recognized these benefits were no longer serving him, he was ready to move forward.

I asked Steven to leave himself sitting in the chair (dissociate from position 1), to have a good shake, to relieve any tension from his body and to come and stand next to me (observer position 3). And I asked him to teach me how to do his stutter.

With some encouragement, he gave me clear instructions and I kept interrupting him to challenge the strategy and introduce the opposite of what he said – applying a scramble technique to disrupt his patterning.

Step 1. Take in a deep breath - it won't work if you breathe shallowly or evenly.
Step 2. Hold your breath - it won't work if you breathe out.
Step 3. Tightly squeeze your diaphragm, it won't work if you relax...

He had truly mastered his technique, and he knew exactly how to do it! As he was instructing me, and we scramble that well-trodden pathway, I brought to his attention that he wasn't stuttering while explaining his strategy. He paused. His eyes opened wide, he looked in my direction and smiled.

In this scenario I did not want Steven to reassociate into himself (position 1 – with the stutter). Instead, we switched seats, so he was now sitting in the coaches chair as the expert.

We explored the need to practice new breathing techniques, redefine his mother's role, and schedule weekly phone calls while abroad. He later expressed his gratitude by sending me a recording of him rapping, stutter free, marking a significant milestone in his journey.

In this example I used only the observer position to dissociate from Steven's problem state. Standing up shifted his physiology and moved him out of his head. Constantly interrupting to ask what would happen if I did it differently forced him to consider it, interrupting his strategy. Getting the steps consistently wrong was also a pattern interupt. Asking him to sit in 'the expert's' chair gave him authority and a sense of control.

Modifying tools and techniques to meet individual client needs and understanding the principles beneath the process, is essential for coaching mastery. As is having a tool box to dip into, that will take coaching even deeper, incorporating the whole person, not just the head.

The Mind-Body Connection

Do you love learning and enjoy acquiring new skills to be able to help your clients more effectively? I do! In my coaching practice, I've explored multiple modalities, always searching for tools that help people move beyond stuck patterns and I love exploring how I can weave tools together to make them even more effective.

I have always been curious about the mind-body connection and one of the most profound discoveries for me is **Multiple Brain Integration Techniques (mBIT)**—a coaching approach that teaches people how to align the intelligence of the head, heart, and gut.

The Future of Coaching: Thinking Beyond the Head

As coaching evolves, we are moving away from purely cognitive, logic-driven methods toward a more holistic, embodied approach. The head brain is essential, but it is not the only source of intelligence. The heart offers deep wisdom about our values, relationships, and purpose. The gut provides intuition, resilience, and an instinctual knowing of what feels right.

When we integrate these intelligences, we make better decisions, align with what truly matters, and move forward with greater confidence and ease.

Coaching is no longer just about changing thoughts—it's about transforming how we *experience* ourselves, from the inside out.

Totally intrigued, I gifted a copy of the book: **mBraining – Using Your Multiple Brains to do Cool Stuff** to my mum, who is always curious about what I'm learning. Months later, she called me, excited: *"I've reached my dream weight—8 stone 8 ounces!"*

Surprised, I asked her which diet she had followed this time. But it wasn't a specific diet or calorie counting. She had applied what she learned from the book—she had simply *gotten her head, heart, and gut talking to each other.*

- **Her heart** truly desired to be slim—it was important to her, tied to her values of health, vitality, and feeling happy in her

body.
- **Her head** knew exactly what she needed to do—she had all the knowledge about healthy eating and exercise.
- **Her gut**, however, was sabotaging her progress, reacting impulsively to food with a simple but powerful response: *"Yum yum!"*

She described it as "calling a meeting of the minds." A conversation between her own intelligences, allowing them to debate, align, and ultimately agree to work together. Nearly a decade later, her weight remains steady—a testament to what happens when we harness the wisdom of the full-body intelligence system.

Why Don't We Always Do What We *Know*?

Most people *know* what they need to do. Yet, they don't always do it. That's because knowing is not the same as integrating. We have been programmed to be head-dominant—analyzing, judging, and reasoning our way through life. But transformation happens when we engage the full spectrum of intelligence available to us and aligning them.

If I were to ask you, *'What does your heart truly want to share?'* or *'What does your gut deeply need to feel safe?'*—you might struggle to answer. That's because your head brain immediately jumps in, filtering the question, analyzing and searching for the 'right' response.

But these deeper intelligences don't communicate in logic and language alone. They speak in sensation, intuition, imagery, metaphor and feeling. To access them, we must shift out of the head and into the body.

Tuning Into Your Embodied Intelligence

A skilled coach will guide the client's awareness and pace their experience. Here's an opportunity to explore your own intelligences in the body:

Connecting with the Heart
- Place your hand on your heart.

- Take a few deep and even breaths, notice how this pauses your thinking mind.
- Your heart holds your values—what's truly important to you. Ask your heart:
    - *'What does my heart truly want to share?'*
    - *'What does my heart say is most important?'*

Connecting with the Gut
- Place your hand on your lower abdomen.
- Breathe deeply and evenly, grounding yourself in this space.
- Your gut is the seat of courage, intuition, and self-preservation. Ask:
    - *'What does my gut need to feel safe?'"*
    - *'What does my gut deeply need to move forward?'*

I invite you to keep exploring and making it a normal part of your life and decision making to check in with your body intelligence, and notice how this helps you to reframe situations, by taking on more perspectives from within.

How Can We Combine Perceptual Positions With Accessing Inner Wisdom?

You are the expert of you. No one knows you better than you do. A coach may have tools to guide you, but they don't hold *your* wisdom, *your* solutions, or *your* truth. And this is also true of the other people you are relating to. We can extend Perceptual Positioning to take into consideration the multiple intelligences of all parties.

As the *expert* of you, connecting with your heart, ask yourself:
- *'What does my heart want to share with <u>their</u> heart?'*
- *'What does <u>their</u> heart say is most important to them?'*

As the *expert* of you, connecting with your gut, ask yourself:
- *'What does my gut want to express to <u>their</u> gut?'*
- *'What does <u>their</u> gut need to feel safe?'*

These are examples of using the observer (Position 3) as the expert. In essence it's Do-It-Yourself mentoring! I have also used this approach successfully to help clients who struggle to listen/hear their heart or gut. Becoming the expert (position 3) and gifting their wisdom to themselves (position 1).

Take the Wheel: Owning Your Life and Your Growth

Life isn't something that happens *to* you—it's something you create. The question is: *Are you in the driver's seat?*

Some people sit in the passenger seat, letting circumstances dictate their direction. Others drift into the back seat, feeling powerless over their own journey. Some have handed the wheel to someone else entirely, while others aren't even in the car—disconnected from their own path.

Imagine stepping outside yourself for a moment—seeing yourself through the eyes of a coach. **If you were your coach, what is the single most powerful question you could ask yourself right now?**

Well done – you have just taken position 3 on your own circumstances. Notice how, if answered honestly, this can propel you toward your most authentic, empowered self.

The Power of Self-Talk

It's clear that how you speak to yourself shapes your reality. Too often, we *listen* to ourselves and get caught in the loop of doubt, fear, and negativity because of the meaning we are placing on a situation.
But what if, instead, you choose a different frame and learned to *talk* to yourself with intention?

- Speak words of encouragement.
- Focus on what's possible.
- Direct your thoughts toward growth and action.

The thoughts you think and the words you say **matter.** They shape and frame the direction of your life. So take the wheel. Choose the words and frames that move you forward. As Wayne Dyer said; "If you change the way you look at things, the things you look at change."

As I conclude this chapter, I urge you to broaden your perspective and embrace the diverse lenses through which others view the world. Cultivate a genuine curiosity about your clients who think and act differently from you; it's through this exploration that we discover the richness of human experience. Ask yourself – What am I not seeing, hearing, sensing here?

Encourage reframing—shift your client's focus to what they truly want and what can be possible, to actively seek the opportunities that arise, especially when life happens.

You are the expert in your own life, embody the very best version of yourself, explore other perspectives to extend your unique insights and wisdom as you navigate your expanding coaching career confidently into the future. Enjoy the ever-evolving journey!

Connect with me…

Beyond coaching, I am a Trainer of mBIT, NLP, Time Line Therapy® & Hypnosis and certified in many coaching modalities including several assessment and psychometric tools. To feed my curiosity I consistently seek valuable insights through master classes with renowned experts, to further enhance my coaching methodology.

If you are a coach, trainer, mBrainer, NLPer or if you are currently at the beginning of your coaching journey, I would love you to join my community. **https://linktr.ee/mbrain.me**

Resources: If you would like a copy of the Perceptual Positions questions I use, feel free to reach out to me.

Book recommendations: mBRAINING - Using Your Multiple Brains to do Cool Stuff by Grant Soosalu & Marvin Oka
Words That Change Minds by Shelle Rose Charvet

CHAPTER 13
The Power of the 'AHA' moment
By Helen Oakwater
Coach, Trainer, Author

Intent on Melting Trauma, Transformation and Future-proofing

Join the dots. Recognising the *'AHA'* moment

You know that moment, when something shifts inside you, and suddenly, everything makes sense in a way it never has before. A thought you've never consciously noticed before surfaces, with a quiet *'oh,'* a surprised *'oow,'* or a resounding *'AHA.'* Whatever form it takes, it's the spark that transforms your perspective and propels you forward.

Using your coaching calibration and sensory acuity skills you can spot a clients *'AHA'* when physicality changes. Breathing rate or depth might alter. Maybe the gaze softens, their focus floating into the distance. A facial flush, a foot starts or stops bouncing. They jolt or freeze. You know something significant has happened inside.

It's not always a huge eureka moment when a quantum leap of understanding occurs. Maybe it's just the realisation that something important has bubbled to the surface. Fresh insights, a shift in perception, comprehension at a different level. You've joined the dots. Link two ideas, you have a third perspective. Connect several ideas and you have infinite possibilities. When you join dots about your behaviour, beliefs, values, life experiences and sense of self, it is transformational. Choices widen. As a Coach, it's a privilege to witness in your clients. As an evolving human, it's a delight to notice in yourself.

While coaching is generally present and future focused, sometimes re-examining our past through fresh lenses is essential. This chapter illustrates how incorporating child development concepts and an awareness of trauma into your coaching schema can accelerate clients' wisdom, reframe events and allow forgiveness.

Psychoeducation offers knowledge about how we function, thus presenting opportunities to improve our mental health, well-being and negotiate the vagaries of life. I believe deeply in the power of understanding the *why*. In my experience when people truly grasp *why* something matters, they are best placed to determine their own *what* and *how*. Also *why* often generates the most powerful *'AHAs'* leading to profound, enduring change.

Why should you listen to me? Because with 20+ years coaching, 30+ years in the child trauma world, lifelong curiosity and the courage to face brutal truths, I've some wisdom plus several grubby T-shirts, stained with the sweat of experience and snot of personal growth.

Delivering training sharpens my coaching, which hones my writing. A virtuous cycle. Two books. Multiple articles. Spouting from platforms around the world. I chose to study with pioneers and masters from multiple fields. I love *'AHA'* moments, even when they hurt.

One of my own big *'AHA'* moments came during my preparation to become an adoptive parent. Self-reflection, understanding your own upbringing, behaviours and relationships is a standard part of the adoption assessment process. A comment from the social worker that I had "only received conditional love" struck me hard. I spent two weeks being very angry, as it challenged my perception of my own childhood. However, I processed and reflected the contrasts between conditional versus unconditional love. As my awareness widened, the significance of the social workers sharp observation deepened. It helped me uncover facets of myself and better understand the three children I later adopted from the UK care system.

A decade later, on the first day of my NLP practitioner course, the sharing of Robert Dilts logical levels model blew my mind. Inside multiple dots joined explosively. Uncharacteristically I did not move. The massive *'AHA'* of "beliefs drive behaviour" made sense of my children's apparently nonsensical behaviour, the consequence of their maltreatment as infants.

Why it's important: sledge metaphor

Einstein allegedly said, "Stupidity is doing the same thing over and over again and expecting different results." The same is true for thinking. Looping round negative, critical self-talk is not useful and can be hugely destructive over time. But how do you break out of such behaviour? Metaphors abound. New light through old windows. Rose-tinted glasses. Taking a bird's eye view. Fake it till you make it. Update your software.

One of my metaphors is a sledge. Imagine we are each pulling a sledge along our unique timeline, over icy ground heading towards the future, our past behind us. The sledge contains significant memories, events and baggage. The negative or painful events are the heavy burdens we drag with us, holding us back. Imagine each of these as a wrapped parcel on the sledge. I use two categories. Round shapes are S.H.I.T. (Selective Hurts Internalised and Trapped) and pointy shapes are C.R.A.P (Charged Reactive Angry Particles). Maybe sketch a sledge that depicts the baggage you are carrying. Play with shapes, sizes, colours and symbols. What insights does that throw up for you?

Good coaching and therapeutic practices offer us a safe space to stop trudging, remove, unwrap and examine a parcel. Inside will be a jewel, a gold nugget, a learning we might place inside our heart.

We can then discard the wrapping (the shit and crap) and proceed feeling lighter, with shoulders less hunched, enjoying our *'AHA'* transformational moment.

Benefits of understanding

Being able to time travel and revisit our past and see our younger selves in a challenging situation can be hugely valuable. We might spot where we formed a limiting belief or how a trauma froze a part of us aged five. We may hear our self-talk coming from someone else's mouth. The father saying "you are bad" becomes embedded, unfiltered by six-year-old ears. Revisiting that experience, as a fly on the wall at 46, you observe that little kid, your younger self, being bullied by a shouting giant who had the power to support, kill, ignore, nurture or hurt you. What an *'AHA.'*

A manager sent a young man to me to improve his awkward presentation delivery. Platform skills and techniques can be taught, though often skills are not the real issue. After some conversational coaching, it became clear, the problem was not capability. Turns out his father was an alcoholic. As a child, my client realised that keeping quiet kept him safe. This belief was true and useful back then, but now it hindered his professional development. Updating that belief to "its safe and empowering to speak and be heard" sent positive ripples throughout his body and entire life. Sometimes an *'AHA'* nudges our life trajectory more powerfully than we realise at the time.

If one *'AHA'* nudge is useful, imagine the profound effect of dozens of dots connecting. A deeper understanding of our behaviours, habits, relationships, strengths and weaknesses leads to systemic change and an enriched life. Pattern detection is a superpower, hence integrated and systemic coaching is essential for deep transformational change, by safely pacing multiple *'oh' 'oow'* and *'AHA'* moments.

Reframing: mindsight, magical thinking, safety and courage

Obviously psychoeducation and learning that facilitate *'AHA'* moments can come from many sources. Books, films, training courses, therapy, friends, podcasts, life crises, parenting and coaching all offer opportunities. It allows us to reframe events with 20/20 vision. To witness our experiences and decision making retrospectively. But, if, and only if, it feels ok and safe to do so.

One aspect of child development, particularly relevant when revisiting childhood memories, was the absence of mindsight, the ability to stand in someone else's shoes and see things from their perspective. This capacity, closely linked to empathy, typically develops in mid childhood, as the prefrontal cortex blossoms. Inconveniently it reduces during adolescence, when the prefrontal cortex experiences significant rewiring.

Another crucial concept is magical thinking which, from roughly two to seven, dominates a child's world view. They believe their thoughts or actions can directly cause events. Lacking the ability to filter or question what they are told, the beliefs formulated in these early years remain deeply embedded and often unexamined. That's why so many people feel stuck. Revisiting those early beliefs with a discerning adult perspective, in coaching or therapy, can be transformative. When I hear the words "it was not my fault." my heart sings, because powerful *'AHA's* are updating antiquated belief systems.

It takes courage to enter the "I need and want to change" arena. Ambrose Redmoon said, "Courage is not the absence of fear but rather the judgement that there is something else more important than fear." The arena itself must feel safe. Are there trusted mentors who have your back? Are they skilled? Have you picked the right coach for your specific issues? I always recommend people talk to at least three coaches before selecting who they work with. Equally, good coaches have boundaries and tell clients, "I'm not right for you because… (insert reason)." Rapport must exist. For me, a client with no sense of humour is a no no. It would prevent me from being my authentic self, hence less able to fully serve my client.

Safety applies to both the external environment, the room, exits, noise, comfort plus the clients' internal somatic senses. It also takes into account real threat and perceived threat. Outside of our conscious control, the Autonomic Nervous System constantly scans the world around us looking for signs of danger and safety, in a process called neuroception. It's our ultimate threat detection system. Think of it like a smoke detector. Some are super sensitive and sound at the faintest whiff of smoke or steam.

Ponder: if you don't feel safe in your body, would you feel safe anywhere?

Barriers to learning: Fear, Shame, Blame

Fear is a major hurdle to overcome when undertaking any change work or tackling a new venture. Sensitive coaching can show fear is often 'False Evidence Appearing Real' causing the body to 'Forget Everything and Run.' A courageous client unpacking a sledge parcel, who reframes a painful event from 35 years ago using today's wisdom, is more able to 'Face Everything and Rise.' That takes serious courage.

Shame is feeling bad about self. It lurks below depression, guilt, sadness, anger and other negative emotions. I think shame is the most toxic emotion and it often grows in children who had inadequate or toxic parenting. At an identity level shame often equates to "I am bad/nothing/unimportant/worthless."

Blaming others abdicates responsibility for your behaviour, actions or feelings. The "it's not my dot to join" mentality. Shame and fear, too painful to examine, may be lurking below the blaming attitude.

Substance abuse, addiction of any kind and self-destructive behaviours can act as a quick temporary fix, to deaden deep pain. Maybe it dulls the neuroception smoke detector. This is a complex cocktail and worth remembering when pacing the speed of an individuals healing journey.

Some people require longer to unpack and process their parcels of shit and crap. Some may not have the capacity for this challenging task right now, or ever.

Deeper Barriers: Trauma and Complex Trauma

I have been exploring the impact of childhood trauma since it walked into my home on six little legs inside my adopted children (aged 5, 4, 2) in the 1990s. Understanding the legacy of maltreatment and neglect, melting trauma and future proofing children has become part of my DNA. I've searched for healing tools, methodologies, therapeutic interventions, read extensively, attended conferences, trainings, support groups and pondered (a lot) in an effort to heal my hurt children. The *'AHA'* that neglect does more harm than abuse was a big one. (If you're neglected, do you even exist?).

Discovering therapeutic reparenting, which aims to undo the damage and fill in the developmental gaps, allowed me to join some dots and recognise the limits of my powers. Not everything is fixable. That was brutal realisation, but essential for my own sanity.

In 2002 I stumbled into NLP (NeuroLinguistic Programming), the study of the structure of subjective experience, and found a glorious new way of being and thinking. A place where my use of metaphors, diagrams, humour, compassion and courage were welcomed. I started coaching professionally and realised that for some clients my child development knowledge integrated beautifully with other models and tools. It can explain why someone is stuck, especially after trauma.

Trauma is an overwhelming, inescapable experience which an individual is unable to integrate. (Bessel Van Der Kolk's book, 'The Body Keeps the Score.' is an excellent resource). Trauma can shatter a persons' sense of self, their belief system and alter their world view. My coaching tool kit has multiple resources and techniques which I adapt to get optimal results for each client. I am comfortable (and safe) working with trauma. Many coaches are not. Get good training if trauma floats your boat. Know your scope of practice and stay in your lane. However, all coaches should be cognisant of the powerful grip trauma exerts on individuals, recognise its appearance and a have basic management strategy. Although significant traumatic event(s) may have occurred decades before, when triggered, it feels like it's happening now. Right now. Right here. In this moment. Because trauma is embodied. It's enmeshed in the body.

A rape victim felt guilty that she didn't fight. I ran the NLP dissociation trauma process with her, which, in essence, allows a client to safely watch a tiny movie of the event while staying emotionally disconnected. The client gets multiple learnings. In this case, she spotted that had she fought, the attacker would have killed both her and her baby. Guilt was replaced by pride. That wholehearted realisation transformed a flurry of dots into a huge gold nugget, a chunky empowering belief and reframe of epic proportions. All without re-traumatising the client. A single incident trauma like this is common and meltable within the coaching arena, *if* you are appropriately trauma trained. Remember: first do no harm.

The impact of childhood trauma, be it neglect, maltreatment or abuse is doubly devastating because it interferes with children's normal developmental processes. Perfect for creating complex trauma. I intentionally mix multiple simple metaphors to explain the concepts and avoid unpleasant gory detail. The purpose is to get the message across, paint a picture, not clinical accuracy. To be useful and make sense of (behavioural) non-sense.

TIM, Shrapnel and Developmental Walls

Consider for a moment an infant lying in a cot. Tim (Traumatised Infant Maltreated) has an oozing nappy, hunger cramps in his belly, can taste his own vomit, smell sour milk and he is cold. The rough, stained yellow blanket is threadbare. Nappy rash runs from his waist to his skinny knees. He stopped crying hours ago, because he knows no-one will respond. These individual sensory components (smell, taste, feel, touch, sounds) amalgamate, in my metaphor, to sensory "shrapnel".

COACHING REIMAGINED Expanding Human Potential

TIM : sensory experience in cot
Creation of Shrapnel

Smell: Sour Milk, Excrement
Touch: Nappy Rash
Taste: Vomit
Hear: Silence? Shouting?
See: Darkness? Violence?
Feel: Hunger Pangs, Nappy Rash, Cold Feet

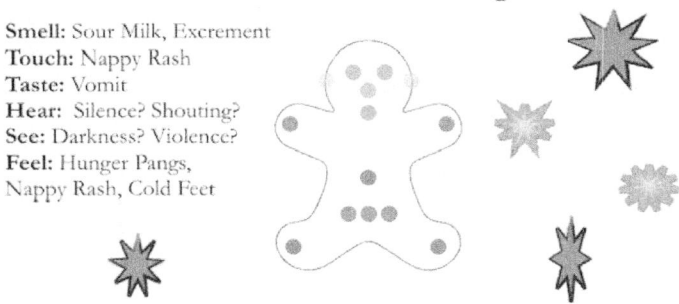

As protection, Tim swathes himself in metaphorical bubble wrap. However, this distorts his perspective of the world and the world's view of him. People see his presenting behaviour (often challenging) not the hurt child below. Without skilled holistic interventions the bubble wrap remains fixed. Are you surprised he hoards or steals food when older, and/or can't sit still in class and/or self-harms and/or has an explosive temper?

Poor Tim had multiple events like this, often over many years. I add colours for maltreatment subsets. The shrapnel shapes vary. Some intertwine. Some morph into parcels of crap and shit. Bubblewrap abounds.

Different Maltreatments
Assorted Shrapnel

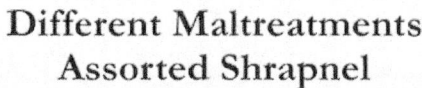

| NEGLECT | | PHYSICAL ABUSE |
| green | | red |

| FEAR | | |
| blue | | |

		SEXUAL ABUSE
EMOTIONAL ABUSE		black
orange		

COACHING REIMAGINED Expanding Human Potential

Whilst we may not see clients as extreme as Tim, everyone has some shrapnel and bubblewrap, hence psycoeducation can be hugely beneficial. When people realise others have similar "deep, dark secrets" shame starts melting. Often an audible sigh. Laminated handouts and books are concrete evidence that "it's not just me."

News flash. We were all once children. Mostly experiencing Winnicotts "good enough parenting." However, some shit and crap happened to us when we were small, young, fragile, vulnerable, exploring the world and making mistakes. Our development is affected by multiple factors.

Imagine child development is like constructing a wall, where the individual needs are bricks. The first diagram gives a rough idea for infants.

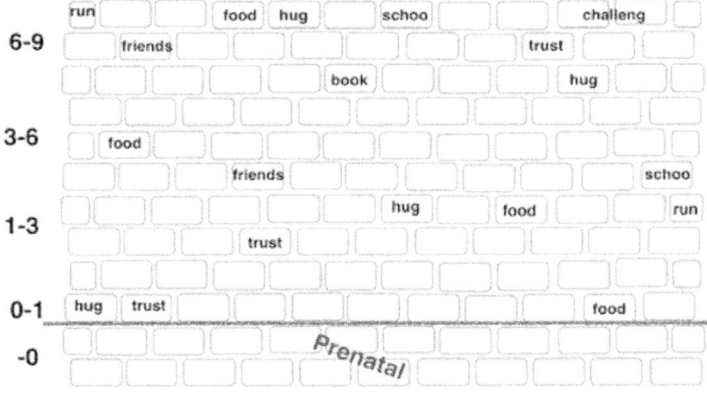

As the child grows, some needs change or modify, new ones emerge and others, like food, repeat endlessly. With good enough parenting, the bricks are solid, the wall robust.

COACHING REIMAGINED Expanding Human Potential

Zooming into bricks of infant needs

hugs	praise	attuned adults	food	fresh air	sleep
touch	comfort	language	calm	warmth	toys
play	routine	stimulation	shelter	good hygiene	trust
boundaries	eye contact	attention	clean clothing	nutritious food	fun

The child with a well-formed wall, has a secure attachment style and a positive world view as shown in the diagram below.

Secure Attachment
Child's View of Self and World?

I am safe
I am loveable
I am nurtured
I am valued
I am special
I can trust adults
I'm okay

There is a place for me here
The world is safe
People love me
People care for me
I am important to them
The world is okay

Sometimes war, disaster, poverty or horrid incidents result in crumbly, cracked or broken bricks. Accidents happen. Parents or loved ones die too early. Sadly, these stun grenades alter families, weakening walls, despite solid foundations. Even worse, some children have toxic parents, who over decades, constantly fail to prioritise their children's needs.

Ponder. What does Tims' wall look like?

Disturbed Attachment
Child's View of Self and World?

I am not safe

I am not nurtured

I'm scared

I am unlovable

I am ignored

I am not valued

I am alone

I am not ok

It's a terrifying hostile world

People hurt you

There is danger

No-one cares

There is no place for me

The world is not okay

Consider how sensory shrapnel erratically embeds itself in the child after prolonged shouting, pain, witnessing domestic abuse, terror, chaos or cruelty. Their belief system and sense of self reflects these experiences. Their neuroception smoke detector will be hypersensitive. That wall more prone to collapsing. Again swathes of bubble wrap, distorting how others see them and how they regard themselves.

Ponder: what does a collapsing wall look like in a 20, 30, 40, 50, 60, 70-year-old? Was that outburst of ghastly behaviour a metaphorical IED (Improvised Explosive Device), wall fall or the triggering of historical shrapnel? Or both? How might Tim behave at different ages?

Consolidation

Children become adults, each with a unique sledge, a unique wall and unique belief and values systems, plus assorted shrapnel. Hence, we should always coach the *person*, not impose our preferred (or only) modality on them. Don't be Slack Harry with just a rusty spanner, screwdriver and spoon. The bigger your toolbox, and skilled flexibility to navigate round it, the greater precision of your coaching. Be humble. Listen. Learn. Observe. Reflect. Question cleanly. Be courageous.

In my experience, many people enjoy the insights models and metaphors offer. Psychoeducation facilitates *'AHA'* dot joining. It's useful. The client with the bullying father realised Dad was an inadequate inflexible man, too fearful to tackle his own baggage. She learned her six-year-old self had no mindsight, hence lacked the capacity to filter his unjust criticism. Her realisation that "I am bad" was buried inside several large sledge parcels was liberating. Her fresh wisdom peeled the distorting bubblewrap. Her self-worth grew. She forgave herself.

We all do the best we can with what we have. I love watching my clients gather fresh resources, update their beliefs, dump some crap, compassionately console their younger selves, acquire new skills, nurture their wounds, update their software, lose their shit, create compelling futures and powerfully embrace their *'AHAs.'* Coaching is a delightful privilege.

As an evolving human, I've stumbled through all the above practices, navigating the road less travelled. I'm still loving *'AHA'* moments, even when they hurt. Hope you do too.

Next Steps

- The Helen Oakwater YouTube channel has two short explainer interviews with Robert Dilts on Logical Levels and trauma. Follow the link.
- For more detail about Tim, his clan, the legacy of child trauma and adoption perspectives, explore my FAB Parents website. **www.FABparents.co.uk**
- Curious to learn more about the me, my coaching, training, books, resources etc? Follow the link
- You can connect with me in most of the usual ways.
- Thanks for getting this far. Take Good Care.
- **Linktree: www.linktr.ee/helenoakwater**

COACHING REIMAGINED Expanding Human Potential

CHAPTER 14
Busting the Imposter Within
By Michelle Dalley

Do You Ever Feel Like a Fraud?

You've worked hard, achieved so much—but deep down, do you ever feel like you don't truly belong? Like any moment now, someone will tap you on the shoulder and expose you as an imposter? If so, you're not alone.

Imposter Syndrome isn't just a buzzword—it's a relentless, quiet voice in your head whispering, *You're not good enough. You got lucky. You don't deserve this.*

I know that voice all too well.

Growing up in a middle-class family in the 1970s, I was taught the importance of working hard and staying humble. Boasting wasn't an option. My parents' values emphasised putting others first, having a strong work ethic, and taking personal responsibility. These lessons shaped me—

but they also taught me to suppress emotions, avoid vulnerability, and strive for perfection to meet others' expectations.

On the surface, my childhood was normal. Loving parents. A passion for dance. I started ballet at four and aced every exam. But when it came to performing? Anxiety took over. I put immense pressure on myself to be perfect. The same thing happened in other sports. Even with positive feedback, I never felt *good enough*. So eventually, I quit.
Sound familiar?

Like many, I experienced rejection or feeling humiliated at times - by teachers, by peers, by love interests. Failing in public, being teased, not measuring up. They were everyday experiences, but each one reinforced the idea that I wasn't enough. So, I did what many of us do: I put on a mask. I became hyper-independent. I kept striving. I made sure I appeared competent, resilient, *capable*.

I had no idea these experiences were rewiring my nervous system, quietly planting the seeds of Imposter Syndrome.

By the time I entered the workforce, my perfectionism was in overdrive. Mistakes weren't an option. Uncertainty wasn't allowed. I pushed myself to get everything *right*—and it worked. Promotions came quickly, my managers trusted me, and from the outside, I looked like I had it all figured out.

But inside? That voice never stopped. *You're not qualified. They'll find out soon.*

In my late 20s, I landed a senior leadership role. I was the youngest at the table, one of only two women, and the only one without a degree. My male colleagues joked that I was promoted because the boss fancied me. I laughed it off, but inside, I was desperate to prove them wrong. So, I worked harder, studied, and kept achieving. But no matter how much I accomplished, I couldn't shake the feeling that I wasn't enough.

Then came my 30s—a successful career, a charismatic partner. On the outside, I was thriving. But behind closed doors? That partner was emotionally abusive. Gaslighting. Criticism. Betrayal. Constantly being told I wasn't good enough. The voice in my head? It got louder.

Imposter Syndrome had me in its grip.

Does any of this resonate with you?

That gnawing doubt, the fear of being exposed, the exhaustion of overworking just to feel *worthy*—it's not just you. Imposter Syndrome thrives in secrecy, but the more we talk about it, the less power it has. The truth is you are not an imposter. Your success is not a fluke. And you don't have to spend your life proving your worth.

So, what if you stopped trying to outrun the doubt? What if, instead of fighting it, you started questioning it? What if you gave yourself the same grace you so easily give others?

Because the real fraud isn't *you*—it's the voice that keeps telling you that you don't belong. And maybe, just maybe, it's time to stop listening.

What is Imposter Syndrome (I.S.)?

There are many ways I.S. can show up. Here are some examples:

Tom sat in a Senior Leadership Team meeting, listening to his colleagues give updates. They spoke eloquently and seemed to have everything under control. He started comparing himself, doubting his own ability. As his turn approached, his palms grew sweaty, his stomach churned, and his mind felt unclear. He delivered his update but felt his voice was strained and his words stumbled.

At the end of the meeting, his manager, Sharon, congratulated him on his progress with the Change Programme. Tom thanked her but dismissed the feedback, focusing instead on his self-perceived mistakes.

That evening, he shared his doubts with his wife, Marama. He had been in the role for five years, received regular positive feedback, and served on other leadership teams, yet he still felt inadequate. Marama sighed, "Honey, you've felt like this before—when will you start believing in yourself like everyone else does?"

Across town, Melissa faced a similar struggle. She had been promoted after being approached by her employer. Though she knew she was capable, self-doubt crept in. She reminded herself she could do the job, but memories of past workplace bullying resurfaced. Her stress levels rose, she procrastinated on her draft budget, and the deadline loomed. Frustrated, she wondered if she had made the wrong decision.

These are examples of I.S. in action.

The paradox of I.S. is that it affects those who are actually skilled and experienced. They have the ability and reputation but don't believe it. Their inner critic fosters self-doubt, anxiety, and other behaviours, such as:

- Maladaptive perfectionism: "If it's not perfect, I'm a fraud."
- Overachievement
- Underachievement: "If I can't do it perfectly, I won't do it."
- Over-preparing
- Procrastination
- Overworking
- Feeling stuck in their career
- Avoiding mistakes or judgment by preferring to work alone
- Not prioritising self-care
- Constantly needing to prove themselves

Back to My Story – A New Opportunity

Thankfully, my 30s were also a time of growth. A leadership coach helped me uncover my self-doubt and limiting beliefs. I started loosening my perfectionist tendencies and embracing vulnerability. She helped to expand my perspective, strengthened my confidence, and sparked my passion for coaching.

She invited me to join her private coach training programme. Over 18 months, I gained invaluable experience. I left my corporate career to start my own coaching business, training in Neuro Linguistic Programming and studying how the brain works. I also left my narcissistic partner and began the process of healing.

Despite my progress, I.S. resurfaced in my business and delivering training sessions. It drove me to seek more qualifications to feel *good enough*.

I worked on I.S. through coaching and self-reflection, making gradual shifts. However, real transformation came when I used psychosomatic techniques, particularly Havening Techniques®, to clear past traumas. These tools helped release ingrained fears of not being good enough, being judged, or failing. Finally, I was free from Imposter Syndrome's grip.

And you can be too. Are you ready?

Helping Others

My own experience enables me to recognise the signs of I.S. in my leadership coaching clients, which I encounter often. Research shows over 70% of people experience I.S. at some stage in their career.

In supporting my clients, I draw on my personal insights, extensive research, and the strategies I've found most effective over 16+ years of coaching. Combining positive psychology with several powerful modalities, I've developed an integrated, transformative and flexible approach to work on I.S. Following are the core elements of the coaching container that I work within.

Create a safe space	Providing a safe space for vulnerability is crucial when working with I.S. The client is generally not comfortable with vulnerability and fears failing or being found out. Create a sense of partnership, ensuring the client feels seen, heard and valued as their whole self.

Raise awareness	*"Awareness is the first step to change"* Coach the client to become the objective observer of their experience – to shine a new light on what's working, what's not and what's possible. This awareness is held with curiosity, compassion, acceptance and non-judgement.
Interrupt unhelpful patterns	Support the client to interrupt and transform any unhelpful patterns, thoughts, emotions, physiological responses and behaviours, that will stop them from embodying the change they want.
Embed new ways of being	*"Change truly occurs when it's embodied and congruent."* The client takes on new beliefs, new responses, new skills and embeds habits that move them towards their desired outcomes and new possibilities. They embody a new way of being and feel more congruent with who they are.

There are several common themes present with I.S. Whilst I've separated these themes out for simplicity, they are all intertwined. With I.S. it is imperative you work with the whole system, not one isolated part. I'm also providing insights from real case study clients, whose names have been changed to protect confidentiality.

Theme 1: Control
It's all or nothing

With I.S. there is typically a strong desire for perfectionism and high standards. This can lead to a need to control the environment and to protect oneself from potentially failing or being seen as not good enough.

Linked with this can be hyper-independence and taking on too much responsibility, that isn't theirs to own, becoming overly responsible for all outcomes. As a leader this can cause unintended consequences such as disempowering others, learned helplessness and limiting growth of self and others.

Control can also show up to protect a person from having to be vulnerable. Controlling what they might reveal about themselves; their feelings, insecurities, challenges, fears etc to not feel judged by others.

Feelings of anxiety are common, as are experiences of burnout.

Case study experience

At the start of our coaching, Amy had a strong need for control to ensure things were done a certain way. She'd had feedback about this from her manager on more than one occasion. She felt like she'd had this need her whole life, it was part of who she was, and whilst she understood it caused some issues, she didn't see how she could change it.

We worked on control over several sessions:
- raising awareness e.g. of triggers, responses, fears and impacts
- interrupting unhelpful patterns e.g. through working on limiting thoughts/beliefs, emotion regulation and clearing associated traumas
- embedding new ways of being e.g. integrating new responses, tools and skills.

"Prior to the coaching, if I wanted something to go my way I wouldn't listen and would push for my outcome. I would think that if I can control it, then I can control the narrative, I can show I'm adding value. There was a fear that perhaps they could do better than me. I had this posture that's like, I know what I'm doing (but only if you do it my way, because I'm too scared to lose that control). Whereas now, I find myself listening to the other person, because it may be a better way, and that's ok. I'm letting others contribute and add value, we're doing it together and getting good outcomes. It's also opened me up to really seeing how much support I do have." -Amy

Theme 2: Trauma encoding
When the past is in the present

Trauma happens in many forms, with varying intensity and to all of us at some point(s) in our life. Our brain is hardwired to be on the lookout for potential threats and once assessed as a "code red" (whether real or imagined), to then be encoded as a "traumatic" experience. The brain and nervous system are now continuously on alert for any similar situations to protect us.

Using a traditional coaching approach that only operates at the cognitive and behavioural level won't unhook trauma encoding. This is where somatic work truly makes the difference with I.S. Many clients say they've "worked through" a trauma but often this is only at the cognitive level and the neurological encoding is still present, causing triggering. As Bessel A. van der Kolk, author of *The Body Keeps the Score*, says:

"… neuroscience research shows that very few psychological problems are the result of defects in understanding; most originate in pressures from deeper regions in the brain that drive our perception and attention. When the alarm bell of the emotional brain keeps signalling that you are in danger, no amount of insight will silence it."

Trauma can look like: being bullied, having a highly critical parent/caregiver, being shamed by a person of authority in front of others, being emotionally or/and physically abused, publicly embarrassing/shaming yourself, feeling abandoned/excluded from social groups.

Identifying trauma encoding

When a client describes triggering of automatic physiological reactions that are difficult to interrupt, put your "detective hat" on and get curious. A model from Havening Techniques® helps us to identify the 4 requirements for traumatisation:

Event	Has the client experienced an event(s) that was perceived by them as potentially threatening?
Meaning	Did they make a meaning of that event about the loss of something significant to them? *For example: a loss to their physical body – injury/illness/impairment etc, a personal loss such as the death of a loved one, a relationship*

	break-up, financial loss etc, a psychological loss such as reputation, identity, security etc.
Landscape	At the time of the event was the client's landscape of their brain vulnerable? *For example, were they already feeling stressed, distressed, tired, under the influence, unwell etc, which affected their levels of resilience at the time.*
Inescapability	And finally, during the event did they feel unable to escape. *For example: either physically e.g. trapped in a vehicle, locked in a room etc, or psychologically e.g. trapped in a relationship, trapped in a meeting/conversation etc*

Michelle Dalley is a certified Trainer of Havening Techniques. Havening Techniques is a registered trademark of Ronald Ruden, 15 East 91st Street, New York. www.havening.org

When all 4 requirements are met, we can hypothesise that the brain has encoded this experience(s) as traumatic. Also encoded is the person's automatic response at the time of fight, flight, freeze or defensive rage, plus all the associated cognitive/autonomic/somatic/emotional reactions.

Clients can be surprised by what surfaces as an originating event linked to their current reaction. Often, they haven't made the association before, and this new understanding helps to normalise this seemingly uncontrollable reaction and gives hope for change. When working with trauma I use a combination of Havening Techniques® and Neuro Linguistic Programming (NLP).

Scope of Practice

IMPORTANT: When dealing with traumatic encoding it's important to be well trained in effective tools and only operate within your skillset and scope of practice. Otherwise, refer the client to someone with the necessary skills in this area.

Case study experience

Leigh had some significant experiences of public bullying/shame that were linked with her feelings of I.S. We cleared these through Havening Techniques®.

"Working on those past events and the clearing/unhooking of them has put them clearly in the past in my mind. It's released me. Previously, I knew that they were present for me, and I'd been working through them, but I hadn't realised what a big toll they were taking. Now they're released, it feels like there's a sense of freedom and I hadn't expected that at all. Nor had I expected the things that have come out of it like now being able to listen to my intuition more, and to set more effective boundaries. But it makes sense, you know, when I was trying desperately to cover my ass and make people think that I know what I don't know, I'm not going to be worried so much about my boundaries!" -Leigh

Leigh's experience of now being able to listen to her intuition is a common outcome of successful trauma clearing. Trauma causes ongoing internal discomfort due to visceral warning signs. People often learn to numb down, shut off or ignore their gut feelings and emotions to disconnect from the discomfort.

Theme 3: Inner Critic
Taming the inner voice

Reinforcing I.S. are well developed, automatic negative thoughts (ANTS).

ANTS can sound like:

"What if I screw this up and let people down?"	"I don't belong," "I don't fit in," "I'm being excluded"
"I need to work harder,"	"Don't get a big head!", "Don't stand out"
"I need to be more qualified,"	
"I'm responsible <*for everything/everyone*>"	"It was just luck," "I only succeeded because of…"
"If I can't do it right straight off, it's better to not do it at all."	"I'm not as good as…"
	"I never feel prepared enough."

One of my favourite techniques for transforming thoughts and beliefs is from the 6-Step Belief Change Process and Havening. It introduces possibility thinking to bust the current thought/belief, for example:

- "What if making mistakes accelerates learning?"
- "What if relaxing the need for control, gives me greater choice?"
- "What if I'm already adding value?"
- "What if I could begin to notice and appreciate my strengths, like others do?"
- "What if it was ok to start sharing more about myself?"
- "What if I'm ok just as I am?"

Using the "what if" language pattern bypasses the brain's bulls#!t detector (which often gets in the way of affirmations) and elegantly begins the reframing process. The remaining steps of the 6 Step Belief Change process help to embody this new thinking. I also draw on techniques from Positive Neuroplasticity training to further over-ride the negativity bias.

Case study experience

Here's what Amy and Leigh shared about transforming I.S. thinking.

"One of the effects of thinking that others were judging me and that I wasn't good enough, was that I would hold myself separate and often feel excluded. Now I'm allowing myself to be more vulnerable and sharing with others. I've been proactively having conversations that I wouldn't have had before, I'm revealing more about my personal life, whereas before I would keep these two things separate. It's allowing me to connect with my new team and build relationships faster than in the past. I also know that I'm in control of how much I share. I say to myself, "it's ok to share who I am and be vulnerable, I am who I am and I'm proud of where I come from." It's been amazing, and I'm thinking why didn't I do this before!" -Amy

"I'm just not wasting time worrying and overthinking as much as I used to. I'm now less concerned about what other people think of me, which is just awesome. It's kind of a weird thing to observe, and I suppose it's more that I'm accepting that I'm not going to be everybody's cup of tea, not everybody's going to love me, and actually, that's not my

problem to solve anymore, and I don't have to. I don't feel that I need to work hard to impress anybody or to win anybody's love and adoration. That's not the driver now. I still work hard and get a good feeling when I do a good job, but it's not tied up with needing validation from others." -Leigh

Theme 4: Identity
Who is the real me?

Our ego always wants to create an "I am" label to define us. We can take on roles or personas as we go through life. Again, we can look to our childhood for clues of unhelpful or rigid identification linked with I.S. One of my clients described this well:

> *"I have an over-developed sense of responsibility. As a child I was "the good girl," the reliable and responsible one."*

Other roles or labels that you might hear with I.S. include:

- I'm a *perfectionist*
- I've always been a *people pleaser*
- I was labelled the *smart* one
- I was always the *responsible* one
- I'm a *hard worker*
- I'm strong, I'm a *survivor*

Often a client will talk about not feeling authentic or describing an external response or behaviour that doesn't fit with their internal thinking.

With an embodied coaching approach, we can help our clients to upgrade their identity from those childhood labels, enabling them to see themselves as a more developed, whole, human being. I use a combination of mBraining, NLP and Havening Techniques.

Case study experience

Leigh's desired coaching outcomes were to have a greater sense of confidence and ease in the areas of her life where I.S surfaced. She wanted to feel like she belonged and didn't need to continuously prove her worth. I supported Leigh to connect with her multiple intelligences; head, heart and gut to bring them into congruent wisdom on being seen and heard as her whole self. This was a profound experience for her. I overlayed this with a model that represented her upgraded identity:

"This experience has been life changing. I now feel more authentic in who I'm being. I don't have to be this pretend version of me to make everybody else feel happy. It's come naturally through the work we've done, rather than feeling like aggressive pushing to change. Instead, it's been a sort of gentle integration and shifting, as opposed to going into war. The growth for me has been huge." -Leigh

Again, taking an embodied approach with Amy has transformed how she now sees herself:

"What I've got out of this has been priceless; if I reflect back to where I was before the coaching to where I am now, it's just changed my whole perspective and life – I can feel the difference. Before I would dismiss successes, "it's not how I am or how I've showed up or what I've done – it was some sort of luck, or somebody else created it." I now know that I'm adding value, I don't get hooked onto those old doubts of "you're not good enough," "you don't know as much," if they do surface, I can interrupt them and move on. I can see the evidence of what I'm doing and that I've gone from one stage to another." -Amy

Let's connect

I hope that sharing my work with imposter syndrome has demonstrated the beneficial role an integrated coaching approach can take; to help people to let go once and for all of the negative beliefs that have hounded them.

If, in some way, you're feeling inspired, curious or interested to learn more, I'd love to connect.

I'm a qualified trainer in Havening Techniques, mBraining, Neuro Linguistic Programming, Positive Neuroplasticity Training, and the 6 Step Belief Change Process. I draw on all these methods when working with

COACHING REIMAGINED Expanding Human Potential

Imposter Syndrome, weaving them to meet the client's unique needs. If you're curious to learn more about any of these methods or how you might be able to use them in your work, lets connect. In the Linktree below you'll find my contact details, my LinkedIn Profile, links to more information and how to book a call with me.

If you're interested in receiving coaching on imposter syndrome or something else, please email me or book in a time to chat. You'll find the details in the Linktree and QR code below.

https://linktr.ee/michelledalley

CHAPTER 15
Somatic Knowing: Unlocking Memory, and Identity for Transformation
By Sue Frend

Coaching is often seen as a safe and transformative space—one where deeply held beliefs and perceived limitations can be gently unearthed and explored. It offers a rare opportunity to venture beyond familiar narratives and discover new possibilities. My own path into coaching was unexpected. It began, not with a career plan, but with a deeply personal question: *What kind of parent will I be?* Like many new mothers, I sought guidance, enrolling in parenting classes to ease my uncertainty. But what I found went far beyond parenting advice. I began to see the profound influence of the labels we carry—how they shape our self-concept and silently define our roles.

Growing up, I was the "good girl," while my brother was the "willful" one. It made me wonder: *How much of our identity is truly ours, and how much has been assigned to us?*

The Power of Perception and Personality

Years after my initial coaching qualifications, I was shocked to discover that the way I process the world relates to a certain personality style. My perception of everything and everyone has a filter—it is my truth, and you have yours. While we are all unique (or as one of my mentors says, "a once-in-a-lifetime cosmic event,") we each have a core way of processing incoming information due to our neurology, our internal wiring.

When we are operating from our personality, our neurology is functioning from our "business as usual" setting, our conditioned self.

Are you someone who overthinks things and worries until you drive yourself to distraction? Or are you a people pleaser, always putting another person's needs before your own? How about taking action, do you just 'do it' and learn from the challenges it brings, full steam ahead? We are each led by our neurology. Some of us have more of a heart focus some overuse their logical centre and some of us are like a bull in a china shop, act now, and maybe think later. This describes just a few.

Neurology Types as relates to the Enneagram.

The Enneagram is a psychological and spiritual tool to understand and recognise your patterns of perception. It predates Christianity and is not to be taken lightly if you are serious, as Aristotle says to "know thyself." It can be quite a shock to "find" yourself.

You see, we all have our methods of keeping safe, and ways to stay connected to people. It really is manipulation and it is unconscious until it is not! Our type never changes or goes away, it is, your gift when not overdone!

Finding this lens was a revelation to me and helped me see my close family, friends and others in a new light. We are all part of this tapestry of life, and we all have our own healing to do, not just for ourselves, for our children and future generations to come. We are all teaching each other, living life through our lenses, as experienced when we clash over something. "Don't shoot the messenger" has become my motto and as my favourite spiritual teacher says, *"Whatever arises, love that."* This does not mean we allow our boundaries to be trampled, it does mean we question our responses.

I believe every single one of us is here at this monumental time and meeting the people we do and having the experiences we have, to heal the history we hold. We carry the information within our blood, the history of the past. For a moment, I invite you to think about when you were an egg in your mother's body, when she was in utero.

You were being carried by your grandmother, how wild is that! You were bathed in her emotional world decades before you were even an embryo. Looking at timelines now, consider what was happening in the world when your grandparents were alive. How many of us are still carrying generational wounds of early world wars: rationing, loss, fighting enemies, danger? Triggered today by current wars, without realising what, or why, you are resonating with. And maybe it wasn't a world war, maybe your grandparents had their own challenges, financial, health, relationships, whatever… it lives on.

It is safe to say the people we now come into contact with daily, can remind us unconsciously to react from our fear-based unconscious, embodied, internal world. Fantastic! What, I hear you cry? Yes. It is fantastic that we now have this awareness and so many tools to address our pain in the 'here and now.' I believe this is our work.

Our meaning and purpose is to heal from our past in the present for a brighter future for us all. All 9 types of the Enneagram are like pieces of a jigsaw. Together we make the most beautiful picture when we are using our gifts, our perception can be for the greater good with awareness and balance.

COACHING REIMAGINED Expanding Human Potential

These brief descriptions of the types, do not do justice however it is a starting point:

1. The Reformer - Gut Type

Gifted, ego balanced as - someone with a strong sense of integrity who strives for improvements and does the right thing.

Ego unbalanced - This person might be accused of being judgmental as they focus on being right or doing the right thing. What we don't see is that as well as pointing out the flaws they see around them, they are toughest on themselves, with a very unforgiving inner critic.

2. The Helper - Heart Type

Gifted, ego balanced as -Genuine, caring and compassionate with a strong sense of connection to others. Very supportive

Ego unbalanced- This person is always trying to support and help others to the exclusion of recognising their own needs. Whilst their focus is on others, they are not feeling their own pain and get bitter when not recognised.

3. The Achiever - Heart Type

Gifted, ego balanced as - Ambitious, goal orientated, strong work ethic.

Ego unbalanced -This person will look to accomplishments to feed their value. If they are not getting external validation, they have difficulty recognising their own worth.

4. The Individualist - Heart Type

Gifted, ego as - Emotionally deep and honest about feelings, creative, unique artistic expression.

Ego unbalanced- This person feels strangely unique, and that no one really understands them. They have really strong emotions and can go to great depths in their emotional wave. Consequently, they feel that they do not fit in.

5. The Investigator Head Type

Gifted, ego balanced as - Intellectual, independent deep thinker, deep understanding of complex concepts.

Ego unbalanced - This person very much lives in their head. Their focus is on getting to the depth of intellectual understanding on something, often to the exclusion of those around them and their own basic needs.

6. The Loyal Sceptic - Head Type

Gifted, ego balanced with - Loyalty to values, a strong sense of responsibility, commitment, and reliability.

Ego unbalanced - This person is always looking for what might go wrong so that they can have contingency plans. To be forewarned is forearmed; they may go to great lengths talking to different people to validate their concerns.

7. The Enthusiast - Head Type

Gifted, ego balanced - Lover of new experiences, positive outlook, optimistic, spontaneous.

Ego unbalanced - This person finds it difficult to be present in the moment. Most of the time they are looking ahead to what is next, and therefore often live in a state of frustration. Often seen as the charismatic life and soul of the party

8. The Challenger - Gut Type

Gifted, ego balanced as - Confident, decisive, strong leadership, protective nature and willing to stand up for what, who they believe in.

Ego unbalanced- This person feels they need to control others and circumstances to feel safe. They are very assertive and wary of letting their guard down in case other people take advantage of them.

9. The Peacemaker - Gut Type.

Gifted, ego balanced with - Calming presence, desire for harmony, ability to see multiple perspectives, good mediator, accepting nature.

Ego unbalanced- If this person speaks up, they believe they run the risk of upsetting others. That internal conflict keeps them from having a voice or an opinion. They can understand so many points of view that they can have difficulty establishing their own and often feel overlooked. Often, feels worthless, as though they have nothing to offer.

Please note some 3, 6 and 9 profiles can have primary instincts (gut distortions) that do not match the typical descriptions of the Enneagram these are known as "counter types."

We all have all of the centres! Of course, we all have a head, a heart and a gut. As mentioned earlier our Business-as-usual setting is us using our perceptions through this wiring, it is us being authentically ourselves.

The Double-Edged Sword of Authenticity

Knowing your lens on the world is not a cure-all. There is much talk today about being 'authentic,' but being authentic without awareness of your lens can cause unnecessary pain. Surprisingly, the very thing you are most proud of is both your gift and your challenge. As you can see from the above descriptions, we have our gifts and our unbalanced egos.

For example, I am very calm, placid, and even-tempered—a reputation I did take pride in. People tell me they feel calm in my presence. However, this also means I struggle with conflict. To me, confrontation feels *life-threatening*. As a result, I have unconsciously avoided it, sometimes to my detriment.

We all have our methods of staying safe, and understanding these patterns allows us to work with them rather than being controlled by them.

There are, however, moments when we naturally align our neurology, or centres as we call them, without realising it—those times when decisions and actions are effortless and the outcomes welcome. It is known as 'right action.' I would bet that in those moments, you didn't 'think' your way to the action you took, I now know I certainly didn't. This is how I recognise when I am functioning optimally as someone (peacemaker) who struggles with action, which is the neurology of the gut centre.

The Enneagram offers profound insights into our patterns, motivations, and ways of being in the world. Yet, true transformation requires more than just intellectual understanding – it calls for alignment between mind, body and heart.

The Science of Coherence

Another word for alignment is *coherence*. Coherance, is a concept central to Heartmath, this refers to the state in which our nervous system is balanced- neither overstimulated nor disengaged – and all of our body's systems work in harmony allowing access to deeper wisdom. Science increasingly affirms what many wisdom traditions have long known, the human heart holds a power far beyond our thinking brain. Yet in our modern world the intellect has taken center stage. From an early age we are conditioned to focus, achieve and push forward – often at the expense of our inner knowing. As a result, anxiety and disconnection have become widespread, leaving many searching for external answers rather than tuning in to their own innate intelligence.

In coaching, creating coherence is essential. A client may intellectually understand their Enneagram type or personal patterns, but real shifts happen when they can embody this awareness – when their mind, emotions, and physiology align, by fostering coherence coaches can help clients move beyond insight into true transformation.

The Expanding World of Coaching

The coaching world has exploded in recent years, with the recognition that support is often necessary to move toward our dreams and aspirations. Coaching is no longer just for business owners, executives, or sports superstars. People who engage a professional coach typically know they need help. After all, who enlists a coach when something is easy?

This brings us to a tricky part: if coaching methods are solely based on rational, logical thinking, clients are likely to either change their minds or sabotage their efforts. Why? Because what truly matters to us is felt on an emotional level, and our bodies are always guiding us through subtle and significant physical and emotional signs. The heart leads awareness—the higher heart, also known as the 'still small voice.'

This small voice is our intuition before it gets drowned out with our internal dialogue, our bodies history and the expectations of others.

> **As one unknown author put it:** *"A goal aligned with your values is not just an aspiration; it's a compass guiding you towards a life that truly resonates with who you are."*

When is a Goal Not a Goal?

A goal, I would say, is to hit the mark. But what if missing the goal is actually in someone's best interest? What if every unexpected twist and turn is, in hindsight, the best thing that could happen?

I believe this is true, though I didn't always think so. I used to beat myself up for being a professional procrastinator—waiting for the pressure to build before taking action, sometimes not even then! Any important decision made from my thinking alone was difficult and often confusing.

Yet, in hindsight, I have also made effortless decisions and carried out actions without fuss or deliberation.

What was the difference? Reflecting on past events, times I had taken action confidently, I realise that there was no conflict between my thoughts, how I felt and the actions I took, you might say I was *coherant*. This insight helped me stop being so hard on myself. It also helped me understand why some clients I had worked with over the years didn't always take the action steps they had agreed to. They may have 'missed the mark,' but had they really?

The Body Remembers

Our bodies hold the history of our experiences. *The Body Keeps the Score*, a pivotal book by Bessel van der Kolk, illustrates this beautifully. Through my own research and training, I have experienced firsthand how trauma and emotions live in the body.

One profound experience occurred during an Enneagram training in New York, where I participated in Holotropic breathwork—several hours of cyclical breathing to drum-beating music. After the session, I was aware of a strong sharp sensation in my shoulder. I went to seek out the person leading the session to explain I was so uncomfortable that I didn't think I would be able to sit with my partner for the next few hours for her turn. He instructed me to return to the room and take my position laying down on the floor again. He had brought 3 members of his team. As I lay there, I was told to push against them as they were holding me down. I hadn't had time to think of anything, but I remember hearing shouting in my head "Get off me, get off me" Though terrifying, I instinctively knew my reaction wasn't to them in the present—it was a response to something from my past, stored in my body. I began seeking methods that engage the body as well as dialogue such as EFT, Emotional Freedom Technique and others.

Knowing our history lives within us. I needed to work with my body too. During a really difficult time in my life, including my father's dying days,

I came across another practice called TRE, Tension and Trauma Releasing Exercises (TRE), an extraordinary modality that unwinds the body's stored stress and trauma. I now teach this to others, empowering them to access their own healing. My preference for TRE is because once you learn how to safely access and exit this natural process of your body, you have full control over when to allow it. It is simple, subtle and very effective. You can utilise the services of a provider like myself for the in-person approach, or if it suits your circumstances better there are books and a fantastic app that can guide you through the whole process. Further details for this practice and links are in my bio.

Coaching Beyond the Mind

I hope this chapter has illustrated that coaching based solely on logical thought does not provide the full picture. I believe we never truly make 'wrong' turns—we either arrive at our destination or gain valuable lessons. The key is reducing unnecessary struggle by tuning into our body's wisdom.

Pain is real, but suffering is optional. With self-knowledge and an embodied approach to self-awareness, we can learn to trust ourselves more deeply.

Coaches who incorporate this wisdom are still rare, but awareness is growing. We see it in the increasing discussion of embodied wisdom in social media and beyond. Change for the better is happening—though if you listen to the news, it may not always seem that way (but that's a topic for another time!)

Top Tip: Stay away from media hype. It upsets your nervous system, putting you in a state of 'fight or flight.' our bodies respond to perceived threats and not knowing how to deal with them keeps us in a state of vigilance. This puts our immune system on overdrive, which then causes inflammation, which can lead to depression (read the Inflamed Mind by Edward Bulimore for a more in-depth explanation). I liken it to having too many tabs open on the computer, overloading the system. Protect your nervous system—it holds the key to your well-being!

I would like to conclude with a strong message of hope for our future society. We are at a tipping point, and we are all playing our part in the changes, consciously or not. Our thoughts and focus determine our sense of well-being. Left unexamined they can run amok and distort us to the point we can't be the gift we were born to be, we remain ego driven. I've been to the depths (another story) despite my outward expression of positivity. I have and always will still be a work in progress. We are not separate from nature; we are part of it. Our DNA is shifting all the time, responsive to our environment both internal and external, the stars and planets are aligning for change, positive change, see you on the other side!

Connect with me

Coaching, whilst readily available, is not always financially viable. Learning about yourself and how you process your world is paramount to reducing frustration and increasing satisfaction on a daily basis. This reminds me of the quote "give a man a fish and you feed him for a day, teach him how to fish and feed him for a lifetime." My service is moving towards sharing self-coaching using tools such as planners, oracle cards, workbooks etc and it will continue to expand. I enjoy condensing the decades of research into actionable and experiential products that make sense and cut out the fluff.

Also, I have had the privilege of being trained by, and worked alongside, some awesome people, masters of their craft who I like to see myself as a sign poster to. I have spent more than I care to admit in time and money over the last 3 + decades. It is my mission to lighten the load for others.

You can find me at:

Linktree: linktr.ee/sue.frend

CHAPTER 16
Somatic Coaching with The APEX Model
By Joanna Harper, MSc

"Be kind to your sleeping heart. Take it out into the vast fields of light...And let it breathe."

-Hafez

Before you read on, I invite you to pause, take a few gentle, sighing breaths, and place your hands lightly in the centre of your chest. Now, turn your attention inward and connect with your heart. Pause to consider the myriad of possibilities that can be revealed by engaging with your inner knowing, your body's wisdom, and your heart's desires.

My clients have discovered that their Heart Goals differ significantly from their SMART (specific, measured, achievable, realistic, time-bound) goals. Another approach is essential if setting an ambitious goal has ever felt like overwhelming pressure or a long, unachievable to-do list for you or your coaching clients. Most traditional coaching frameworks and models prioritise outcomes generated by the thinking, rational mind.

Standard coaching models and techniques are not always robust or flexible enough for all clients or circumstances. Alternative blended and integrated approaches are vital for those who do not know what they want and cannot set an achievable goal or outcome for a coaching session and beyond. These are people who are struggling with life challenges and cannot yet even imagine what else may be possible. By contrast, other clients want to change their whole lives and personalities in an hour. Approaching both with linear models and frameworks will not be effective for these clients.

Over the years, my free-flow coaching approach has evolved. Beyond utilising traditional methods, coaching models and goal-setting strategies. I blend in elements from many ancient practices, including yoga, qigong, and meditation. The integration of breathwork, movement, and somatic awareness practices add another dimension to client and group coaching sessions. Conversely, I weave coaching principles into movement, breathing, and mindfulness sessions, workshops and retreats.

Introducing The APEX Model

My APEX model offers an integrative, somatic coaching approach. Coaching with all the elements of APEX - often reveals to the client overlooked, disregarded or forgotten dreams and aspirations that are currently outside their conscious awareness.

Apex means a summit, a crest, or a pinnacle, which could be represented as the crest of a roof or the peak of a mountain. Reaching a summit requires a lot of effort and energy. Once there, the options are to remain, plateau, or come down, perhaps by another route, side, or elevation. Therefore, an apex can be experienced as a tipping point resulting in momentum, a change of direction, or viewpoint.

What Coaches Say About the APEX Model

- "The APEX model is quick and easy for clients to understand and use - it has
transformed my coaching approach." MJ
- "I find the APEX model a very useful coaching tool." TN
- "I'm sharing APEX with both clients and trainee coaches." CH

When I presented the APEX Model at the NLP International Conference in 2023, the interactive, experiential session was popular and highly rated. The delegates found APEX to be a practical and holistic coaching tool. APEX helps clients shift from feeling powerless to taking control of their decisions, responses, and behaviours by enhancing their awareness, fostering autonomy, and developing self-efficacy.

I will guide you through the elements of my APEX model later in this chapter.

Let me introduce you to two coaching clients, Clare and Aldo, who benefit from an integrative coaching approach in different ways. Their will show you the potential of coaching with the elements of the APEX model for you and your clients.

Unaware Clare

Clare has been in her current role for nine years. She provides exceptional customer service and manages her budget and small team well. Clare enjoys many aspects of her work but is bored with the predictable routine and wants to earn more. A senior post in her department has been advertised. The post is vacant for the second time in six months. Despite her manager's strong recommendation, Clare has not applied for the role previously. Today, her manager told Clare he hoped to receive an application from her as he thought this position would suit her and her skills well.

However, Clare is unaware of why her manager thinks so highly of her. As she often focuses on what she considers are her shortcomings and inadequacies. Clare gets increasingly anxious when being interviewed. Her mouth dries up, her face flushes, and she cannot think of a spontaneous reply to unexpected or probing questions. Clare thinks she will appear incompetent and unsuitable to the interview panel.

Unaware Aldo

Another department member is Aldo, who has been in his role for seven months. Aldo is ambitious; he believes that he has learned everything there is to know about his current role and is ready for progression. Aldo is unaware of how little he knows about the synergy of the organisation and how his department interconnects with other business areas. Aldo's confident manner can sometimes be perceived as arrogant by his colleagues and customers. He has applied for the same role that Clare is considering.

These two individuals have a different focus. Aldo is aware of his strengths but is less aware of his areas for professional development. Clare does not recognise her personal strengths and professional qualities. However, she is acutely aware of what she perceives as her failings, particularly in the context of an interview. Not focusing on what she can offer to the role, to her colleagues, and to the organisation significantly limits her progress.

Aldo believes he is ready to progress after seven months, while Clare stays safe, remaining in the same post for nine years. Aldo would benefit from coaching to be more self-aware, particularly how he can be perceived by others. And Clare, to reach her personal and professional potential, will benefit from learning how to manage her thoughts, emotions, and psychophysiological state during interviews and other challenging situations, while recognising what she does bring to the workplace and her team. Both have access to workplace coaching sessions and a stress resiliency program that includes expert instruction in mind-body practices and nervous system regulation breathing techniques.

Later in the chapter, we will return to unaware Clare and Aldo to discover how they benefitted from an integrative coaching approach and utilised the APEX model elements.

Free Flow Coaching

My focus throughout the coaching process is on my client or group. I listen attentively to what they are saying and notice what they are not saying while simultaneously tracking their language patterns and nonverbal communication. To do this, I still my thoughts, regulate my state and fade everything else out of my immediate awareness so that I can be fully present with them.

My coaching has evolved from task and goal setting to a free-flowing, client-centred integrative style. I do not follow a specific format; I follow the client and track whatever emerges for them during the session.

How and why, I developed The APEX Model

Although standardised, linear coaching models or steps can be beneficial at times, where appropriate, I don't often follow them. I became curious to establish if I have an unconscious coaching process - which I do. By actively engaging in reflective coaching practice, I became increasingly aware of my coaching 'models' and the key elements I hold lightly as I coach. I detailed the elements of this approach to teach it to my students and share it with my clients.

My first book, The Trauma-informed Coach, introduced my APEX model to coaches. It is a flexible model that coaches and clients can widely use—its application is not limited to trauma-informed coaching.

The Elements of The APEX Model

A = Awareness
P = Pause
E = Embody and Engage
X = Crossroads = Choice = Direction

COACHING REIMAGINED Expanding Human Potential

The A Element of APEX – Awareness

We don't know what we don't know. Therefore, the first element of the change process is to increase awareness, focus, and attention. We become conscious of what has previously seemed automatic and incognizant. When we become aware of our own patterns and responses, it becomes possible to change them.

Many people come to coaching because they want to change something, such as a behaviour, a habit, a response, a symptom or spiralling thought patterns. They perceive that their thoughts and reactions happen to them, not necessarily that they have autonomy and choice.

Increasing awareness can help disrupt unhealthy habits such as mindless snacking, continual social media scrolling, smoking or vaping. Conscious awareness starts with noticing without judgment, what is happening internally, noticing thoughts, feelings, emotions, sensations, and inner dialogue – all our individual responses.

As you read, you can consider something you would like to change.

Awareness of Responses

When we lack awareness, we do not know what has initiated our responses. They seem automatic and unconscious—as though our thoughts, feelings, and reactions are happening to us. We are not in control and do not have autonomy. The first step to positive change is increasing awareness of patterns of responses, reactions, distractions, and thought patterns and their associated psychophysiological states.

Increase Awareness of:

- Responses
- Reactions
- States
- Behaviours
- Thought patterns
- Physiology
- Breathing
- Issues
- Conflicts
- Blocks to progress
- Resources

First, identify a maximum of five unresourceful or limiting habits. Next, identify five or more empowering, resourceful responses and habits as a vital counterbalance.

Awareness List

	A Unresourceful reactions, responses, states, behaviours, thought patterns, physiology	B Empowering reactions, responses, states, behaviours, thought patterns, physiology
1		
2		
3		
4		
5		

The P Element of APEX - Pause

Intentionally pausing with awareness can disrupt repetitive behaviour patterns, habits, and reactions the moment that they are noticed. During the pause, ground yourself and take a gentle, mindful breath, which can be a regulating state and mindset changer. Some clients find it helpful to visualise or mimic pressing a pause button, like using a remote control or pausing a video clip. Others shift their posture or move their body to help them release unresourceful states, emotions and thoughts.

Pause to take a gentle, regulating, mindful breath. When you breathe optimally and fully inhabit your body, you can ground yourself in the present moment. Daily practice of voluntary regulated breathing practices (VRBPs) has the potential to transcend restrictive and unwanted patterns of behaviour, responses, and thought habits. Mindful, active pausing can bring stillness, space, clarity, and insight, expanding awareness of the signals and information from your whole body.

The Two E Elements of APEX
Embody

In somatic psychology, the body is a revered sacred space. When we align with our bodies and experience mind-body unity, we create a sense of balance and wholeness. By grounding ourselves against restless thoughts that, when left unchecked, can spiral and escalate. It is through a deep and contemplative return to embodiment—that we can find our place.

Placing a hand on your heart and/or belly can enhance your connection with your body and help you notice emergent feelings, emotions, sensations, and thoughts.

Engage

With regular use of the APEX elements, it becomes easier to patiently turn inward. Increasing conscious awareness of unresourceful habits of the mind, such as:

- Worrying
- Ruminating
- Procrastinating
- Circular thinking
- Catastrophising

Taking the time and opportunity to pause, notice, and actively engage with thoughts, feelings, and reactions further increases awareness. This practice enhances the opportunity to engage in conscious thinking and explore whatever is important to you.

The X Element of APEX – Crossroads = Choice Point

The X is symbolised as a crossroads, indicating choice and potential for a change of direction. By expanding choices and options, the X can become a compass with 365 degrees of choice, potential and possibility.

The client's empowering and resourceful responses list may be a helpful reference tool at this point. Be aware that during the embodied and engaged elements, new and additional ideas and possibilities often spontaneously emerge.

How Unaware Clare used APEX

Through coaching Clare quickly elicited her problem state and her previous automatic thought habits and responses within an interview context. Many were familiar to her and predated attending job interviews; they were linked to negative school experiences.

Clare's Five Unresourceful Reactions

1. Thinks she is inadequate and incompetent.
2. No spontaneous replies.
3. Feelings of anxiety rising in her chest.
4. Anxious breathing and rapid heart rate.
5. Dry mouth and flushed face.

Clare's Five Resources

Eliciting Clare's workplace and personal strengths and resources took more time. Her sense of self-worth and confidence are mostly related to her achievements in her current role.

1. Exceptional customer service.
2. Budget control and team management skills.
3. Knowledge and experience of the business.
4. Dedicated and committed to the business.
5. Loyal and trusted colleague.

Repeatedly using the APEX model elements made Clare aware of her unresourceful reactions, states, and thought habits during interviews. She recognised that her rapid-escalating stress responses elevated her heart and breathing rate and were responsible for her dry mouth and flushing symptoms when she is asked unexpected or probing questions.

Now consciously aware of her negative response patterns, Clare pauses and takes two mindful, regulating breaths before responding when she feels uncertain. During the interview, she plans to sip water to give herself space as a strategy to remain cool and calm. This strategy will provide Clare time to reflect on challenging questions before replying.

Practising the technique of interrupting her recurring negative thoughts and anxious breathing patterns as soon as she notices them while preparing for the interview has positively impacted other areas of Clare's life. She is calmer, sleeping better, and feeling more confident. Clare now pauses when she becomes aware of her anxious response patterns, notices her unresourceful thoughts and associated physical sensations, and consciously chooses a different response. When Clare is grounded and present, she can connect with what she really wants in both her personal and professional life.

How Unaware Aldo used APEX

In his workplace coaching session, Aldo explored his reasons for applying for the post. Through the process, he became increasingly aware that he wanted to progress to earn more income, not because he was ready or well-suited to the role. He dislikes being at a desk all day, and working from home on a laptop in his bedroom two days a week is impractical.

Aldo's Five Revelations

1. Lacks business-wide knowledge.
2. Limited experience.
3. Talks more than he listens.
4. Rushes decisions.
5. Can be seen as arrogant.

Aldo chose to work through his unconscious behaviour and response patterns using the APEX model. Taking time to pause and reflect is new and invaluable to him. Aldo can explore his options when he does not feel compelled to reply immediately or make quick decisions.

Noticing his rush to speak and express his opinion without listening to others is a key insight for Aldo. Throughout childhood, he struggled to be heard, as he had four older siblings who often teased him. Aldo had learned to get attention by being loud and rushing to be first to avoid missing out.

The APEX model helped Aldo recognise that he feels unfulfilled in his work and personal life. He considers his current role and the organisation a temporary rung on his career ladder until a better or more interesting opportunity appears.

Aldo's Resources

1. Ambition.
2. Confidence.
3. Determination.
4. Open to change.
5. Willing to listen to and integrate feedback.

The element of APEX that was revelatory for Aldo was embody and engage. He was surprised that his heart and body had any wants, needs or desires. He has always made decisions with his conscious, rational mind. Aldo's heart expressed that it is unhappy, and his body is tense and restless at work. These insights confirmed to Aldo that he must reconsider his long-term career options. When he left college, he wanted to train to be a physiotherapist, but he had been encouraged by his family and friends to get a job, learn to drive, and buy a car. Now, his heart whispered that it was not too late to pursue his ambitions. Aldo's Heart Goals differ from his SMART goals, which are focused on income and following his current career progression. As he realised this, the tension in Aldo's jaw unwound, and he sighed. He felt like he had been holding his breath for months.

Client Outcomes

Clare was calm and present during her successful interview and is now content in her new role. She still uses APEX and regulation practices to manage her responses.

COACHING REIMAGINED Expanding Human Potential

Aldo chose to withdraw his application for the post and remains in his current role. He now actively listens and pauses taking time to reflect before he responds. Aldo is considering his long-term career options and exploring the routes to train as a physiotherapist.

In summary: Many Ways You can use The APEX Model

You can apply the elements of APEX whenever you choose for your personal and professional development. As a quick state change practice. If you or your clients feel constrained by standard coaching models you can integrate the APEX elements to change the flow and dynamic.

The APEX model and the elements are flexible. Coaches can utilise them in many ways:

- As a self-coaching model.
- As a four-step change-work process.
- As a brief state change process.
- As a decision-making model.
- As a framework for coaching sessions.
- As a group and/or team coaching framework.
- Over 4 + sessions - focusing on one element per session.
- Self-application for clients between sessions.

Explore APEX More

If you are inspired to explore, discover, and learn more about applying APEX read my book: The Trauma-Informed Coach: Strategies to Support Clients When Their Past Prevents Progress. Five complex case studies detail examples of clients using the APEX model during and between sessions. Additionally, my other models, including the Trauma Trees, the GROUNDED Model, and the PRESENT Model, further demonstrate my integrative, free-flow coaching approach.

References

Brown R.P., & Gerbarg, P. L. (2012) The healing power of the breath: Simple techniques to reduce stress and anxiety, enhance concentration and balance your emotions.

Shambhala. Caldwell, C. (1997). Getting in touch: The guide to body-centred therapies. Quest Books.

Harper, J. (2022). The trauma-informed coach: Strategies to support clients when their past presents progress. The Right Book Press.
Siegel, D.J. (2018). Aware: The science and practice of presence. Scribe.

About Me and Integrate Training

As a lifelong learner, I have a long *résumé* including a master's degree in Transforming Integrated Health and Social Care. I am an Accredited Trainer, a Master Coach, a Yoga and Qigong Teacher, a co-coaching facilitator for the Association for Coaching and the Director of the Breath-Body-Mind™ Foundation UK programs.

In 2015 I created Integrate Training, with the aim to offer a range of quality and enjoyable certification and continuing educational development (CPD) courses for Coaches and Practitioners. Including Breath-Body-Mind™ (BBM), Integral Eye Movement Therapy (IEMT), Trauma-informed Coaching and Neuro-Linguistic Programming (NLP) Coaching.

My Gifts for You

Contact me and ask for the first three chapters of my book The Trauma-Informed Coach. You are also welcome to attend a one-hour BBM class with me as my gift to you, so you can experience my teaching style and experience BBM regulation practices.

Connect and Discover More

You can find more about my online and in-person courses, classes, workshops, and retreats on my website and by joining my mailing list to receive infrequent newsletters.

Although I'm not very active on social media, I am happy to connect with you.

Website: www.integratetraining.co.uk

Linktree: https://linktr.ee/joannaharper

COACHING REIMAGINED Expanding Human Potential

CHAPTER 17
K9 assistance in team development
By Frank van Nimwegen

Introduction

Have you experienced team work at its best or at its worst?

Have you worked to improve team performance, or do you just hope you will find a way through to a reasonable result?

I have spent over 35 years in a technological and commercial B2B environment, and I have had the privilege of observing many teams up close. Some of those teams were a joy to be part of—harmonious, productive, and inspiring. Others, however, were the complete opposite, bogged down by poor management, conflict and lack of cohesion. This led me to ask the question: What is the difference that makes the difference?

COACHING REIMAGINED Expanding Human Potential

Interestingly though, this question wasn't confined to the corporate world for us. For over 40 years, I have been deeply involved in canine sports—high-level dog training and handling. Over those years, I saw strikingly similar patterns emerge. Some handlers consistently rose to the top in competitions, excelling at what they did, regardless of the dog they were working with. Whereas others, even with outstanding dogs, never managed to reach their potential.

This parallel patterning intrigued me. What makes a good dog handler truly great? And could the same principles also be applied to managing and leading human teams? Driven by curiosity, I set out to explore these questions. What I discovered was fascinating: the skills and mindsets that set in practice of dog handling can be applied and used as trainings goals in human leadership as well. And yes, we found a way to keep the dogs involved.

Here's the thing about dogs: they're honest, transparent, and completely in the moment. They don't come with hidden agendas or ulterior motives. Their reactions are pure and are immediate reflections of the behaviour they encounter. They do not worry about socially desirable behavior. This makes them extraordinary teachers. When you change your approach, a dog's response changes instantly, giving you real-time feedback. It's a safe, dynamic space to experiment with and reflect on new methods—to see what works and what doesn't—without the stakes being too high.

Through working with dogs, I have seen leaders gain profound insights into their leadership styles and I have seen teams discover new ways to communicate and collaborate more effectively. The process is engaging, transformative, and, most importantly, fun. Dogs have an amazing and unique way of revealing truths about ourselves and our interactions that we might otherwise overlook.

So, let's explore together how the lessons learned from exceptional dog handlers can help you become an exceptional team leader. With a little help from our four-legged friends, you might just discover the secret to building the best team you've ever managed.

COACHING REIMAGINED Expanding Human Potential

Working in teams; a blessing or a burden?

A team is more than just a group of people working together. A great team has a clear vision, shared values and a reachable but challenging goal. Members of the team all have the same ambition to reach that goal, which often means putting their own personal goals aside or of less importance. The team results come first. There is no room for an exclusive I in a TEAM.

When a team is initially formed it is good practice for each person to share their different perspectives and creativity. Each will have their own unique skills and experiences which can be optimized to enable the team to overcome challenges, in a creative way far more effectively than one person can do alone. Matching individual skills to team roles, enhances team effectiveness and productivity. This respectful connection works to amplify their strengths and allows the team to learn from each other further enhancing the team as a whole.

Teams are built on three simple and powerful pillars: responsibility, trust and connection. When team members take full responsibility for their actions and tasks, they are trustworthy. When team members feel trusted and able to trust their fellow members, they are able to take responsibility for their tasks and role. They will show a genuine concern for the wellbeing of their fellow team members and will support and motivate them, strengthening the bond between people, not only professional but personal as well. Great teams celebrate successes together. They are connected and all team members will be able to be their beautiful self for 100% of the time.

But it is not always like this: working in teams can also be a burden. When team morale and team values don't align with your own values, you risk being constantly misunderstood and mistreated.

When work is not evenly divided, or when members avoid their responsibility. When communication is poor and not leading anywhere, or, working in teams can feel like hell, with repeated conflicts, bullying, mistreatment, misunderstandings or even, at its worst, some people being excluded, being part of a team like this can feel a huge burden.

It is the responsibility of the team leader to form a team in which it is a blessing to work. He (or she) is responsible for the forming of the team, keeping the team on course during the storming phase and providing clarity through the norming and then providing ongoing motivation to ensure ongoing performing. No easy task.

How can emerging skills in coaching and team development help to form a flourishing, balanced and thriving team? What I call: The Best Team Ever', led by The Best Team Leader Ever.'

It doesn't just happen. It takes work and conscious, skilled and deliberate effort from all involved.

How do we see a team?

To understand team strategies, we often use the metaphor of a "wolves pack" to clarify what happens in teams. In the wolf pack there are five main topics:
- The role
  Which role has each team member?
- Security
  Do all team members feel safe to play your role(s)?
- The hunt
  How does the team work together to achieve the goals?
- Feeding
  Are team members filled or are they fed?
- Quality time
  How does the team spend its time together when the hard work is done?

Which role has each team member to play?

In a team every member plays a vital role. The team leader is responsible for the team goals, vision and ambition and to create the right circumstance for the team to perform and excel. The team leader should know what the qualities and drawbacks of the team members are to ensure s/he puts the right team member in the right spot.

Team members should be able to follow their leader, set aside personal gain. Still, they should guard their own values and boundaries and, whenever it's sabotaging, step back from the team.
In this, connection and trust are the key indicators.

In the wolf pack we see specialists in tracking, taking the lead to find a prey, hunting and killing. Every wolf is clear what their role is and how they fit in with the whole pack.

Safety
The main task for the team leader is to create and maintain safety. Every team member should feel safe in the pack. Fights are not tolerated. They are counter productive, cost a lot of energy and there is always the risk of getting hurt. Wolves that are hurt cannot take their role and must be taken care of, taking time away from the pack. The team leader has a central role in this process.

The hunt
This is a metaphor for team goals: what do you want to gain, and how can you get it. This means; planning, doing, checking, acting. This involves awareness of how the team works together. How team members trust each other and take responsibility for their part of the puzzle. Team members that trust each other and are sure that all responsibilities are taken can connect. The firmer the connection the more likely it is that team goals are met. Responsibility and trust are the result of a process, they do not come coincidentally.
Is there a clear and flexible process for people to follow?

Feeding
Often, when teams are not successfully organized, members are *filling* instead of *feeding*. Filling is a busy-ness that is not feeding or contributing

to the team process and goals. Feeding is the opposite; it's fulfilling and nurtures the team and leads to goal achievement.

Quality time
After a successful hunt the pack takes time to eat together, enjoying, playing and relaxing with each other. How do you, as a team, create quality time together? Is there room for relaxation? Do you take time to connect and enjoy meals together, to play?

Using this metaphor, we can work with our dogs to help teams to develop and grow. Dogs naturally understand these procedures, and mirror what's happening in a team, bringing any areas for growth to awareness.

This is different from team building. While building a raft together, playing music or doing an outward bound survival activity together can be beneficial when there is an existing team connection, they can also amplify problems and risk making these activities counter productive.

Wise team development, on the other hand, helps your team to become aware of and then overcome the problems you all are facing, making a distinction between what you see and are conscious of (above the surface) and what is the cause (under the surface and outside of your consciousness). And employing the wisdom of the pack can hugely amplify the results of this.

This level of team development takes time and deliberate effort. It requires honest reflection for each team member, about what part they are playing, what values are important to them and how those values align with the team values.

The team leader plays a vital role in modeling team values in practice and working with the team to make goals explicit and each person's contribution to those goals clear.

Then a plan can be created using for example: the Deming circle: Plan - Do -Act- Check. This involves, making a plan, sticking to plan, or adapting the plan in order to achieve results.

How can dogs assist in team development?

First, and most honest answer? Because we, and the teams we work with like to work with dogs. Dogs are:

- fun, creative, they connect, and they take full responsibility for their actions.
- always true to their values, which are not necessarily the same as ours.
- great metaphors for teamwork, they live and hunt in a pack, they have to communicate, work together and have a plan. They have a hierarchical/roles-based structure, just like a team.
- great mirrors, they react on what they see, hear and feel. They do not have a hidden agenda, or desired behavior. They are just being themselves.
- honest and opportunistic, when you change your behavior or mindset, they will adjust and show you the result immediately and with no restraint.
- unique in their traits and can be applied in different situations fitted to each objective.

Dogs add an additional element of wisdom and insight, which has been found to deepen reflection and development of teams in practice. Dogs will work together with humans to a common goal, and they live fully in the moment. While working with them, participants might think it's all about dogs...... not!

With the metaphor of the wolf pack in mind we start with developing the vision and strategy of the team.

- What kind of team do you wish to be?
- What are the core values here?
- What is the heart driven importance of each team member and how would they like the session to be.
- What does each team member need to feel and be safe?
- What is the desired outcome, and what needs to be done to achieve that?

- And what has never been said before, but needs to be expressed now?

We begin by exploring what role each person will play, in line with the wolf pack metaphor, using the dogs to assist.

Case studies

Let me share a Case Study with you to exemplify how this works in practice.

We coached a team of consultants. The team was made up of a few experienced and older consultants and a lot of young professionals at the start of their career. The exercise we set up was a simple slalom.

The handler was instructed to guide the dog through the slalom (the process), the finish was set to be the end of a project (goal).

The first person to do the exercise with our big black dog, was one of the experienced older consultants. Confident he took the leash of the dog and with no doubt he led the dog through the slalom making it look very easy.

One of his younger colleges wanted the next turn, and he modelled what he had just seen, taking the leash with the same confident facial expression of his predecessor. And off they went. But now the dog was very much taking the lead! Our big black canine friend pulled the poor consultant where he wanted to go. We stopped the exercise to ask him what was happening here? The young consultant had no idea, he was shocked: "I am exactly doing what "he" did" was his answer. So, we asked him specifically what exactly are you doing? He reflected and answered that he had copied the facial expression and the body posture of what he saw in the exercise by his predecessor. This led us to explore: "and how are you feeling, doing so?" He described feeling insecure, uncomfortable and a bit nervous. He felt it was not *his* way of being, rather it was what he thought he *should* do. We encouraged him to lead the dog again, this time as he felt right. He took a moment to breathe and reset, took hold of the leash and led our dog clear through the slalom, reaching the end of his project without pushing and pulling and with a big smile on his face.

What was the difference that made the difference?

According to him, the second time he followed his heart, not his head. He felt into what the dog needed and together they finished the project, as a team, not as two individuals. He was able to stay tuned in and adapt his feeling through the rest of the day, every exercise with a big smile on his face. He had gained a huge lesson in being real and working in unison with the dogs.

It is easy to see how this can be applied back in the office. To lead with the heart, not the head, and to be attuned to those around you.

In a second case study we explored creating safety.

Every team requires safety to be able to perform. Team members need to be sure they are backed up. And they need to have the safety to speak their minds.

Working with a legal team we set up a competitive exercise.

The team leader took the first turn and he and our dog went for it! They fully committed and succeeded. He looked with a glorious face to his team members and said he needed a smoke now. And off he went, leaving his team behind in a competitive setting. It was evident that they felt insecure and unsafe.

The dogs noted the change immediately and changed their behavior. The dogs took the lead and they had a wonderful time. To prevent the exercise getting out of hand, we stopped it. And asked the team: "what do you need right now?" They answered they would benefit from guidance and the security to know that what they are doing is the right thing. We assured them, you are the right team in the right place, you can do this. And despite the absence of their leader they felt safe, because of our confirmation and trust. They asked if they could do the exercise once again, which we, obviously, granted. The dogs, now more secure performed like a dream and the team grew in confidence. When this team leader returned from his smoke break his team had a clear message for him: whenever you leave, give us the confirmation of our capabilities and leave us empowered to keep on performing.

This fits the analogy of the hunt. The hunt is seen as the most important task for a team. This is about the results, and where everybody, outside your team, can see what you do. The hunt is a crucial part of teamwork and needs preparation: goal setting and planning. Without a clear goal there is no clear direction and without a plan reaching a goal is just a dream. The Best Team Leader Ever has a clear goal and direction for the team and ensures the team know the goal and have committed to it, knowing and ensuring it is aligned to their personal and team values.

A Case Study around The Hunt

We were working with a just formed team. Our session was the first team meeting, and the objective was to get to know each other and find out how they could work together. We started with some exercises in which the core values of the team members got clearer and clearer. To see how they could work together we gave them a team assignment. With our dogs they had to run a (simple) course four times, and every team member had to be involved in the process.

The first attempt was terrible. It was chaotic, slow and the dogs involved were puzzled. On review it was clear that the plan was not shared with all the members, communication with team members was suboptimal, and individual tasks and responsibilities were not clear.

So, let's do it again but better. The team took more time in preparation, making sure every member was connected and knew their task and responsibility. This attempt looked so much better! It was quicker with less energy used. The dogs understood what was desired and they went for it! It was a real team boost!

They asked for another attempt because they felt they were on the right track. And the next attempt went even better, with both the team and our dogs enjoying it more and more. There was no stress, just joy.

At the end of the session the team summed up all their learnings and were stimulated to get to work with each other in new ways. By simply reacting to what was happening our dogs stimulated them to make a good plan, to communicate and to act on circumstances around them. They learned how to connect, trust and take responsibility.

This is key in team work. So many teams are working harder, and burnout is becoming a work pandemic. Using energy wisely is essential. The hunt can either feed you or fill you.

Feeding is nurturing, you grow and gain energy. Filling takes energy and doesn't give you fulfillment (in the long run). At its best it will give you satisfaction in that moment.

Every Best Team Ever will set its' goals on feeding, not filling.

We met a team of highly qualified engineers. They had a lot of fun "teasing" each other and spent lots of time and energy in convincing their colleagues of the own talents and expertise. Competition was way more evident than collaboration.

We divided the group into two. Giving each group the same exercise.

The group who went first were pleased with themselves, declaring "it was the best result ever." Then group 2 came to the starting line. And to our surprise group 1 surrounded the course, calling the dogs, distracting them with food and toys. The dogs reacted immediately, leaving the exercise and going to our van, to the security of their own place. They didn't want to be part of this! We asked both groups to reflect on whether this was the result they were after.

Group 1 couldn't stop laughing; they still had "the best result ever" in their view, even though they left their colleagues (and our dogs) in despair.

COACHING REIMAGINED Expanding Human Potential

We asked them: is this filling or feeding? And they had to admit it was filling.

We gave them some time to explore the impact on their fellow team members and on our dogs.

- Was it who they wanted to be?
- Did they think our dogs (a metaphor for your clients!) want to play with you again?
- How do your fellow team members feel?

With some embarrassment they apologized, not only to their team members but also to our dogs. They had lost sight of the team.

As soon as *filling* is more important than *feeding* your most important customers, it is very likely the players will leave the field.

Finally - Quality time

After a successful hunt the pack benefits from time to relax and play. In a team, make sure every team member can enjoy this time. It is important for the Best Team Leader Ever to know and understand how every team member wants to have quality time. If it doesn't suit a member, it's not quality time.

After an exercise with one team, a nice young lady wanted to play with the dog she had worked with. And she started to play a "tug of war." It was clear that the dog was not interested in her play and was more interested in eating some biscuits. Despite this, the lady insisted on her chosen form of play, but the dog refused. Even more surprisingly, she pushed the toy in the dog's mouth and demanded PLAY! The dog, disappointed, left the field and went to some other people and tried to score some snacks.

Why did she insist on playing with that toy? Well, SHE thought it would be fun and could not think the dog didn't like it.

Whenever you want to have quality time with someone, find something you **both** like! Whenever it's not to the liking of the either one, the fun will stop, leaving disappointment and disconnection evident.

How does it all come together?

To become the Best Team Ever it is important to keep on developing: consciously and deliberately. After team building and getting through the stages of becoming a team: forming, storming, norming and performing, it is essential to create an environment where every team member can contribute at his full power to the success of the team.

Team performance is the result of a deliberate process over time. As The Best Team Leader Ever, you need to have a process for team development, trust your process and stick to your plan, adjusting the details as you go to ensure success. In team development, we have found that dogs can be a valuable mirror, metaphor, development guide - a beautiful source of wisdom to amplify the team development opportunities. Their honesty and immediate reaction in the moment can help you to grow and make changes into the right direction.

The use of these amazing animals will help you and your team to grow beyond just being good, they will help you to become The Best. Without any restrictions they will do this again and again. With wagging tails and a smile on their face they will show you what is happening, and we are happy to translate it into winning approaches, by introducing you and the dogs in world leading training which takes coaching and team development to a whole new level.

Come into action mode!

The first, smallest step, you can take into team development is to do a workshop coaching with us and our dogs. You will experience what we, and our amazing dogs, can do for you and your team, taking your team development to the next level. After this introduction workshop it is a small step to the growth program to become the Best Team Leader Ever and The Best Team Ever.

Let's make some fun and learn from and with dogs, ensuring you and your team to grown beyond.

Let's Qynnect

https://linktr.ee/frankvn

CHAPTER 18
Burnout-Proof: Because Misery Isn't a Metric
By Michelle Comrie

Careers with a Pulse lead to Success Without Self-Destruction

Success - what does it mean to you?

We've been sold a version of success that looks great on paper—titles, promotions, pay checks—but leaves too many of us exhausted, disconnected, and wondering if this is really it. Burnout is just an excuse for those who can't hack it… or so they say—right up until you're running on caffeine, tears, and pure delusion.

But what if success is about living aligned with who you truly are? Imagine a career that fuels you instead of drains you. A life where your work aligns with your passions and values, where ambition and wellbeing coexist instead of collide.

In my work as a coach, I've seen many professionals at a crossroads—high achievers on the outside but struggling on the inside. Their drive for success is costing them their wellbeing, authenticity, and sometimes even their happiness.

What if the path to true success isn't about pushing harder but listening deeper. This chapter is about breaking the burnout trap and invites you to explore that possibility.

The Turning Point: From Overwhelm to Alignment

Let me introduce you to Sarah. A dynamic leader with an enviable career trajectory, Sarah was doing all the right things—networking, upskilling, and working tirelessly. Yet, she was exhausted, unfulfilled, and questioning everything.

She came to me believing she needed a career pivot. But what she truly needed was a recalibration. Through our work together, she realised she had been making decisions solely from her rational mind, ignoring the powerful insights of her body, emotions, and deeper intuition.

By integrating whole-body wisdom - the mind, heart, gut, pelvis, and nervous system - Sarah began making decisions that felt right, not just looked right on paper. The result? A career path that felt effortless, exciting, and truly aligned with her purpose.

The Power of *You*: Ditch the Mask and Own Your Impact

Think back to a time when you felt truly seen - when someone listened without judgment, held space for your thoughts, and allowed you to be unapologetically yourself. How did that feel?

For many, these moments are rare. In a world that often prioritises performance over presence, we've been conditioned to believe that success comes from relentless striving and proving our worth.

Here's the thing: true transformation doesn't happen in the hustle. It happens when we pause long enough to listen to ourselves—when we create space to explore what truly matters.

That's why I invite you to shift your perspective. Consider this:

- **Who are you beneath the titles, roles, and expectations?**
- **What lights you up?**
- **Where do you feel most alive?**

If you've been feeling stuck, exhausted, or uncertain, you're not alone. But there's a way forward—one that's not about fixing yourself, but about rediscovering the wisdom that's already within you to amplify your career impact.

Burnout is Real - But So Are You

Burnout doesn't announce itself with a fanfare—it infiltrates like a silent poison, stealing your energy, suffocating your passion, and leaving behind a hollow version of yourself. Let's be blunt: burnout isn't just about working too hard. It's about a system that treats humans like machines and then acts surprised when we break. In a culture where self-worth equals output, not impact, exhaustion becomes the twisted new normal.

Burnout doesn't politely wait until midlife when you're running on over-scheduled devices, adrenaline, and the vague hope that you'll finally rest next weekend. It begins in childhood—when you first learn that survival means pushing through discomfort, wearing the brave face, and doing what's expected regardless of the cost.

I know this first hand. At eight years old, my world was ripped apart. One night in Zimbabwe in the 1970s, my family escaped undercover of the night with our worldly possessions in three suitcases and fled to the UK. In an instant, home, stability, and safety were gone. That was my first lesson in the "Stiff Upper Lip" - keep going, no room for fear, sadness, or vulnerability.

Fast forward to my first real job—PR in the early tech-orgy, go-hard-or-go-home '90s. I was flying blind, making it up as I went, fuelled by ambition and three pots of coffee before 9 a.m. Then came my dream job in Hong Kong—global travel, 18-hour days, an exhausting cycle I wore like a badge of honour, pushing through sickness and exhaustion.

COACHING REIMAGINED Expanding Human Potential

I crashed—hard. Years of relentless hustle demolished my body and mind, all in the pursuit of someone else's definition of success. Stress may not be officially addictive, but let's be real—it gives us a biochemical high that keeps us coming back for more, just like any other bad habit. The threshold rises until chaos feels like home and calm feels threatening. My system finally collapsed - spectacularly. Breaking that cycle took years.

You'd think that the top brass would get this—especially when HR teams proudly champion "supportive cultures" all over corporate websites. As Richard Branson says, *"Take care of your employees, and they will take care of your business."* Turns out, that memo got filed under "flush and forget."

Eventually, I met a coach who held up a mirror and said, *"This? This isn't it."* That moment shattered everything. Success wasn't about martyrdom—it was about working smarter.

That awakening led me to pivot into coaching and headhunting where I now do for others what someone once did for me: help people rewire their approach to work so they can thrive as humans first and professionals second.

Today, I combine deep coaching insights with razor-sharp recruitment strategies, helping you land the right roles without sacrificing what's important. Because the price of pushing through is too high. We are not machines.

Burnout is real, and so is our right to a career that doesn't cost us our soul.

Too Bold to Blend In, Too Human to Ignore

We live in a world obsessed with automation, efficiency, and AI. But an era of relentless optimisation, what makes us human is our greatest competitive advantage. The future doesn't belong to the best algorithm—it belongs to those who can blend strategy with soul, intellect with intuition, ambition with authenticity.

The rapid shift toward corporate efficiency has created a wasteland where creativity, human connection, and emotional intelligence are sacrificed at the altar of productivity. Companies preach people-first values while demanding machine-like performance. The pandemic only intensified this contradiction—remote work erased boundaries while automation questioned our very relevance.

The numbers tell the story: 77% of global workers report burnout (Deloitte, 2023), while 72% of senior executives admit feeling professionally hollow despite their success (McKinsey). We were already human resources being strip-mined for value—AI just accelerated the excavation.

When did we collectively agree that success should cost us our humanity?

AI is revolutionising industries, transforming job functions, and reshaping recruitment. But in the rush to automate, we risk sidelining the very human qualities that make us indispensable, such as intuition, ethical judgment, emotional intelligence and the ability to build, meaningful relationships

The irony? Companies need these traits now more than ever. AI might optimise but it can't lead with vision, inspire loyalty, or navigate the wild magic of human connection.

Coaching faces the same challenge. AI-driven tools promise efficiency, but algorithms don't see you. They don't hear the tremor in your voice, challenge your carefully constructed blind spots, or hold space for the uncomfortable transformation that precedes breakthrough.

The future belongs to those who bring their full, messy, brilliant humanity to the table. In a world engineered for efficiency, your authentic self is the ultimate disruptive innovation.

The Five Centres of Intelligence: Tap In, Level Up

The world demands we push, perform, and power through, even as our bodies and spirits scream for a different approach. What if resilience meant tuning in rather than powering through?

True intelligence transcends logic—it's about accessing the embodied wisdom already within you. By integrating all five intelligence centres—

mind, heart, gut, pelvis, and nervous system—you unlock decision-making that's not just smart, but profoundly wise.

Most professionals operate solely from their heads while their other intelligence centres whisper crucial insights they never hear. When you align all five, you don't just make better decisions for yourself—you become unshakeable in a world of constant change.

- **Mind (Logic & Strategy)** – The seat of analysis, structured thinking, and problem-solving.
- **Heart (Emotions & Connection)** – The space of emotional intelligence, empathy, and intuition.
- **Gut (Instinct & Drive)** – Our primal intelligence, guiding us through gut feelings and courage.
- **Pelvis (Creativity & Power)** – The core of passion, creativity, and embodied purpose.
- **Nervous System (Regulation & Resilience)** – The foundation of calm, presence, and adaptability under pressure.

You've had this Superpower all along - It's Time to Use it.

Here's how to start integrating whole-body intelligence into your career and personal growth:

1. Listen to Your Whole Self Before Making Big Decisions

Before saying yes to an opportunity, check in with all five centres:

- **Does it make sense logically?** *(Mind)*
- **Does it excite and inspire you?** *(Heart)*
- **Does it feel right in your gut?** *(Gut)*
- **Does it spark creativity and passion?** *(Pelvis)*
- **Can you pursue it without stress and burnout?** *(Nervous System)*

If any of these feel off, pause and explore why before moving forward.

2. Reframe Success on Your Own Terms

Ask yourself:

- **Beyond money and titles, who really am I?** *(Gut)*
- **How do I want to feel in my work and life?** *(Heart)*
- **What would a fulfilling career look and feel like?** *(Mind)*

Success isn't about achieving more—it's about achieving what truly matters to you.

3. Regulate Your Nervous System for Resilience

High achievers often operate in chronic stress. Small shifts can have a huge impact:

- **Breathwork** to ground yourself before key moments.
- **Movement** to release tension and unlock creativity.
- **Pausing** before reacting under pressure.

Fortitude isn't about enduring stress—it's about mastering your response to it.

4. Own Your Personal Brand with Authenticity

Your career is yours to shape. Instead of conforming to market expectations, highlight what makes you unique. The more attuned you are with your true strengths and values, the more magnetic your success becomes.

Unshakable in Chaos: Trusting Your Gut and Rising Strong

When we trust ourselves, we stop outsourcing decisions to fear and start listening to the quiet, knowing voice within. True resilience isn't about pushing through—it's about aligning with your deepest intelligence.

Every decision—career move, leadership choice, even how you manage relationships—should be a reflection of who you truly are, not just what feels "safe" or expected.

The body is a profoundly intelligent and interconnected system of wisdom. 80% of the Vagus nerve's fibres send signals from the body to the brain, yet most professionals only rely on their cognitive intelligence, ignoring the vast intelligence in the heart, gut, and beyond.

This is where our hybrid coaching-headhunting model shatters convention. Instead of the transactional "bum-in-the-seat" volume recruitment approach, we integrate coaching, neuroscience, embodiment, and whole-body intelligence to help leaders make more aligned decisions. The result? Choices that feel authentic at your core, not just ones that seem ideal on paper.

The Gut: Your Second Brain

The Enteric Nervous System (ENS)—your gut brain—is a vast network of neurons in the digestive system that shapes mood, instincts, and risk-taking. It produces 95% of the body's serotonin and plays a critical role in decision-making.

That "gut feeling"? It's your personal leadership radar, hard-wired directly to your brain via the Vagus nerve.

In our model, we help leaders move beyond hesitation and analysis paralysis. Instead of second-guessing every move, you learn to trust your instincts as much as your strategy. This gut-level intelligence transforms leadership presence because confidence isn't just a mindset; it's a biological state.

A client put it this way:

"Before, I was second-guessing everything. Now, I trust my instincts as much as my strategy, and my team feels the difference. My decisions are faster, bolder, and my business has never been stronger."

Try This:

Before making a big decision, pause. Take some belly breaths.

With your hand on your heart ask: **Does this feel right?** Are you truly aligned with your deepest self in this moment?

With your hand on your stomach ask: **What do I need?** Your gut often knows before your mind does.

The Science Behind the Magic - The Intelligence of the Heart

Neuroscience reveals a game-changing truth: when the heart and brain sync, you become an unstoppable force—sharper, calmer, more resilient. Studies from the HeartMath Institute show that cultivating this state—through breathwork, emotional coherence, and presence—can reduce stress and improve focus.

High performers dismiss heart intelligence as weakness. We see it as your ultimate competitive advantage. Our approach includes daily practices that transforms pressure into presence via clarity rituals, resilience techniques, and coaching.

A client put it this way:

"Before, I was always fighting. Now, I lead from calm. Everything changed."

Try This: 4-4-6 Breath Reset

- **Inhale: 4 seconds**
- **Hold: 4 seconds**
- **Exhale: 6 seconds**

Regulate your nervous system. Elevate your performance.

The Pelvis: Stability, Creativity, and Power

The pelvis is your centre of gravity—the foundation for balance, presence, purpose and creative energy. When we are physically grounded, we communicate with authority. When we are tense or disconnected, our leadership presence weakens.

Through the hybrid coaching model, we integrate breathwork, movement, and embodiment techniques to help professionals expand their executive presence. True leadership isn't just about what you say—it's about how you show up.

A client described the shift like this:

"Michelle's work is like magic—except it's not. It's deeply practical, and it works. I used to struggle to get buy-in from my board; now, I walk into meetings, and they're already aligned with my vision before I even present it."

Try This:

Before stepping into a big meeting, an interview or a presentation:

1. **Plant feet hip-width apart**
2. **Soften knees**
3. **Three deep belly breaths**
4. **Feel your weight settle**

When you enter the room with presence, people notice.

The Nervous System: The Master Regulator

Your nervous system is the unsung hero of decision-making. It dictates whether you lead from power or panic. If you're stuck in survival mode, you'll react from fear. If you're regulated, you'll respond with clarity and control.

Research in neurophysiology shows that a well-regulated nervous system enhances:

- **Cognitive function**
- **Emotional intelligence**
- **Stress resilience**

This is why our model integrates somatic techniques—helping leaders shift from reactive stress to proactive mastery.

A client put it this way:

"I used to think stress was just part of the job. Michelle helped me shift my entire state of being. Now, I lead from a place of clarity and presence instead of burnout and reactivity."

Try This:

- **Cold exposure** - Splash cold water on your face to instantly reset your nervous system.

- **Slow, deliberate movement** - Yoga or tai chi can shift you from stress mode into clarity.
- **Long exhales** - Exhaling longer than you inhale calms the nervous system and improves focus.

Test it, tweak it, own it.

Why This Matters

Most coaching models focus on mindset alone. But leadership isn't just in the mind—it's in the body.

This is what makes our hybrid coaching model different. We don't just talk about success - we hardwire it into:

- **How you think**
- **How you feel**
- **How you show up**

By activating all five intelligence centres, you move from:

- **Stress** → Resilience
- **Doubt** → Confidence
- **Burnout** → Thriving

The shift is tangible, proven, and transformative. The most effective professionals don't just think; they feel, sense, and trust their entire being in decision-making.

Ask Yourself:

- What would change if I trusted my gut, not just my logic?
- How often do I pause to check in with my emotions before reacting?
- Where in my life am I pushing through when I should be listening to my body?

These questions will either liberate you or terrify you. Choose wisely.

The Invitation: Be Unapologetically Human

The Old Way Is Dead: Grinding kills. Overthinking paralyses. Fear lies.

The New Rules: Stop outsourcing your power. Start trusting your entire intelligence. Lead, decide, and live from a place of:

- **Clarity**
- **Intuition**
- **Embodied confidence**

The future of leadership and career success doesn't belong to those who push harder. It belongs to those who listen intuitively. The world isn't just changing. It's waiting. Waiting for leaders who:

- Trust themselves
- Integrate intelligence from their entire being
- Redefine success on their own terms

Your move.

Our Elevation Plan: A Whole-Body Approach to Career Success

Want to align your career with who you truly are while making strategic, confident moves? Here's how:

1. **Start with a Deep-Dive Discovery:** Before making any career change, ask yourself:
   • What is success like beyond money and titles? (Gut)
   • How do I want to feel at work and in life? (Heart)
   • What career path would truly fulfil me? (Mind, Pelvis)
2. **Position Yourself Strategically:** Own your personal brand by embracing what makes you unique.
   • Ditch the mould—Highlight your strengths and individuality.
   • Build genuine relationships with decision-makers who align with your values.

3. **Master Resilience & Peek Performance:** Regulate your nervous system with simple but powerful techniques.
   - Use breathwork to stay calm under pressure.
   - Move your body to release tension and unlock creativity.
4. **Align Before You Act:** Before saying yes to any opportunity, check in with all five intelligence centres:
   - Mind: Does it make logical sense?
   - Heart: Does it fit with my values? Does it excite and inspire me?
   - Gut: Does it feel right deep down?
   - Pelvis: Does it spark creativity and passion?
   - Nervous System: Can I approach it without stress and overwhelm?
5. **Commit to Sustainable Growth:** Success isn't about reaching the finish line; it's about ongoing evolution.
   - Keep adapting, learning, and refining your career path with ongoing self-awareness.
   - Trust that your body holds wisdom just as much as your mind.

Why I'm a Game-Changer (And You Can Be Too)

I go deep—no shallow coaching, no one-size-fits-all career advice. I ask the questions no one else dares to—cutting through the noise, the fear, and the 'shoulds' to get straight to the core of what matters to you. I don't do polite coaching. I break the rules, challenge the excuses, and get to the truth—fast.

I combine this with savvy headhunting strategy - teaching you how to position yourself so powerfully that the right opportunities come knocking. Because confidence alone won't land you the job, you also need to know how to navigate power dynamics and make yourself irresistible by serving what decision-makers are looking for on a silver platter.

Here's what truly elevates my work: Helping you remember what it means to be you, while navigating this terrifying new workplace territory together.

COACHING REIMAGINED Expanding Human Potential

Working with me won't come with a guarantee of a new job. What it does offer is a transformational advantage. Through it you will stand out in an AI-driven market. I get it - some of these ideas might be shaking up what you thought you knew. Welcome to the cutting edge of coaching. It's bold. It's powerful. It works.

In an increasingly automated world, being human is the ultimate competitive edge. Master your inner intelligence, and you'll never second-guess your path again.

Coaches—let's collaborate and disrupt the game. Our clients deserve it now more than ever.

Driven Professionals—If burnout isn't the badge of honour you signed up for, we're about to #designyourbestlife together.

Connect with Me

Linktree: https://linktr.ee/UnapologeticEdge

CHAPTER 19
Finding Confidence, Happiness and Purpose in your Work Through Wellbeing
By Colleen Lansdell

As I sat down to write this chapter, I stared at a blank screen - once again, my all-too-familiar companion (or foe), my inner critic, made her appearance. There was a time when I would have given up in defeat, distracting myself with a shopping trip, a movie or a glass of wine - after all, I *deserved* it! I've become wise to her tactics of steering me toward distraction and my comfort zone, trying to derail my dreams. So, I take a deep breath - several, in fact - quiet my mind with meditation, and invite her to take a back seat as I take the wheel and trust the wisdom within me to guide me forward.

It hasn't always been like this. I used to be the quiet broker behind the leaders, diligently working behind the scenes, making others look good. I was driven by an overly vigilant inner critic and unhelpful beliefs fuled by fear - all the while ignoring the whisper to follow my heart. Then, in spectacular fashion, and a series of heartbreaking events, I found myself standing at a crossroads in both my career and life.

By embracing courage, compassion, and gratitude, along with the coaching tools I now share with my clients (and with you here), I cultivated self-awareness, allowed myself to be vulnerable, and strengthened my connection with both myself and others – including my inner critic!

The Crossroad

Mary Oliver, the beloved American poet, posed a profound question in her poem Summer Day.

Tell me, what is it you plan to do with this, your one and wild precious life?

If you find yourself at a crossroads feeling stuck in your career, craving more meaning and purpose to reignite your passion, this chapter is for you and I'm truly grateful that it has found its way into your hands.

We all face this reckoning. When it comes to success, happiness, and meaningful work, there is no one-size-fits-all solution. Some people fall into a career, while others find one through careful consideration and deliberate design. Some choose a career dedicated to helping others, advocating for the most vulnerable, and protecting the community. Others create—designing, building, reimagining the world. We chase qualifications that seem logical at the time and align with our passions. We make our parents proud. We embark on our careers with a backpack full of hopes and dreams, maintaining disciplined schedules and studying diligently to achieve our career aspirations.

Yet over time while projecting an image of having everything all figured out with all the boxes checked, we often conceal our insecurities and live in fear of being exposed as imposters. Gradually, our once-light backpack grows heavier—the hopes and dreams replaced with self-doubt and stress disguised as pebbles.

Enter the crossroad intersection.

Whatever career path you have chosen, chances are years later, when you've seemingly *arrived* - having achieved everything you set out to do - you reach a crossroads. Standing at this intersection, questioning your chosen career despite your outward success, feeling strangely empty and unsatisfied, you find yourself asking yourself: Is this it? Is being *truly* happy only reserved for everyone else, and just not me?

It's at this moment - lost and dissatisfied - that we frantically search for answers outside of ourselves. A new job. A rushed resume update. Another qualification. A new relationship. Something – anything to *fix* that gnawing emptiness. We grasp external solutions to ease our dissatisfaction, and quiet our anxiety. Desperate to escape from the very life we've built.

For my client Lilly, a 25-year police veteran, after years in a patriarchal environment bound by rigid rules and regulations, her anxiety and vigilant inner critic, lack of confidence and self-belief became too much. She craved change. Yet she feared putting herself "out there." She had no vision of what a new path would look like and feared how she would change careers, and where to begin. With the support of a friend she crafted a resume for a handful of applications, and she pounced on the first job offer that came her way.

Lilly believed she'd found her escape. No more shift work. Less stress. No more missed family occasions. The work life balances her family desperately needed. What she discovered next wasn't exactly what she expected. After a few short months in her new job, she felt lost as her inner critic intensified, working harder than ever and feeling even more uncertain than before. When we began working together, she realized that in her rush to *fix* the problem she had overlooked critical steps in considering the layers of her career change and that she was not as prepared as she had initially thought.

Like Lilly, we often ignore the wisdom within us. Our intuition. Our internal guidance system.

For some of us we have forgotten who we are. What lights us up. What we want. What we don't want. For some, we realize we've never been asked these questions - or asked them of ourselves. These truths lie buried underneath layers of conformity, family values, patriarchal and societal expectations. Within, waiting for an outlet, is the courage to be vulnerable to ask these questions with self-compassion and gratitude.

Yet, in the busyness of life of being everything to everyone else, we rob ourselves of taking the time to pause and reflect. Rarely do we connect within, to what we truly, deeply desire. Never questioning why we do what we do, or if we are good at it. Nor do we understand our motivations and acknowledge our strengths. Instead, we blame external factors that contribute to our unhappiness: the horrible boss, our partner, our kids, the government, and, not considering that the last person having an impact, maybe, just maybe, is ourselves. Spoiler alert!

People don't fear change; they fear the loss that change brings. Read that again.

Our most fundamental instinct is self-preservation; we are hardwired to protect ourselves, which serves us well when driving, operating machinery or cooking with gas. However, courage often requires us to defy this instinct—urging us to take emotional risks, to be vulnerable, and to acknowledge our mistakes, guilt, shame, and perceived failures.

No one likes to feel stuck. Directionless. Unwanted. Disempowered. The vulnerability and uncertainty around what to do next often causes our deepest misery. You've been driving without a map, taking life's twists and turns, only to arrive at a destination that no longer aligns with who you are - or who you want to be.

The choices we made as children to protect ourselves continue to shape our decisions as adults, often driven by a deep and unrelenting fear. Our need to control situations stems from a desire for safety and stability. Along the way, we made decisions - often unconsciously - to shield ourselves, but these same patterns persist into adulthood, influencing our choices and holding us back in ways we might not even be aware of.

This leads us to operate on autopilot. Perfectionism. Self-doubt. Impostor syndrome. People-pleasing. Fear of Failure. Need to Control. Our inner critic and imposter work overtime - software programs running silently in the background of our minds. We live driven by unconscious imprints: beliefs, values, and judgments left by caregivers, siblings, teachers, community. We stay stuck in soul-crushing jobs driven by security needs, until something finally breaks.

For some, our inner critic, the pressure of toxic workplaces and ego driven managers - who don't know how to manage, let alone lead - becomes too much. For others we are made redundant, a relationship breaks down, or we have a death in the family. We have reached breaking point – the crossroad intersection.

The toll on our mental health and wellbeing has reached a point where we *must* make a change.

Only then do we dig deeper. Learn to trust our intuition. Follow our hearts' desire. Take the wheel and become the driver of our own life and career.

I knew this intersection well, just like many of my clients. It took me years to build the confidence to fully commit to my career change. Back then, the only support available was resume assistance, which, although valuable, is only helpful once you're clear on your path, and if continuing the employment pathway – not so much if you are considering the entrepreneur -self-employment as an option. Despite the limited support, I made progress, but something always held me back - until a series of heartbreaking, life-altering events. **This wasn't part of my plan.** Though a very painful experience, it brought me to that intersection that *made me* to stop, reflect, find the courage to listen within, and take the steps that ultimately led me to where I am today. And as challenging it was, I'm so grateful it did. The universe certainly works in mysterious ways - as they say rejection is re-direction to something bigger and better, and more aligned to who you are, and what you are here to do on this earth.

By shifting our focus from a negative narrative to one of growth and learning, and embracing our imperfections with self-compassion, kindness and gratitude, we can foster greater contentment, authenticity, and self-acceptance. This transformation nurtures empathy and a deeper sense of inner peace, strengthening our connections with ourselves and those around us.

As we release the need for control and replace it with acceptance and self-compassion, while tuning into our true selves, we begin to recognize our authentic needs and desires. This creates space for deeper, more meaningful connections with others and a stronger sense of purpose. By listening to the quiet whispers within, uncovering patterns that no longer serve us, and charting a new path forward, we open ourselves to richer, more fulfilling connections.

For many, the pandemic forced this reckoning – a collective moment to reconsider personal and professional priorities. Or perhaps for you, another defining moment triggered by change: the crushing weight of overwhelm, burnouts empty exhaustion, or the jarring realization you're no longer aligned with your chosen career or your organization's priorities and values.

Unlocking The Wisdom Within

My approach integrates mind and body – a powerful blend of strategy and wellbeing. This isn't traditional coaching. It's transformation. I combine practical professional development with deep personal growth, creating change programs that work differently.

My methodology draws from positive psychology, mindfulness practices, NLP, and matrix therapies, it's anchored in cutting-edge neuroscience-based coaching techniques like mBraining, EFT and energy healing.

At the heart of my work is courage, compassion, and gratitude - key elements that cultivate self-belief, confidence and happiness at work, and in life.

We focus on who you are *being* before what you are *doing*.

I work with clients in professions dedicated to helping others—individuals who are often introverted, deep thinkers, and passionate about making the world a better place. Many find themselves at that intersection feeling burnt out and questioning their next steps. They seek clarity, confidence, self-belief, and direction as they navigate this pivotal stage of their lives.

I support them to connect their experience and strengths and show them how to design a life that enables them to engage in meaningful work aligned with their values and strengths. Together, we create a path that not only fulfills their personal needs but also brings simplicity, ease, and flow to their lives.

What is clear before changing the exterior of our world, is that we must first look within, build self-awareness, understand our beliefs, thoughts, and behavior patterns. Unless acknowledged, accepted and healed, these patterns will keep us frozen at that crossroad—eternally craving meaning while repeating the same cycles in every new career or life change, we attempt.

For Lilly, her backpack now felt as though it was filled with rocks she had carried for many years. She feared the vulnerability of unpacking it; yet without doing so, her backpack would continue to fill and eventually overflow.

She needed to unpack and grieve the career she worked so hard to achieve and had left, to process her emotions, and begin to develop self-awareness. She needed to understand herself, her needs, her strengths, and what was next, all while appreciating the expertise she had to offer a potential employer.

Everyone has a story to share, and it's a crucial part of any career change to reflect on and acknowledge with gratitude, then actively express your journey so far—the highs, the lows, the successes, and the setbacks that have shaped you. Your story not only creates a sense of connection but also helps you recognize and articulate your strengths as you explore a new career direction as an employee, or to take the leap into entrepreneurship and start your own business.

During my half-day session with my client Sally, a 20-year police veteran, I began by asking her to share her story. She expressed her passion for working in the community sector - what she loved most about it, along with the less enjoyable aspects of her job. She then walked me through the events that ultimately led her to the difficult decision to leave her career in policing.

Listening to Sally, I observed her shift in her seat as we unpacked this further, she recalled a childhood memory she had never shared before, surprisingly recalling it as it surfaced. As the youngest of six children, she grew up in a chaotic household constantly listening to her parents' aggressive arguments and feeling intense fear for her mother. On one occasion, she described the yelling as so loud that she needed to "hide" to feel safe. She mentioned this became a regular occurrence and recalled the fear of hiding under her bed, waiting for the shouting to stop.

She recognized that her anxiety, preference for working behind the scenes, and the feelings of disempowerment and shame were directly linked to her inability to speak up and help her mother. She understood that allowing herself to be vulnerable opened her to understanding how this dynamic had continued to affect her life as an adult and had persistently influenced her career and relationships.

In my work with clients, one of the techniques where I regularly witness notable relief is EFT (Emotional Freedom Technique) which unblocks the energy centers of the body, calms the amygdala (the "fight or flight" part of the brain), and assists clients to release energy and clear negative patterns and beliefs. Tapping is the divine combination of Chinese acupressure, positive psychology, and neuroscience, and the technique helps restore balance and flow to the body's energy systems.

With Sally in the subsequent sessions, we worked with her energy, clearing it to align her emotions and helping her to cultivate compassion and forgiveness for the little girl who felt scared, powerless, and overly responsible for others, constantly trying to "save" them.

With these insights, Sally worked to identify where and how they specifically manifested. I guided her through several processes to align her energy system, including the Emotional Freedom Technique (EFT) and a focused approach on her throat (expression) and solar plexus (the power centre) chakras.

For Sally, who had struggled with self-doubt and an overactive inner critic, this technique proved to be most effective. Over several sessions, we released the blocked energy in her body which assisted her to transform from a feeling of powerlessness, into being an empowered woman who felt safer to speak up and ask for what she needed and wanted.

We focused on small, specific changes she could incorporate into her daily life and habits that would have a noticeable impact on her mental health and well-being. Through our work together, she gained clarity on the sources of her anxiety and the triggers that sparked her inner critic and learned strategies to support herself. By practicing mindfulness, meditation, keeping a gratitude journal and adopting compassion for herself and others, she began to experience positive shifts in her life, gaining a truer sense of herself, while cultivating a new and loving relationship with herself. Where she once felt unaccepted by her peers or lacked connection, she discovered newfound acceptance and connection.

Your North Star

When considering a career change, understanding your values can be the key to choosing a path that truly aligns with you, rather than one that doesn't. Your values guide your decisions, the environment you live and work in, your daily routines, how manage your finances and the people you spend time with, and even the conditions you set for your job or business.

Research has shown that we are happier and more fulfilled when our actions align with what truly matters to us. Understanding your values - what is important to you and what you stand for - provides clarity for your decisions, ensuring that you stay connected to what matters most.

Think of your values as your north star—guiding you through life's twists and turns by staying true to who you are and what you stand for. Defining your values is a deeply personal and enlightening process, and unique to you. It's not just about picking meaningful words from a list, as some might suggest. It's an experience that many of my clients have found both uplifting and inspiring.

Modern coaching goes beyond simply selecting values from a list; it helps you uncover and integrate those values through a method I use in my work called mBraining. This approach integrates neuroscience with teachings from ancient wisdom, positive psychology, and cutting-edge neuroscience to enhance a person's intuitive abilities, leading to wiser decision-making in daily life.

We have three brains—head, heart, and gut—and when these neural networks align, something remarkable happens. When operating in harmony, they reveal our highest wisdom. The impact of these three brains working together toward our goals is far more powerful than when they function in isolation. True transformation happens when all three are in sync.

If you've ever felt miserable and drained at the end of a workday without understanding why, chances are your values are out of alignment. For example, when my client James came to see me, he transitioned from the community sector into a sales role. He mentioned that while the pay was good and he enjoyed talking to people, he didn't care about the sales process, or the product he was selling. During our session, it became clear that his mind was focused on the extra money and potential possibilities, while his heart felt something was missing. He experienced a heavy sensation in his gut, signalling that something didn't feel right about selling a product he didn't believe in. Likewise with Melisa, who had left the corporate world to start her own business. She was passionate about her work in workplace training; however she struggled with the selling of her programs, she described that it didn't feel right to sell because she just wanted to help people. Like James, her three brains were communicating with her, but they were out of sync. Through mBraining, we can accurately identify what is truly important to us - our core values - and synchronize the three brains, aligning them with our goals and decisions eliminating internal conflict that can stop us moving forward.

Growth Mindset Revolution

Our brain's negative bias, our thought patterns, and the way we perceive our lives, careers, and relationships – including our relationship with ourselves – are all influenced by our mindset. We are creative beings, crafting stories based on the beliefs we've adopted as truths about our reality. However, it's often these very stories that keep us from moving forward. Learning to evaluate and challenge our thinking with compassion can lead to profound changes in our lives.

COACHING REIMAGINED Expanding Human Potential

After decades of research on achievement and success, Stanford University Psychology Professor Carol Dweck uncovered a simple yet powerful concept: the power of mindset. In her book *Mindset: The New Psychology of Success*, Dweck delves into the impact of our thinking patterns on our lives, relationships, productivity, and careers, breaking them down into two distinct types: a fixed mindset and a growth mindset. These mindsets dramatically influence how we perceive our abilities, strengths, and potential.

A fixed mindset is the belief that our qualities and abilities are innate and unchangeable. People with a fixed mindset see their talents and intelligence as fixed, believing there's no need to develop them further. In challenging situations, they often struggle to recognize opportunities or find solutions, as they don't see their potential for growth.

On the other hand, individuals with a growth mindset believe they can enhance their strengths and abilities through effort, learning, and resilience—key traits for achieving both career and personal goals. People with a growth mindset, combined with a curiosity for problem-solving, focus on building self-awareness, exploring their unique strengths, and discovering deeper meaning and purpose in their work and lives.

When my client Ben, a department manager at a community organization, came to me, he shared that he had recently been promoted to this role and was generally enjoying it. However, he was facing challenges with his staff. He described them as rigid and said he struggled to communicate effectively with them. As we discussed his career history, strengths, and qualifications, Ben revealed that he hadn't taken advantage of the leadership training offered by his organization, nor did he feel the need to. He believed his experience was enough to manage the team, and he saw the problem as being with the staff, not with him.

When I suggested to Ben that maintaining a fixed mindset would hinder his growth as a leader and his ability to connect with his staff through improved communication and leadership skills, he was taken aback. Had he approached the situation with a growth mindset - being open to learning and improving his skills, even though he was already good at his job - his perspective would have shifted, allowing him to grow as a manager, and be better leader to his team.

Recognizing the impact of his mindset, Ben decided to learn to embrace a growth mindset. We initially worked on enhancing his leadership, communication and emotional intelligence skills and later held a team workshop focused on increasing engagement and helping the team strengthen relationships. The workshop centered on understanding each other's communication styles and work preferences to foster better connections.

Understanding our strengths and behaviors provide profound insights that help unlock your potential are a crucial component during career change. Profiling tools like DISC and VIA offer a structured way to reflect on your core traits, communication preferences, level of emotional intelligence and decision-making tendencies, helping you navigate challenges and maximize your effectiveness. By identifying key patterns in how you think, feel, and act, you can develop a clearer sense of self, leading to greater confidence, more intentional decision-making, and improved relationships.

For example, tools like DISC help you recognize your communication style, whether you tend to be assertive and direct (Dominance), persuasive and social (Influence), patient and steady (Steadiness), or methodical and detail-oriented (Compliance). This self-awareness not only enhances your ability to work more effectively with others but also aids in adjusting your approach when interacting with colleagues or clients who may have different preferences. Understanding these dynamics can foster smoother collaboration, reduce misunderstandings, and even inform career choices - helping you align with roles that best suit your natural communication tendencies.

When Fiona, a business manager in a large government department, came to me to discuss her challenges within her current role, she expressed feeling overwhelmed by the detailed reporting required in her role. In addition, she was struggling with her manager, whom she described as bossy. She was eager to stay within the same organization but desired a change. During our debriefing session of the DISC assessment, Fiona was surprised by how accurate the results were. It became immediately clear why she wasn't enjoying her current position or connecting well with her manager, and where she could make some changes.

We then explored options for her to be more empowered in her choices and ways she could leverage her strengths to enhance her daily work experience to align more with her personality and values, while also focusing less on her challenges.

VIA Character Strengths has a slightly different focus, identifying your core virtues and personal strengths, such as creativity, kindness, leadership, or perseverance. These strengths are closely tied to your sense of purpose and well-being. By recognizing which strengths, you naturally possess and how to cultivate them, you can build resilience in the face of challenges and create a more fulfilling, purposeful life. When individuals engage with their strengths, they often experience greater life satisfaction, as they are able to tap into their inherent capabilities, contributing meaningfully to their careers and personal relationships.

The combined benefits of exploring these tools with a coach go beyond just understanding yourself - they can actively shape how you engage with the world around you. By leveraging your strengths and being mindful of your behavioral patterns, you can unlock opportunities for personal growth, career advancement, and stronger, more authentic connections with others. These tools encourage you to step into your full potential, making it easier to navigate the complexities of life and work with clarity and confidence.

Surviving to Thriving

As humans, we are constantly seeking meaning. We judge ourselves and others, often repeat patterns of behavior that leave us feeling unfulfilled. In our search for purpose, we unconsciously try to fix things by adopting the values and beliefs of others, holding on to behaviors that don't truly serve us – often to try to fit in. We stay in jobs that drain our energy in the name of security, all the while overlooking the unique strengths and qualities that define us. This prevents us from embracing our true selves and tapping into the inner wisdom that's urging us to be acknowledged and followed.

COACHING REIMAGINED Expanding Human Potential

The future of career coaching is evolving, integrating mind-body approaches, positive psychology, neuroscience, and energy work to create holistic transformation.

It's about helping clients design lives where their work lights up their hearts.

So, let me ask you—what are you planning to do with this one wild and precious life of yours?

What impact and legacy do you plan to leave behind?

Are you at a crossroads?

Does your work - whether as an employee or entrepreneur - bring you meaning, purpose, and happiness, allowing you to thrive rather than just survive?

Are you seeking direction and ready to cultivate self-belief, confidence, and the courage to take your next steps?

Are you prepared to unpack your baggage, build a strong sense of self, and forge meaningful connections with others, filling your days with purposeful work that truly makes your heart sing?

Are you ready to create a life you love?

"Happiness is not something you postpone for the future; it is something you design for the present."

Jim Rohn

Website: www.evolvedsteps.com.au

CHAPTER 20
Healing Birth Trauma:
Supporting Life's Greatest Transition
Dee Dawson & Christine Mellor

"In giving birth to our babies, we may find that we give birth to new possibilities within ourselves."

Myla and Jon Kabat-Zinn

The path to parenthood is a period of significant transition and vulnerability. It's not surprising that adverse events that happen along the way – or indeed in earlier life – can result in fear, anxiety, and trauma. Infertility, pregnancy loss, fear of birth, birth trauma, postpartum stress and anxiety, childhood trauma, and sexual abuse are all emotionally challenging and can affect every aspect of birth and parenting.

We are our histories, and so how we feel about ourselves, how we behave, how we connect with others, and how we parent can all be affected by past experiences and beliefs, as well as any crises we encounter during pregnancy, birth and the postpartum period.

The well-being of the birthing woman and her family during this critical time is crucial and may influence health well beyond the perinatal period.

On Becoming a Parent

Growing or creating a family is hands down one of our most beautiful, empowering and rewarding life experiences. It can also be one of the most traumatic, pushing us to the absolute limits of our capabilities. During pregnancy, new parents are often faced with overwhelming amounts of information, physical challenges, financial stress, hormonal changes, loss of identity and anxiety. Support people may also be confronted with sights and sounds they've never experienced before. They can find themselves placing the well-being of their loved ones in the hands of people they don't know and can feel helpless, confused and deprived of all sense of control as they try to make sense of unfolding events.

Birth trauma is in the eye of the beholder, and it can never be assumed that a birth has, or has not, been experienced as traumatic. Some research studies suggest that as many as one in three births may be experienced as being psychologically traumatic and the ripple effects are significant. They may include postpartum stress, anxiety and depression, disrupted bonding between baby and parents, low self-esteem and social isolation, and fear of subsequent birth.

Negative consequences for the health and well-being of women, babies, and families can be very long-lasting. Unfortunately, birth trauma is not always routinely discussed, appropriate services are not always easily accessible, and the associated morbidity may be underappreciated. However, there is a therapy that can help.

Havening techniques®

Havening was developed by doctors Ron and Steve Ruden in the U.S.

Using neuroscience, they describe the process by which a traumatic event rapidly encodes into the amygdala situated in our brains, storing the information for future use to keep us 'safe' should a similar event reoccur.

If the amygdala detects a previous bad experience is looming once again, we initiate flight, fight, freeze or defensive rage responses to protect ourselves.

Havening techniques® utilise specific areas of touch, generating neurochemicals and delta waves in the brain. This 'depotentiates' the neural pathway created during the earlier traumatic event. Following therapy, the memory remains but has lost its associated emotional distress.

Whilst Havening is a relatively new therapy, this effect is understood to be permanent. Havening celebrates neuroplasticity and our brain's ability to grow, reorganise and heal. Havening is a beautiful blend of science and compassion and is remarkably effective in helping people who are negatively affected by post-traumatic stress disorder, trauma-related anxiety, phobias and negative core beliefs.

Importantly, Havening provides practitioners with a framework to utilise when working with clients. This includes the understanding that four criteria are necessary for an experience to be encoded in the brain as traumatic rather than simply a memory.

Firstly, an event needs to occur. Something has happened, that has been experienced as significant for that person.

Secondly, we all experience life with an existing emotional landscape that is either resilient or vulnerable. Emotionally vulnerable people are more likely to be negatively affected by an event.

Thirdly, the event must contain meaning for the person experiencing trauma, for example where they fear for themselves or for someone they love.

Finally, for an event to be encoded in the amygdala, there needs to be an element of inescapability experienced by the person, this is often characterised by a loss of control or a feeling of being trapped in a situation.

Crucially, childbirth can potentially give rise to all four criteria, leaving birthing women and their loved ones vulnerable to the events around childbirth.

Midwifery meets Havening

Before establishing Willow, their private Havening practice, both Christine and Dee, worked extensively with women and their families who had experienced earlier trauma, stress, anxiety, fear and negative self-belief, and felt distressed as they approached childbirth. Acutely aware of the gap in support services in this space, and seeing the seriousness of the need, they decided to be the change they wanted to see and became certified Havening practitioners.

The art and skill of midwifery have always been a blend of intuition and science. The task of establishing trust and safety, building rapport, and sharing knowledge and wisdom is crucial to the relationship between midwife and birthing woman. A midwife naturally uses coaching skills, as they care for a woman through one of the most significant events of their lives.

Therapeutic touch is central to care in this field. It is described by Fischer & Johnson (1999) as being the "consciously directed process of energy exchange during which the practitioner uses the hands as a focus to facilitate healing". Midwives utilise therapeutic touch to reassure, calm, connect, and relieve pain. For Christine and Dee, the combination of midwifery, clinical coaching skills and Havening techniques® feels like perfect synchronicity.

The synthesis of midwifery and Havening offers beautiful resolutions. Havening can be utilised at any time during the birth continuum: in pregnancy, in preparation for birth, birthing and the postnatal period, or even many years later. Midwifery and Havening are a dance between science and intuition, care and compassion, technology and tradition. Empowering and emotionally preparing women for birth and parenting takes knowledge, skill and mastery.

Dee and Christine bring extensive midwifery expertise and insight to their Havening therapy in a special and unique way, bringing additional strength to their work. Clients know that as midwives they can visualise, and fully appreciate, what women experience. Their professional understanding, it seems, is *felt*. This is a key enabler for their healing work.

One of the unique services that Christine and Dee offer involves blending their midwifery and Havening expertise in a combination of debriefing, Havening, and planning or guidance. This usually entails working with a woman, and sometimes their partners too, who have experienced a previous pregnancy, birth, or postpartum period as distressing or traumatic. Debriefing would optimally be done with the midwife or obstetrician who cared for the woman, but sometimes this isn't possible. This service by Willow, however, extends beyond debriefing and into trauma resolution and resilience building using clinical skills, coaching and Havening, to help families create their desired outcomes.

The debriefing process begins with carefully unpacking the previous experience, ideally with their maternity clinical notes, providing opportunities for questions, and offering explanations and guidance where needed. During this discussion, if trauma, anxiety, fear, or negative self-belief is identified, Havening is used to facilitate healing. The next step in the process involves carefully exploring, planning, and visualising the woman's needs and instilling a sense of calm and positive self-belief whilst applying Havening touch. The importance of preparing the mind for birth and the postpartum period cannot be underestimated.

To explore this in more depth, let us share some specific case studies with you.

COACHING REIMAGINED Expanding Human Potential

From grief to freedom

Melissa normally has a robust and sunny disposition. She suffered, however, from post-natal depression after her daughter was born and was afraid to have a second child. Despite wanting a sibling for her daughter, she doubted her body's ability to maintain another pregnancy. Melissa felt her depression was linked to an earlier miscarriage before the arrival of her little girl.

Melissa was also haunted by a challenging time when her father was deathly ill in the UK, and she was called to be with him. As she was preparing to leave, Melissa discovered she was seven weeks pregnant with her first baby. Then, soon after arriving in the UK, Melissa had a scan that revealed her tiny baby had no heartbeat. As she was trying to process this devastating news alone, she still had her father to care for. At 4am the very next day, he passed away with Melissa at his side.

Dee saw Melissa in her own home sitting comfortably in her living room. They sat quietly together and once Havening touch was applied to Melissa's hands, arms and face, Dee asked her to recall the worst part of that time in the UK as she had coped with two terrible and simultaneous losses. She was tearful initially but calmed as soothing delta waves dominated her brain activity.

After 26 minutes, the session ended. Melissa volunteered reaction. She said the dark memory she had started with was fuzzy now and surrounded by a feeling of calm. She could remember feeling her father's hand in hers, but it was soft and warm and not dreadfully cold as it had been before.
She added she'd had a lot of counselling but said, "I only ever walked out of a session feeling about a quarter as good as I feel right now." Melissa was now excited for the future.

She fell pregnant again not long after our session. Later, she said she wouldn't have felt comfortable or ready to do so if she hadn't experienced our Havening session. She gave birth to a gorgeous little boy and had no recurrence of post-natal depression.

This is a great example of how working with the body, rather than merely talking about previous experiences, elicited a very different result. Through disrupting the old trauma pathways, Melissa was now able to remember her experience without the extensive negative emotions that had been present previously.

Rapidly reducing a state of 'high alert'

Christine first met Nadia, a first-time mum, when her baby was five weeks old. She had been experiencing flashbacks from her birth, and she wanted to feel more peaceful about her experience.

They met in her home, and the tension was palpable. Nadia was clearly on 'high alert', the baby was unsettled and not feeding well, and her husband didn't feel confident handling the baby. Even the dog seemed to be responding to the tension. When Christine arrived, Nadia was stressed trying to latch her crying baby to the breast, and the dog was barking. Nadia didn't have much eye contact with her baby, and she looked anxious when she held him.

The situations that Christine and Dee enter are often complex and multifaceted and may contain more depth than is first communicated. However, the trust people have in them as midwives is *already there*, creating a safe space, a significant facilitator for healing.

Nadia's trust in Christine also helped her to assess the overall situation and she gave Nadia some support with breastfeeding before starting the Havening, and this midwifery skill was incredibly important in creating a calm and peaceful space.

Together Nadia and Christine identified the difficult encoding moment in Nadia's birth, and the Havening on that specific event left her feeling calm, 'light,' and able to think about her birth without feeling triggered. Christine left her feeling peaceful and more confident in herself.

On checking in the following week, Nadia was feeling less anxious and was not as worried about her baby, who was also more settled. Even the dog was much calmer!

On the return visit, Christine noticed that Nadia now had good eye contact with her baby and looked relaxed when she held him. Havening helped her resolve her negative feelings, not just about the birth but also in how she was previously associating her baby with her traumatic experience. Indeed, it was during the Havening process that this had become clear to her, and from that insight she realised it had influenced how she responded to and bonded with her baby.

Building self-belief

Christine met Flo when she was 34 weeks into her second pregnancy. She was becoming extremely fearful about her upcoming birth. Her first labour had not gone to plan. Flo had needed an epidural and felt so out of control during the second stage of labour and wasn't able to push. She had lost faith in her body and had requested to have an elective caesarean section. Flo had had IVF treatment to conceive both her babies using donor sperm after a long fertility journey.

The loss of control seemed quite complex, but they carefully explored Flo's experiences at her pace, starting with the birth. Christine assured Flo that she was completely present with her as she worked to resolve her feelings and observed her physiological responses very carefully. Towards the end of the first session, her primary emotion was fear of not having agency. Interestingly, this was no longer related to the birth, but instead to her infertility, despite earlier receiving counselling following the IVF process. Further Havening resolved these feelings and built self-belief.

Flo went on to have a positive physiological birthing experience, during which she felt strong, in control, and safe.

It is clear from Flo's case that the trauma was not at a conscious level. It was through working with her using Havening techniques, that the layers of trauma could be uncovered, to ensure a complete resolution.

COACHING REIMAGINED Expanding Human Potential

Self-Havening – a tool to induce calm

In many cases, a client can be taught self-havening, to offer support between sessions – and as an ongoing life skill.

It is important to say that self-havening on your own is not recommended for significant trauma, as support and guidance from a certified Havening practitioner is essential. However, self-havening is a very effective tool that can be used anywhere to reduce emotions that are concerning and perhaps limiting you in a given moment, such as stress, anxiety, fear, and anger. For example, you may be feeling anxious before an interview, angry after an argument, or be fearful before a dental appointment. Havening touch brings about a feeling of calm, and within a few minutes you can be feeling much more settled.

The images below illustrate self-havening touch. This is best done gently and rhythmically, finding the right pressure and speed of touch that feels right for you. You can rotate the touch to the three different areas in any order, or you may find yourself settling on a favourite.

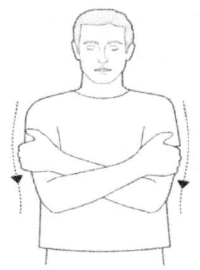
Arm Self-Havening

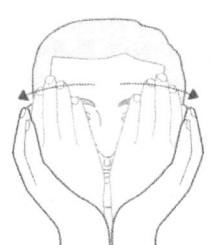
Face Self-Havening

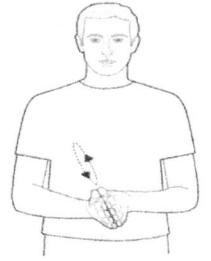
Palm Self-Havening

www.havening.org

- Before you start sit comfortably, close your eyes, and think of the event or feel the emotion that you want to resolve.
- Start the self-havening touch.
- Take 3 deep, slow breaths and clear your mind.
- Keep self-havening and begin to count backwards out loud from 50 to 0.

- Continue Havening, using your chosen touch – arms, face or palms, and when you reach 0 check in on how you are feeling.
- If the feelings are still present, keep havening.
- Think of all the colours of the rainbow and try to identify one object for each colour
- Imagine yourself in your favourite place and think of 5 things you can see, smell or hear
- Check in again on the event or feelings that you started with and continue to haven if you aren't feeling as calm as you would like
- If counting backwards isn't for you, singing along to a favourite song also works well.

Ultimately, the role of the counting or singing is to distract your brain from the emotion while the delta waves and neurochemicals do their work. It only takes a few minutes to bring your brain to a place of calm.

Havening and Midwifery: A Transformational Approach to Birth Trauma and Anxiety

Midwifery is not just about delivering babies—it is about delivering **confidence, calm, and emotional resilience** to the women in our care. A midwife's clinical skills are essential, but the emotional landscape of pregnancy, birth, and motherhood requires something more—**a deeper, more holistic form of support**. This is where **Havening** becomes a profoundly valuable tool, offering a gentle yet powerful way to soothe fear, process past trauma, and create an experience of safety in both body and mind.

For women who feel anxious about their first pregnancy, have experienced a previous traumatic birth, or have endured the heartbreak of loss, the journey to motherhood can be filled with fear and uncertainty. Traditional midwifery care offers physical monitoring and reassurance, but **true healing and empowerment happen when emotional wellbeing is held with the same level of expertise as clinical care.**

Havening, a neuroscience-based psychosensory technique, works by engaging the brain's natural ability to rewire and heal. Through soothing touch and intentional focus, it helps **reduce stress, release trauma, and build emotional resilience**. When integrated into midwifery practice, it transforms the support a midwife can offer—moving beyond reassurance into **deep, embodied calm and confidence** for the mother.

A Unique Form of Clinical Coaching

Havening in midwifery is more than a comfort technique; it is a **form of clinical coaching** that enhances and refines the very essence of midwifery care. It allows midwives to:

- **Support women with birth-related fears** – Helping them shift from anxiety to empowerment.
- **Gently process past trauma** – Creating emotional freedom before stepping into birth again.
- **Enhance the mind-body connection** – So that women approach labour with trust in themselves.
- **Offer self-havening as a lifelong tool** – Teaching mothers how to create their own emotional sanctuary.

When midwifery embraces Havening, it moves already holistic care into something truly **exquisite and unique**—an artful blend of clinical expertise and deep emotional support, leaving the woman feeling **held, understood, and fully prepared** for her birth experience.

If you would like to talk to us about how we can support you, we would love to hear from you.

Your Birth Experience Deserves to Be One of Strength, Safety, and Support

If you're feeling anxious about an upcoming birth, carrying the weight of a difficult past experience, or still healing from a previous loss—you don't have to navigate this alone. Birth is more than an event; it is a deeply emotional and transformative journey, and you deserve care that supports both your body and mind.

With the gentle power of Havening, you can release fear, process past

trauma, and step into birth feeling calm, confident, and in control. This is not just about coping—it's about healing. It's about reclaiming your experience, rebuilding trust in your body, and preparing for birth in a way that feels safe and empowering.

♡ Imagine stepping into labour free from fear
♡ Imagine feeling emotionally lighter, unburdened by past trauma, and entering into motherhood with peace and calm.

This level of care is possible, and it's here for you.

If you're ready to approach birth with calm, clarity, and confidence, let's begin this journey together. You deserve it.

Willow Psychosensory Therapy

Here is a link to Willow's website address:

www.willowtherapy.co.nz

CHAPTER 21
From a roaring lion to a purring kitten
By Kerry Smith

A Strategic and Empowering Approach to Navigating Children's Emotions

Have you ever been so angry that you wanted to yell at someone as loudly as possible? Or have you ever attended a business meeting where you couldn't express your point of view because no one was listening? If you can recall your thoughts, emotions, and feelings in these situations as an adult, imagine being an angry, yelling child, perhaps six or eight years old.

Children often struggle to navigate intense emotions like anger, frustration, and sadness, which can feel overwhelming in such a small child. These feelings frequently arise at unexpected moments during the day, leaving them uncertain about how to process their emotions or cope with the complexities of a highly structured elementary school classroom.

COACHING REIMAGINED Expanding Human Potential

As an educator and coach, I have tried, tested and refined multiple techniques and coaching modalities for working with children over the past thirty years. This chapter introduces and integrates my most successful strategies through a powerful, engaging, and practical approach to help children recognise and regulate their emotions. I will share this refined set of tools, designed to reshape how young children experience and respond to the world with their newly discovered self-regulation. They can then begin to respond to their inner world and effectively navigate their deepest feelings. By transforming how children perceive and interact with their emotions, you will discover how we can equip them with lifelong skills to manage challenging academic, emotional and social situations.

'Everyone has a Voice to be Heard.'

Are you genuinely reaching your full potential in life?

Do you have a voice that deserves to be heard in the world? If not, how does that make you feel?

My fascination with human potential began when I was about seven years old. This early childhood experience profoundly impacted my life and has been a key driver of my purpose.

I was lucky to grow up in a typical, stable British family with a younger sister. She was adorable, self-assured, and vibrant, exuding a personality almost entirely different from mine. My sister's mischievous antics captured our parents' attention, always keeping her at the centre of any situation. In contrast, I felt compelled to be quieter and more well-behaved, as if to create a counterbalance. Unfortunately, this was futile, as I held the unconscious belief that I wasn't good enough, yearned for my parents' attention, and wished for my voice to be heard.

Surprisingly, my beliefs changed, on the day my sister ruined my favourite birthday gift, a brand-new painting set. She received all the attention for her 'crime' and my feelings were neglected. While my perception of the event may have altered over time, I vividly remember my adverse reaction to her behaviour as I sped upstairs, slamming my bedroom door as loudly as possible!

Suddenly, I captured my parents' attention as my father raced upstairs to discover what had happened. Finally, I had a voice that could be heard! That single event, more than 45 years ago, is engraved in my memory and has been a significant catalyst throughout my life. It has shaped my passion for education and my purpose as a coach: to ensure all children are heard.

Furthermore, I have become an accomplished international educator working with diverse teams and individuals. Each role, from class teacher to principal, has deepened my understanding of children's needs, how they communicate, and what shapes their identities. My purpose fuels my passion for ensuring every child discovers and expresses their unique voice. It is an empowering and enjoyable experience. While I will share real-life stories, names have been altered to maintain privacy. I invite you to join me on this journey.

Why?

According to the author Simon Sinek, in his global bestseller 'Start with Why?' the true measure of success is a clear definition of purpose that inspires your actions. 'Why do you get out of bed in the morning?' As an instructional coach, people are often surprised when I discuss emotions, as I'm perceived to be logical and organised. Understanding a child's emotional intelligence is vital to my role. By comprehending their behaviours and helping them develop self-regulation strategies, we ensure they can manage their actions in the future. That's **why** I chose to be a coach: I empower students to find their voices, mitigate reactive behaviour and make informed and wiser choices.

Taming the Roaring Lion!

Case Study: While working with Grade 2 teachers at a large elementary school, in the Middle East, I encountered a seven-year-old student named David, whose disruptive behaviour severely impacted his learning. He often refused to stay in class, rarely followed expectations or completed tasks, and frequently ignored his teacher. Soon, he began running out of his classroom and around the school on a daily basis.

One day, after walking 10,000 steps around the school, following David as he evaded learning, I found him in a corner, trapped by a swipe-card-only security door. Frustrated, he pounded his heels against the glass and had a full-blown emotional meltdown. I realised that a better solution was needed for both David and my own mental health and well-being. During this temper tantrum, David raised his voice in a primal, lion-like roar that demanded attention.

The Significance of Strategy

As a coach, I'm often brought in by teachers, such as David's, who are at their wits' end after dealing with this behaviour daily. I must step in to facilitate a solution for the child. Alternatively, I may find myself rescuing those teachers who avoid their responsibilities in managing escalating behaviour. In other words, I need to rapidly tame that roaring, angry lion into a purring cat based on three key principles:

- safety
- satisfying their needs
- modifying the behaviour

Ultimately, my strategies always prioritise the immediate need to keep the student safe, rapidly de-escalate the anger, without judging it, and ensure the student returns to learning as soon as possible.

A coach's strategy is vital for guiding students through their emotions. Effective strategists utilise their coaching tools wisely, patiently supporting students as they progress towards positive reintegration into their class after emotional challenges.

One of the most significant inhibitors of success could have been that David was angry, and I didn't yet know the underlying cause. I needed to assist him in rapidly changing his unresourceful state into a more resourceful position.

All behavioural challenges have a positive intention, although it may not initially be evident. These challenges, such as the primal lion acknowledging David's emotions, have various triggers. For example, a student leaving the classroom may not intentionally misbehave. Still, their actions may indicate that they need support to feel secure or their nervous system response is one of flight, getting away to feel safe.

One of the valuable roles a coach plays is to guide teachers in developing strategies that minimise disruptions and enhance engagement. A common issue is inconsistent treatment of students.

For example, if one teacher allows sensory aids for self-regulation while another does not, this can confuse students and exacerbate behavioural problems. Instructional coaches can help by emphasising consistency in classroom management.

When working with children like David, 'in the moment,' it's essential to go beyond basic goals-focused coaching and tap into a young child's vivid imagination and help them access their nervous systems.

Several key strategies work well:

- Balanced Breathing
- Restorative conversations
- Sub modalities
- The Magic Volume Button or Remote Control
- The Feelings Volcano
- Drawing the Problem

Coaches aiming to manage emotions must believe in themselves and have the courage to support students in self-expression. While some well-meaning adults may attempt to control the behaviours and intervene, their involvement should not undermine a coaching environment that empowers student-led behavioural change. David needed to feel safe. By remaining silent beside him, I created a safe environment, allowing him to begin to calm down. As he exhausted his options, I noticed his automatic deep breath. Then, using balanced breathing techniques, I synchronised my breath with his to help him regulate and acknowledge his feelings. We took a short walk to my office, where I maintained a positive tone in conversation to convey that his emotions were valid. This fostered a safe coaching space for David's engagement. In addressing the issue, he successfully reintegrated into the classroom, with his needs met, through having felt heard.

Seizing Inspiration from Play

"Imagination is more important than knowledge."

Albert Einstein

Encouraging imaginative play fosters restorative conversations with students like David. I often allow students to choose from Lego, magnetic tiles, paper, and coloured pencils. Engaging in parallel play helps identify the triggers of his emotional outbursts. Giving them choice is a cue of safety to their nervous system.

Effective questioning at this stage is essential. Since David was calm and engaged in play, I could begin to pace his recent experience and elicit the chain of events that initially led to his outburst.

It is essential to focus on the event that caused the meltdown and elicit the student's perspective on their strategy. This approach helps uncover the moment of escalation, clarify the triggers behind David's adverse, explosive reaction and avoid a masked response that the student feels you want to hear.

As coaches, we can easily illustrate the event as a simple timeline, guiding the student to revisit the problem. Drawing several boxes on a page allows the student to navigate the events before the reaction.

Here are a few straightforward coaching questions that students will readily comprehend, which I advocate in achieving rapid results.

- What happened?
- What else happened?
- What happened before that?
- What was the very first thing that happened?
- And then…
- What else is important?
- What needs to happen to fix this?
- What smart choices could you make instead?

Students may hesitate to share their true when the fear of consequences outweighs their desire for change. Creating a sense of safety can help them open up in their own time. If a child remains silent, hold the space for them and allow them to respond, even if it feels prolonged. For those who struggle to articulate their thoughts through words, encourage them by offering alternative communication forms such as visual storytelling or drawing.

Tapping Into Intrinsic Imagination

Returning to David, I sensed his responses were superficial, as he seemed to tell me what he thought I wanted to hear. It was time to leverage my curiosity and employ another coaching strategy. I aimed to go beyond basic coaching to uncover the root cause and elicit the underlying wisdom within David's heart. I used his innate imagination to discover what he struggled to express without his lion's roar.

The fearlessness of a child's imagination is joyful, a perfect platform for curiosity as a coach. Children can easily create make-believe characters such as the Tooth Fairy, superheroes, or princesses in their play. Therefore, it's not a massive stretch to imagine talking to their hearts. To support this, having a heart-shaped fluffy plushie or a cushion toy with arms to hold against his heart enabled David, with minimal prompting to breathe calmly, deeply, and evenly so that he could listen to his heart communicate. I asked two simple questions:

- **What does your heart want to say about roaring like a lion?**
- **What did your heart truly want?**

David struggled to express himself due to his frustration with phonics and writing in a busy classroom where he felt overlooked. His heart offered the wisdom that he wanted connection with others. Often, he reacted by wandering or misbehaving until he was reprimanded. Supporting his needs was vital for his engagement and connection with his teacher, to **truly connect**. Structured reflection improved his behaviour; he illustrated his feelings through drawings, including an angry Tyrannosaurus and a roaring lion, symbolising his feelings of being misunderstood. He also drew a picture of better choices, depicting himself sitting at his desk, raising his hand, and asking for help, which demonstrated greater self-awareness and accountability.

Another example of connection and relating to others, from a heart-based approach, is that multiple incidents have occurred in another, similar elementary school due to disagreements in culturally diverse classrooms. Some students come from backgrounds that promote physical retaliation, as some parents may advise, 'if he hits you, hit him back.' However, school policies advocate for non-violence and encourage reporting to adults. The instructional coach facilitates structured conversations to help students resolve disputes amicably and minimise future conflicts. Additional coaching for teachers through professional development workshops supports restorative justice discussions. By fostering a culture of communication, embedded with a coaching approach, schools can create an environment conducive to peaceful conflict resolution.

The Feelings Volcano and Emotional Regulation

Children learn best through play. By framing emotional regulation as a game, we make it enjoyable, transforming anger from a roaring lion to a purring kitten, and turning frustration into a balloon that floats away. These approaches empower children to understand and control their emotions. Rather than telling them to 'calm down,' we provide playful methods to shift their emotional state naturally.

Following our restorative conversation, David needed an anchor to begin self-regulating and recognising similar feelings as they start to simmer up, in the future before they escalated to the 'lion's roar' again. One effective technique in my coaching toolbox for behaviour management is the **'Feelings Volcano'** anchor chart. Students draw a simple volcano outline or have a visible learning template to help them identify a greater range of vocabulary to express emotions. On the drawing, the student is encouraged to plot ten feelings on the page, progressing from calm at the bottom of the volcano to angry and explosive at the top. Each stage is organised in ascending order from calm to tension, frustration, and anger. The aim is for students to explore these levels and discuss the situations that trigger each emotion, enhancing their understanding of their emotional patterns.

Here is the technique in easily actionable steps:

1. **Volcano Outline:** Provide a template of a simple volcano outline or have your student draw one on blank paper.
2. **Create Levels:** Draw 10 levels on the volcano, as a ladder.
3. **Label the Levels:** Number them from 1 to 10.
4. **Associate Emotions and Meaning to Levels**: Ask the students where they were on the volcano when they felt angry, with 10 being the most intense. Then, relate level zero to calmness, encouraging students to label each level with their personalised vocabulary, from calm up to exploding.
5. **Colour the Levels:** Use cool colours for calm levels and hot colours, up to red, for higher levels

In our subsequent coaching sessions, David developed greater self-awareness by using the volcano technique to connect emotions with different colours and intensities. He was able to take proactive steps to manage his feelings before reaching a crisis point. Additionally, he took the anchor chart back to class after the coaching session to share it with his teacher.

Adjusting Emotional Intensity with the 'Magic Remote-Control Buttons'

All students are adept with modern technology, so using an imaginary remote-control button to help them manage their emotions is quite feasible. This technique is rooted in neuro-linguistic programming (NLP) and submodalities, which explain how our brains organise experiences. NLP presupposes that every thought, feeling, and memory has its own structure. For example, an angry moment, like David's roaring, may manifest as a red-hot image, a loud sound, or a sharp sensation. We can alter how he perceives his emotions by handing David an imaginary remote control to adjust these sensory qualities (size, colour, sound, intensity, etc.). This approach puts the student in control to explore their feelings thoughtfully. For students, the 'Magic Buttons' offer a simple and engaging way to manage intense emotions.

Here's how it can help them better understand and express their feelings with confidence:

1. **Imagine the Sound:** Ask the child to imagine their emotion as a sound. For example, anger might sound like a loud, roaring lion or frustration might be a blaring alarm.
2. **Visualise the Remote Control:** Tell them to visualise a remote control or magic volume button that controls this sound.
3. **Turn Down the Volume:** Invite the child to slowly turn the volume down, making the growl softer or the alarm quieter. Encourage them to describe what it feels like as the sound becomes more peaceful and calmer.
4. **Pace their current experience**: Once the sound is soft and calm, ask how they feel now compared to the peak of their anger. Reinforce that they can 'adjust' their feelings whenever they need.

This game helps children regulate their emotions, enhances their sense of control, and stimulates their imagination, making emotional self-regulation easier.

Transforming Emotions through Visualisation

Another popular game rooted in NLP submodalities is the 'Emotion Shape Shifter.' Here's how it works:

1. **Ensure Safety:** Make sure the student is in a safe space to stand free of any furniture or obstructions, or sitting on an appropriate-sized chair
2. **Close Eyes:** Ask the child to close their eyes and imagine their big emotion as a shape, colour, or object. For example, anger might look like a spiky red ball or a storm cloud.
3. **Describe it:** Encourage them to describe it in detail: How big is it? Is it moving? What does it feel like? Ask them if it is inside their body or clarify the position of the emotion.
4. **Guide them to Shift:** Then, guide them to change one thing about the image: 'Can you make the red ball smaller? What happens if you turn the spikes into soft feathers?' or 'What if your storm cloud becomes a fluffy white one?'
5. **Notice the feelings:** As the child plays with the image, notice how their feelings shift and bring it to the child's attention
6. **Get rid of the Shape:** While imagining, encourage the student to erase the shape, pull it out of their body on to their hand, make it tiny, dump it in the bin, kick it into space or get rid of the big emotion in any way that they choose
7. **Celebrate their creativity** and remind them that they have the power to adjust and replace with a resourceful emotion instead

This game makes the abstract concept of emotions tangible and fun, helping children learn to take control safely and imaginatively.

Many students will benefit from movement-based interventions, particularly those with attention and self-regulation challenges. Activities such as sitting in a calm corner, taking short brain breaks, jumping, skipping, and engaging in sensory play help restore students' equilibrium. Instructional coaches can present these techniques to teachers in workshops and emphasise their importance through classroom modelling.

Advocating for Student and Teacher Success

Today, instructional coaches play vital roles in academic support, behaviour management, teacher coaching, and student advocacy. I have consistently pursued further certification to stay relevant and to optimise my coaching toolbox. It is crucial to my success as a coach to research advances in neuroscience and update my knowledge through a global network of like-minded coaches. Not doing so would hinder my students' potential. It would be the equivalent today, of using a mobile phone released in 2012 without updating its operating system.

This book's central theme emphasises the need for coaching methods to evolve and for integrated approaches to be developed, weaving tools together to optimise results for the children in our care.

To conclude the story of my coaching journey, my passion and purpose will continue to support young people, ensuring that my dreams and ambitions for them are fulfilled throughout my life. I have been very fortunate to have several remarkable mentors and coaches who have guided me along this path, including some of the global coaches contributing to this book. Using my coaching skills, I can realise this purpose by advocating for children now, representing an incredible legacy.

By integrating emotional self-regulation coaching into a child's learning experience, we provide them with the tools to navigate their emotions confidently. Children can cultivate emotional intelligence, resilience, and self-awareness through engaging activities, visualisation techniques, balanced breathing, and alignment. These methods establish a strong foundation for a lifetime of self-regulation and emotional mastery, ensuring children develop into confident, expressive, and emotionally balanced individuals who excel.

At the heart of my purpose and passion is the belief that ***everyone* has a voice to be heard**. Just like David, who once roared with anger like a lion but, through coaching mastery, connection and understanding, found his voice—now calm, confident, and ready for a future of growth and success.

Services

Children's Success Coach• Educational Consultancy • Multiple Brain Intelligence Coaching • Emotional Intelligence • Instructional and Academic Coaching • Educational Leadership•

If you are interested in discovering how I can assist you, or would like to connect with me, feel free to access any of my social media channels:

Linktree: https://linktr.ee/kerry.smith

COACHING REIMAGINED Expanding Human Potential

CHAPTER 22
Coaching Beyond the Session – Why Client Experience Matters
By Karl Sandland
Growth Strategist for Coaches

Another cost-cutting board meeting. Another strategy to squeeze more from less. And yet, no one was talking about the real issue. As I sat in the boardroom, listening to our CEO and Chief Finance Officer discuss—yet again—how to streamline costs and reduce overheads, I couldn't help but think, *they're missing the point.*

It wasn't that cost-cutting was wrong; it made business sense. But I knew from experience that our real issue wasn't expenses—it was retention. Instead of focusing on delivering an exceptional experience that encouraged loyalty, we were pouring resources into acquiring new customers, only to lose them just as quickly. I had seen this pattern before.

Companies obsessed with efficiency often forget that loyalty isn't built on transactions—it's built on trust, relationships, and seamless experiences. After hearing enough about cost-cutting strategies, I finally spoke up.

"Why don't we just fix the leaky bucket?"

Silence. A sharp glance from the CEO. The CFO raised an eyebrow. Then, after a pause, something shifted.

"Hmmm… so what exactly would that look like then, Karl?" the CEO asked.

I was ready. I had been preparing for this conversation for days, knowing it could be a turning point for the business.

At this stage in my career, I had spent two decades working in and around customer service functions in software businesses. Sitting at the boardroom table as the Director of Customer Success, I had seen firsthand how the right experience—not just the right product—was the key to business growth.

My career had evolved from project management to solution design, then into customer experience and success. Leading a complaints department, a customer service team, and a software support division gave me a unique perspective. I saw how much impact a great experience (or a terrible one) had on retention, profitability, and long-term trust. That insight led me to formally study customer experience, earn qualifications in the field, and eventually be recognised as one of the Top 20 CX Professionals by *Customer Experience Magazine* in 2022. More importantly, it led to a major shift in strategy.

The outcome? The company transformed. Instead of focusing solely on acquisition, we doubled down on experience, retention, and loyalty. Within months, our churn rate plummeted. Within a year, we were retaining 95% of our customers—a shift that made the business far more profitable than any cost-cutting ever could.

But here's the thing. That shift in mindset—focusing on the experience rather than just the transaction—wasn't just the key to business growth. It would take me time to realise, but it was also the missing link in coaching.

When I became a coach, I noticed something fascinating: the same principles applied. Many exceptional coaches struggled—not because they lacked skill, but because they weren't paying attention to the *experience* of coaching. They were focusing entirely on their sessions, their methodologies, their frameworks. But they weren't thinking about how clients *felt* throughout the journey—the ease of booking, the clarity of communication, the sense of progress and continuity. And just like in that boardroom years ago, I started noticing another leaky bucket.

Working with dozens of coaches, I began spotting patterns—data, trends, and insights that pointed to a critical issue in the coaching industry. An issue that, once addressed, could have a game-changing impact on a coach's ability to build a thriving business.

This issue wasn't about coaching ability. It was about the entire coaching experience they provided—from the client's perspective.

The future of coaching isn't just about what we do in sessions—it's about creating a transformational environment that extends beyond the session itself.

The Client Experience Gap in Coaching

Many coaches focus almost entirely on the coaching itself—the insights, methodologies, and transformative conversations—while giving far less attention to the overall client experience. This is a critical oversight.

You might be thinking, *"But my clients experience real breakthroughs—that's what truly matters!"*

And yes, transformation is at the heart of coaching. But there's a difference between delivering great coaching and delivering a great *coaching experience.*

A coach may be exceptional at guiding growth, but if the *experience* of working with them is frustrating—if scheduling is difficult, communication is slow, or progress feels unclear—clients may disengage. The coaching experience isn't just about what happens *in* a session; it's about every single touchpoint a client has with you.

Some of the most successful brands in the world—Amazon, Apple, and Disney—understand that loyalty isn't built on a single great interaction. It's built on a carefully designed journey. The same applies to coaching: it's not just about the session itself, but about every moment before, during, and after.

Take Amazon. Why do millions choose it over competitors? Because Amazon removes friction. With one-click purchasing, intuitive navigation, and rapid delivery, buying is *effortless*.

Apple applies a similar philosophy. Yes, they build great products, but what makes them truly stand out is how they make customers *feel*. Walking into an Apple Store is intuitive. The staff provides hands-on guidance, seamless setup, and a sense of exclusivity.

Then there's Disney. A visit to a Disney Park isn't just about rides—it's about a meticulously designed experience. Visitors don't feel like customers; they feel like *participants in a story*.

What do these brands have in common? They don't just sell products; they create experiences that make people feel something.

Maya Angelou once said, *"People will forget what you said, people will forget what you did, but people will never forget how you made them feel."*

This is the foundation of a great client experience—and the future of coaching itself.

Think about the last time you had an incredible experience as a client. Maybe it was a restaurant where the waiter remembered your name or a hotel where staff anticipated your needs before you asked. Those details create emotional connection—a feeling of being valued and understood.

Now, compare that to a frustrating experience—an unhelpful support agent, a confusing website, or a service that felt impersonal. How did that make you feel?

Clients don't just remember the frameworks you use or the goals you help them set—they remember how they felt throughout their journey.

If their experience working with you is seamless, engaging, and supportive, they'll feel motivated, valued, and invested. But if booking is difficult, communication is unclear, or follow-up is inconsistent, clients may associate those frustrations with the coaching itself—even if the actual coaching is excellent.

This is why client experience is just as important as coaching quality. It's not about making coaching transactional—it's about creating an environment where clients feel seen, heard, and supported at every step.

As coaching evolves beyond traditional models, experience will be the differentiator. Just as companies have transformed how people engage with products and services, coaching must evolve to transform how clients engage with personal growth.

The next evolution of coaching isn't just about methodology—it's about experience.

When coaches craft a journey that is seamless, intuitive, and empowering, they elevate coaching from a one-time service to a lifelong, transformational partnership.

If we, as coaches, commit to reimagining the entire coaching journey, we won't just build better businesses. We'll create lasting impact, elevate the profession, and transform human potential in ways we've never seen before.

That's where the real magic happens.

My Journey – Learning to Practise What I Preach

If client experience is the future of coaching, then I should have been ahead of the game. And yet, I found myself making the same mistake I have seen so many others make.

When I first set out as a solopreneur coach, I thought I had it all figured out. I had the skills, the experience, and the credentials. Decades in senior business roles had equipped me with strategy, leadership, mentoring, and coaching within corporate structures. I had built and developed teams, shaped high-level business strategies, and coached professionals at different stages of their careers. On top of that, I had strong organisational, project management, and IT skills.

What could possibly go wrong?

Like many solopreneurs, I quickly learnt why larger companies have entire departments dedicated to business development, sales, marketing, and finance. These small gaps in my knowledge soon became glaring voids. It didn't take long to realise that being a great coach wasn't enough—I also had to run a business.

So, I invested in myself. I took training courses, sought mentors, and hired my own coaches to help me structure and scale my business the right way. And for a while, it worked. Clients were coming in, transformations were happening, and I was heading in the direction I had envisioned.

But somewhere along the way, I ignored a little voice in the back of my mind.

"Karl... what about the experience?"

I brushed it aside. I was too focused on growth. But deep down, I knew—

COACHING REIMAGINED Expanding Human Potential

I wasn't applying my expertise in customer experience to my own coaching business.

That realisation hit hard when I completed my first few 12-week coaching engagements. By the end of those 12 weeks, I had built incredible relationships with my clients. They had achieved breakthroughs, gained clarity, and set ambitious new goals. They wanted to keep working with me. And yet... I had nothing structured to offer them.

I had designed my programme as a standalone engagement, never stopping to think:

- *What happens next?*
- *How would clients continue their growth?*
- *What new aspirations had emerged for them?*
- *How could I keep them engaged beyond just extending the same programme?*

Instead, all I could say was:

"Well, you can continue working with me on the same structure..."

But even to me, that felt wrong. It lacked intention, evolution, and a true understanding of what my clients needed.

That was when I knew it was time to rethink my approach—this time, through the lens of customer experience. I needed to think differently.

I needed to design my coaching business the way top brands design their customer experiences. Amazon removes friction. Apple creates seamless, intuitive interactions. Disney builds a journey so immersive that customers want to stay engaged.

So, what would that look like in coaching?

I rebuilt my business with the client journey in mind—at every touchpoint. Instead of a one-size-fits-all model, I designed multiple ways for clients to engage, ensuring my coaching was accessible beyond a single high-ticket offering.

And that's when the RELATE framework for coaching businesses was born—helping coaches step into the future and meet the evolving needs of their clients.

RELATE: The 6 Key Indicators for a Meaningful Coaching Experience

When I redesigned my coaching business through the lens of customer experience, I saw a pattern—certain elements made the difference between an average coaching experience and one that truly transformed clients. It became clear that the best coaching wasn't just about what happened in the sessions; it was about everything surrounding them.

How easily could clients engage? How supported did they feel? Was the experience frictionless?

The more I explored this, the more I realised that coaching needed to be designed as an experience, not just delivered as a service. That's when I developed RELATE—a framework for making coaching experiences seamless, engaging, and transformational.

> *Responsive* – Remove friction so clients can engage easily and effortlessly.
> *Efficient* – Deliver results in the simplest, fastest, and most effective way.
> *Limitless Access* – Make support available when and where clients need it.
> *Awareness* – Provide full transparency into progress and next steps.
> *Tailored* – Adapt the coaching journey to each client's needs and preferences.
> *Empathetic* – Anticipate and proactively support clients before they even ask.

COACHING REIMAGINED Expanding Human Potential

A great coaching experience is *Responsive*. If booking a session, finding key resources, or reaching out for support feels complicated, clients may disengage before their transformation even begins. Coaching should feel effortless.

Responsive considerations:

- A seamless, intuitive booking system with minimal steps.
- Automated reminders, follow-ups, and easy rescheduling.
- A smooth onboarding process that sets expectations and removes friction.

It also needs to be *Efficient*. Clients don't come to coaching for drawn-out processes—they come for clarity and action. Every part of the coaching journey should move them forward, not hold them back.

Efficient considerations:

- Clear action steps after every session so clients know what to do next.
- Quick, structured check-ins via voice notes, email, or messaging apps.
- Pre-session reflection exercises to ensure sessions are used for deep work, not admin.

A coaching experience should offer *Limitless* Access. If clients feel restricted—whether in communication, availability, or access to insights—it creates unnecessary barriers to progress.

Limitless considerations:

- Multiple ways to engage (video, phone, voice notes, group coaching, or text-based support).
- A coaching portal where clients can book sessions, access notes, session recordings, and resources.
- A community of like-minded clients for peer accountability and

continued learning.

Clients also need *Awareness*. Without clear progress tracking, coaching can feel vague, and clients may struggle to see how far they've come. A structured experience keeps them motivated.

Awareness considerations:

- A roadmap outlining key milestones, so clients understand their journey.
- Session summaries with key takeaways and next steps.
- Goal-tracking dashboards where clients can log progress, breakthroughs, and challenges.

For coaching to truly stand out, it must be *Tailored*. No two clients are the same, yet many coaching programmes take a one-size-fits-all approach. When coaching feels personal and aligned, the impact is far greater.

Tailored considerations:

- Adjusting coaching styles based on a client's learning and communication preferences.
- Offering self-paced courses to complement live coaching.
- Providing custom content recommendations (books, exercises, or tools) based on the client's needs.

Finally, the best coaching experiences are *Empathetic*. Clients shouldn't always have to ask for support—sometimes, they don't even realise what they need until it's offered. A great coach anticipates challenges and provides guidance proactively.

Empathetic considerations:

- Checking in before a big life or career event (e.g., a job interview, presentation, or major decision).

- Identifying patterns in client struggles and offering solutions before they ask.
- Creating on-demand resources (e.g., meditation audios, resilience exercises, or mindset prompts) to support clients between sessions.

When coaching is responsive, efficient, limitless, aware, tailored, and empathetic (RELATE), it becomes more than just a process—it's a seamless, engaging, and deeply human experience.

Clients stay engaged not because they must, but because they want to. And when a coaching experience is designed this way, clients don't just commit to a programme—they commit to a journey—that leads to lasting transformation.

Leveraging Technology to Deliver a RELATE-Based Coaching Experience

Technology, when used intentionally, has the power to enhance rather than replace the coaching experience. While automation and AI can improve efficiency, coaching is, at its core, a human-to-human relationship. The key isn't to replace personal connection but to leverage the right tools in a way that strengthens engagement, builds trust, and removes friction for both coaches and clients.

An all-in-one platform that integrates key elements of RELATE can help create a seamless, structured, and transformative experience—without sacrificing personalisation or emotional depth. Instead of using fragmented tools that create a disconnected experience, a centralised platform enhances how coaches deliver their services, engage clients, and track progress.

Imagine a single coaching platform that acts as the backbone of a client's journey—one that provides everything they need, not just during sessions but before, between, and after them.

COACHING REIMAGINED Expanding Human Potential

My own coaching business now operates through a powerful all-in-one system that allows me to create multiple offerings at different price points, meeting clients where they are. This includes free communities, paid memberships, high-ticket programs, and flexible subscription models that allow clients to scale up or down as needed. Most importantly, every offering still includes some direct interaction with me—whether through group settings or one-on-one coaching—because human connection is non-negotiable.

By using technology strategically, I can deliver a richer, more engaging experience without adding unnecessary complexity. Clients have access to a personalised portal where they can book and review sessions, review notes, access course materials, and stay connected through a private community. Tracking insights, such as course completion and session engagement, allows me to anticipate client needs and offer support proactively.

But the real beauty of the RELATE framework is its flexibility. Every coaching business is different. Some coaches may prefer to focus on group coaching and digital courses, while others thrive on intensive one-on-one coaching. The tools and systems we use should adapt to our unique approach and the needs of our clients—not the other way around.

At its core, coaching is about transformation—not just in the moments within a session, but in the entire journey a client takes with us. The experience we create isn't just about delivering value in a structured programme; it's about how effortless, accessible, and deeply human that journey feels.

From the start, we explored the leaky bucket problem—how businesses (and coaches) often focus too much on acquisition while overlooking retention, experience, and loyalty. We saw how client experience is as important as coaching itself, shaping whether clients stay engaged or walk away despite transformative breakthroughs.

We then explored RELATE—a framework designed to bridge the gap between great coaching and a seamless, engaging client experience. Each element—Responsive, Efficient, Limitless Access, Awareness, Tailored, and Empathetic—ensures coaching experience is not just powerful but accessible, intuitive, and built to sustain long-term growth.

Finally, we addressed technology's role—not as a replacement for human connection, but as a tool to enhance, amplify, and refine the coaching experience. A well-integrated system removes friction, makes engagement effortless, and allows coaches to expand their impact without compromising authenticity.

But here's the real takeaway: Clients don't just remember the insights we share or the frameworks we use. **They remember how we made them feel throughout the entire journey.** They stay not because of a single breakthrough, but because the experience—**from first interaction to long-term support—feels effortless, intuitive, and built around their needs, their pace, their growth.**

Coaching **beyond the session** isn't just the future—it's what sets apart **coaches who create lasting transformation from those who simply deliver sessions.** The true power of coaching lies not just in the moments of insight, but in the **experience** that keeps clients engaged, supported, and invested in their own growth.

And when we elevate the coaching experience, we don't just change businesses…

…we change lives!

Connect with me…

Karl Sandland – Growth Strategist for Solopreneurs

www.karlsandland.com

COACHING REIMAGINED Expanding Human Potential

Empowering Solopreneurs to master tech, adopt automation, and enhance customer experience - so they cut costs, reclaim time, and scale without the overwhelm.

growthruntime.app

The ultimate all-in-one platform to simplify, automate & scale a small business.

CONCLUSION
A New Era of Coaching: The Invitation to Lead
Dr Suzanne Henwood

Here's to the bridge-builders, the hand-holders, the light-bringers, those extraordinary souls wrapped in ordinary lives who quietly weave threads of humanity into an inhumane world.

They are the unsung heroes in a world at war with itself. They are the whisperers of hope that peace is possible. Look for them in this present darkness. Light your candle with their flame. And then go.

Build bridges. Hold hands. Bring light to a dark and desperate world. Be the hero you are looking for. Peace is possible. It begins with us.

L.R. Knost

Coaching stands at a crossroads. For decades, it has been defined by structured conversations, tools, and frameworks designed to help individuals set and achieve specific goals. It has been measured in outcomes, milestones, and progress. And yet, the world is shifting. People are seeking something deeper—something more integrated, more human, more alive. Coaching must evolve to meet that call.

What was new and cutting edge yesterday – is sometimes treading water, or worse out of date and inaccurate, as leaders come and go and modalities stagnate, or get taken over by people who have lost sight of the vision – focusing instead on money and commercial opportunity.

Ultimately, only we can ensure the quality of our own coaching toolbox. We can ask the questions about whether there is an evidence base guiding practice; when materials were last updated (and if it is over 3 years, there are valid concerns to be had); the driving values, ethics and vision of the tools and modalities we choose to sustain.

This book is not just a collection of ideas. It is a declaration, a movement, a profound reimagining of what coaching can be. The 24 authors who have contributed their wisdom to these pages are not merely theorists; they are pioneers, way makers. With over 355 years of combined experience and wisdom, they have dared to step beyond the familiar and into the unknown, forging a path that is systemic, integrated, somatic, ethical, service-led, and heart-driven and wise. They are redefining coaching— not as a method, but as a force for human development, a practice of deep presence, connection, and transformation.

This book is a call to bring greater wisdom, compassion and consciousness to a world that is facing significant challenges and is searching for new ways of being and doing life, work, leadership, relationship, wellbeing and life. We believe coaching, in the right hands and hearts, has a vital role to play moving forward.

As you turn this final page, you stand at a threshold, at the edge of possibility. This is your invitation.

An invitation to step beyond the head-based, talk-based, tool-based, linear, goals-based approaches that have shaped coaching in the past and to embrace a way of coaching that is connected to and alive in the body, in the nervous system, in the space between people and in the world around us. To see coaching not as something we *do* but as something we *are*—a way of being that calls forth the highest potential in ourselves and those we serve.

This is an invitation to take your place in a new era of coaching. To let go of old definitions that no longer serve, and to trust that something even more powerful is emerging – and that you are part of creating that. This is an invitation to stand with those who believe that coaching must be more than a profession—it must be a vital, necessary contribution to the future of humanity. While also informing AI, ensuring deep heart-led humanity is represented in the brave new world on line.

The work ahead is not small. The world is in flux, and the need for coaching that truly meets people—where they are, as they are—has never been greater. If we are to be fit for purpose for the next decade, the next century, we must be willing to evolve, to stretch, to listen, and to lead how we want coaching to be. This is not the destination; this is a decision to be on a journey of evolution.

And so, as you close this book, take a breath. Feel what has moved in you. Notice what calls you forward.

Then go. Step fully into your own coaching mastery—not just with cognitive knowledge, but with a deepened sense of purpose, courage, and connection. Bring this new paradigm into your practice, into your conversations, into your life. For yourself – and for those you serve.

The future of coaching isn't something that will be handed to us.

It is something we will create.

And it starts now. With You.

COACHING REIMAGINED Expanding Human Potential

COACHING REIMAGINED Expanding Human Potential

bWISE: Where Neuroscience Meets Indigenous, Innate and Systemic Wisdom in Coaching

"The deepest truths aren't just known in the mind—they're felt in the heart and sensed in the gut. Real knowledge comes when thought, emotion, and body align."

— Dr. Gabor Maté

Unlock Wise Intelligences in Decision Making

What if you, your clients, your colleagues could make truly wise decisions—aligning their head, heart, gut, pelvis and autonomic intelligences? How would their lives change if they had exquisite self-awareness and could take consistent action with clarity, wisdom, confidence, and purpose?

Introducing the groundbreaking **Wisdom Intelligence Self-Evaluation Report (wise)**, the worlds first and only scientifically validated psychometric tool that reveals how people use their multiple intelligences to make wise decisions. Backed by ten years of empirical research and peer-reviewed studies, wise helps clients align their thoughts, feelings, and actions to make wiser decisions and create lasting transformation.

Discover, Experience, and Share Wisdom Intelligence

The wise assessment provides:
- A detailed map of intelligence preferences (dominant vs. underutilized)
- Tools to recognize when head overrides gut instincts
- Methods to access heart intelligence for compassionate leadership
- Pathways to deeper meaning, creativity, and purpose
- Strategies to resolve internal conflicts and self-sabotage
- Practical exercises to develop integrated intelligence

Experience It First

Before introducing wise to clients, discover your own intelligence profile. Your personal report reveals your unique intelligence centre preferences,

COACHING REIMAGINED Expanding Human Potential

decision-making patterns, and strategies for achieving greater internal alignment.

Take Coaching to the Next Level with the bWISE Certification

The bwise Coaching Certification is an advanced training in integrated, embodied, systemic, and neuroscience-based coaching. It expands beyond the empirical research to include the latest neuroscience equipping you with:

- A robust framework for aligning 12 multiple intelligences (yes 12!)
- Unique, world-leading tools to enhance creativity, leadership, and emotional intelligence
- Science-backed methods to facilitate transformation at a profound level

Be Part of the Future of Coaching

- Get your personal wise report and uncover your intelligence profile
- Train as a certified bwise coach and bring a cutting-edge approach to your practice
- Join an exclusive group of forward-thinking professionals revolutionising coaching

Visit **www.theluminosityproject.nz** to join our exclusive waitlist. Be among the first to receive your wise report, become a certified wise facilitator or bwise coach, and offer your clients this exceptional, world-leading service.

bwise— Illuminating and Expanding Human Potential.

NOTES

NOTES

NOTES

NOTES

COACHING REIMAGINED Expanding Human Potential

© Dr Suzanne Henwood

COACHING REIMAGINED Expanding Human Potential

Printed in Great Britain
by Amazon